DATE DUE

DEC 1 2 2005	

LIVE FROM THE
GATES OF HELL

LIVE FROM THE
GATES OF HELL

An Insider's Look at the
Antiabortion Underground

JERRY REITER

 **Prometheus Books**

59 John Glenn Drive
Amherst, New York 14228-2197

Published 2000 by Prometheus Books

Inquiries should be addressed to
Prometheus Books
59 John Glenn Drive
Amherst, New York 14228–2197
VOICE: 716–691–0133, ext. 207
FAX: 716–564–2711
WWW.PROMETHEUSBOOKS.COM

04 03 02 01 00   5 4 3 2 1

Library of Congress Cataloging-in-Publication Data

Reiter, Jerry.
    Live from the gates of hell : an insider's look at the antiabortion underground / Jerry Reiter.
        p. cm.
    Includes index.
    ISBN 1–57392–840–2 (alk. paper)
    1. Pro-life movement—United States. 2. Abortion—Moral and ethical aspects—United States. 3. Abortion—United States—Religious aspects. 4. Terrorism—United States. I. Title.

HQ767.5.U5 R454 2000
363.46'0973—dc21   00–044569

Printed in the United States of America on acid-free paper

CONTENTS

Although I am a journalist by training, this book is more of a personal memoir than a journalistic account. Parts of the story are based on taped interviews, published reports, or court documents, while other parts are my recollections of events and conversations I observed or participated in firsthand. Therefore, some of the quotes are not verbatim, but rather my best recollection based upon notes taken at the time.

In some instances I have used composite characters, merging a few of the many interviews, both formal and informal, I conducted with various persons into one strong interview for the purpose of drama and brevity. I have also taken the liberty of changing the names of individuals who are not public figures where it seemed wise to do so for their protection.

I should also say that I do not pretend to be an objective reporter in this book. Quite the contrary, I openly talk about my feelings and reactions to many of the violent and shocking events I witnessed, and I add my own analysis in an attempt to put the story into some kind of context. However, I have tried to describe events as much as possible rather than interpret them, in order to let the action show the reader the social reality at the time rather than simply talking about it.

PART ONE

THE MYSTERY AND THE MURDER TRIAL

ONE

February 15, 1994

The evening sun flooded the glass-walled TV and radio studios where I worked as the day's rush hour wound down, and a night I would always remember began with deceptive calm. I could feel the warm rays on my face, even in one of Houston's "cooler" months. I had moved to the growing, hot, and humid new city from chilly Buffalo, New York, to get a fresh start after my involvement with the Religious Right had temporarily derailed my broadcasting career.

The fifth-floor suite of offices from which we broadcast belonged to my employer, Shadow Broadcast Services, a traffic service that had recently expanded to include news, weather, and sports information in most of the nation's top radio and TV markets.

During the time I worked for Shadow, I was an on-air reporter for all these different categories, serving as a traffic reporter on KTRH news radio and as a news reporter on multiple FM stations. I continued to freelance for national news services, including Shadow's own national network, and the BBC. I had learned how to get freelance assignments while at the ABC radio affiliate in

11

Buffalo, where Ray Marks, a kindhearted veteran of broadcasting, took me under his wing and explained the procedures for becoming a regional radio news stringer for ABC National News.

On this particular evening I was going to do a little research for the upcoming freelance assignment. I was to cover the trial of Michael Griffin, the man accused of murdering a doctor who provided abortion services.

I took my notebook, filled with details about some of the radicals from various fringe groups, into one of the small news cubicles. I sat down to make what would turn out to be a fateful call to Rev. Donald Treshman, the founder of Rescue America, a group that advocated both legal and illegal activities to prevent women from getting abortions.

Treshman's phone rang four or five times, and then his machine picked up. I could hear his deep, stern voice on the recording. When the beep-tone went off, I introduced myself, told him I was working on a book, and gave him my number. Then I mentioned what would be a crucially important detail, the names of my former pastors, the twin brothers Paul and Rob Schenck.

Suddenly, Treshman picked up. "Yeah, I know the Schencks. Tell me again, who the hell are you?" His blunt style and staccato delivery startled me a little, and I stammered, "Oh, yeah, my name's Jerry Reiter. I was a member of the Schencks' church two years ago when Randall Terry [fiery founder of the antiabortion group Operation Rescue] announced right after the huge Wichita rescue that he was bringing his next national protest to Buffalo."*

"How'd you get hooked up with the Schencks?" Treshman asked. I told him that back in 1989, my wife got a job teaching at the school affiliated with the Schenck brothers' church. "We started goin' to church there, too," I added.

"Are you a born-again Christian?" Treshman inquired.

"Yeah," I replied, "I was raised Catholic, but became a born-again Christian in high school. One of my good friends from those days became the music minister at the Schencks' church. He introduced me to Paul and Rob. I knew they were involved in Operation Rescue, but

---

*At the 1991 Wichita rescue, two thousand arrests were made in seven weeks.

I never took part in any of the rescues myself because of my job, but I had friends who got arrested, and I'd been introduced to Randall Terry by the Schencks."

Treshman mumbled something about Terry that I couldn't make out. I hesitated. "Go on," he barked.

I replied, "Well, I knew right away that the protest coming to Buffalo was going to be a problem for me because I was working as a news reporter for the local ABC affiliate. When the Schencks were announced as the local leaders of what was dubbed the Spring of Life rescue, I went to my news director to tell him who my pastors were and offer to remove myself from covering the story. He just about fell off his chair."

Treshman laughed, breaking the tension, and said, "I bet he didn't like that one bit."

I said, "I think he was not only shocked, but embarrassed 'cause he had just come into our news staff meeting and said, 'I think Randall Terry and the Schencks and all these antichoice protesters planning to come to town are nuts. They're total whack-jobs! Now . . . we're gonna cover this thing 100 percent objectively.' "

Treshman relished the irony. "Yeah, that's our 'objective' press, all right. The damned liberal media at work!"

I told him that my boss informed me that station management decided to take me off of all news duties for as long as the protest lasted. "I couldn't cover any stories at all, not a town board meeting or a homicide, nothing at all no matter how unrelated to the protest it was. And I was mad!"

Treshman sympathized, "There's so much anti-Christian bias in the media these days it isn't funny."

"Yeah," I said, "later on my story got written up in [televangelist and former GOP presidential candidate] Pat Robertson's *Christian American* newspaper about how I had put my career on the line for the pro-life cause. But, getting back to the protest, what happened was that when I told Paul Schenck about the way the station was gonna take me off all news duties during the weeks of the protest, he said maybe that was God's way of making me a nonjournalist so I could help the pro-life side. He asked me to join him in the headquarters of Operation Rescue as a media coordinator, helping write press releases, schedule interviews, and so on. I went into the secret communication center, and did not only that, but radio interviews in every city except Buffalo, so I could go back to work as a journalist."

Everything I told Treshman was true, but I left out most of the things that I didn't like about the rescuers—for example, the way the Schenck brothers repeatedly said from the church pulpit that the rescue movement was committed to peaceful nonviolence, yet soon after I entered the secret command post of Operation Rescue, I was given books on dozens of not-so-peaceful activities, including a book by Rev. Michael Bray advocating the bombing of abortion clinics. Bray wrote the book while in prison for practicing what he preached. He had been convicted on conspiracy charges in the bombing of nine clinics.

But even Bray's controversial tome had stopped short of calling for murder. His thesis had been that since abortion is murder, it is justifiable to commit arson, bombings, chemical attacks, or anything else that would destroy the property used to "kill babies" through abortion. But then the radicals had gone even further with a shooting in Pensacola, which some of the pro-life leaders were calling "justifiable homicide."

My investigation into the shooting in Pensacola was the reason for my call to Treshman. One of his most trusted underlings, Rev. John Burt, had been a type of mentor to the shooter in the weeks before the assassination. I hoped he'd be helpful in researching what had happened back on the day of the murder, but I didn't have any forewarning of the huge hint that Treshman was about to drop regarding the future.

Thanks to Don Treshman, I was about to enter the deepest and darkest hardcore web of radical right-wingers which would include militia members, "Christian" bombers, and "pro-life" killers. Of course I didn't know yet how close the radicals ties to 'respectable' conservative leaders would be. That would come later.

As it happened, I stumbled into something that would get Treshman to start opening up to me. As we talked about the specifics of the protest in Buffalo, I happened to mention that I thought Randall Terry had made a serious miscalculation when he had come to my radio station and announced, several months before the fact, that the Buffalo event would happen in the spring of 1992, giving the pro-choice side time to be ready. Treshman grabbed the thought like a hungry fish would grab bait.

"Randy's always shootin' his mouth off; been that way since the beginning, back in the early days of the rescue movement when we were takin' over the movement from the Catholic ladies. Randy was always givin' his hellfire-and-brimstone speeches. He thought he was the center of the universe; we thought he was just a clown, but he was good at drawin' people in, so we let him. It was a big mistake 'cause he couldn't work with anyone else. We had a great group goin', but then Terry broke off and launched his own group, and now his group [Operation Rescue] gets all the attention even though they're just a split-off from us. But we're the ones who are going to make the difference; we see the big picture. And the future belongs to us."

I was stunned by the intensity in Treshman's voice as he spoke about Terry. I hadn't expected to find such animosity sparked by intra-movement rivalry and jealousy. But my criticism of Terry seemed to make Treshman feel more of a kinship with me than the fact I had put my career on the line for the cause.

Treshman asked me if I was going to be in Pensacola for the trial of Michael Griffin. I said I was considering it, and Treshman said that I ought to definitely go because I'd get to see what was being planned.

"What kind of things?" I asked.

Treshman chose his words carefully, "I'm not in a position to give you specifics right now, but let me just tell you that if you go to the trial, stick around the following weekend for a special event." He explained that the National Coalition of Abortion Providers was going to hold a special event, a conference in Pensacola on the one-year anniversary of the death of Dr. David Gunn at a time that, if early estimates held up, would also happen to coincide with the termination of the court proceedings against the slain man's murderer. This meant that hundreds of abortion providers, feminist leaders, and pro-choice activists would be gathered in the same place on an emotionally charged date in memory of the martyred man.

Treshman told me, in a deep, dark voice, to make sure I didn't leave

Pensacola too quickly at the end of the trial because *"somethin' big, some-thin' really big, is coming!"*

There was something in Treshman's tone that made me instantly certain he was not talking about a march or a protest. As far as what form the "something big" would take, I had no idea yet. I only knew that if my suspicions were on target, violence could be part of the package.

I had seen from the inside of Operation Rescue's headquarters the slippery slope of the Machiavellian morality that had set the stage for the nation's first murder in the name of life. Those who had started down the path of illegal activity by trespassing and blocking clinic doors now no longer had the moral authority to stop those who wanted to go to the next step, and the next step, and so on—until bullets started to fly at the clinic entrances that served as the front line in the nation's culture war, what the radicals had dubbed "The Gates of Hell."

If I was going to prevent any further tragedies in Pensacola, I'd have to figure things out very quickly, because there was so little time. I couldn't go to the cops because I had so very little evidence. The clock was ticking, and unless I had completely misread the situation, lives were hanging in the balance. It was up to me to do something.

TWO

February 28, 1994

The sky was ablaze with brilliant pink, purple, and orange-tinged hues in layers of hazy gauze illuminated by the breaking dawn as I approached the outskirts of Pensacola, a compact city neatly tucked away in the northwesternmost corner of Florida. My body ached because I had driven my little red Chevy all night long to make the five-hundred-mile trek from my home in Houston, Texas.

Wiping the bleariness of the last ten hours from my eyes, I suddenly noticed a huge white cross of vapor trails in the sky above me; it somehow seemed to be an omen of things to come. The cross in the sky struck me as a perfect symbol of a religiously significant event; but then again, this one had been formed by modern technology, probably from jets flying out of nearby Eglin Air Force Base or the Pensacola Naval Station. So, if it was an omen, what was it supposed to mean? Surely it was not the mighty military making a mystical metaphor for a militant murderer.

I shrugged it off, realizing that that was always the problem with omens; they only existed in the eye of the beholder. It was time to clear the cobwebs from my mind and focus on what lay ahead. The murder trial of formerly obscure chemical worker Michael Griffin was about to begin, almost exactly one year after he allegedly shot Dr. David Gunn three times in the back.

But this was obviously no ordinary homicide, no routine story. It was the nation's very first abortion-related slaying, committed by a self-confessed assassin who failed to see the irony in his fanatical action, the ultimate oxymoron—a "pro-life" killing.

Ostensibly, I was there as a radio news reporter. I would be sending taped portions of the trial up to the BBC radio newsmagazine *File Four*, getting paid for my coverage of the event; but there was potentially much more to this story than just another freelance opportunity. I had received that mysterious tip from the leader of one of the nation's most radical right-wing groups about "something big" that was supposed to be coming. I thought about the ominous tone in Don Treshman's deep, dusky voice when he gave me the tip on the phone just two weeks earlier; now I was here to find out what he was talking about.

The national and international media circus was already brightly glittering in its full-color pageantry and three-ring insanity as I pulled up to the scene of the action. Antennas and satellite dishes protruding from garishly garnished trucks and hastily assembled broadcast towers sent words and pictures out to an eager public. CNN, ABC, CBS, NBC, PBS, and countless newspapers from around America, as well as far-flung foreign news organizations had assembled their front line of truth seekers to undertake their massive descent on the harsh brown squares of steel and stone known as the M. C. Blanchard Judicial Building, the Escambia County Courthouse.

The semimodern complex had none of the charm of the nearby historic portion of the port city along the verdant Gulf of Mexico, an area dubbed the "Emerald Coast" because of its wide array of green trees, bushes, and grasses. Indigenous loplolly pines, with their long, soft needles and sparse branches, far outnumbered palm trees and exotic orange-winged bird of paradise flowers, two better-known symbols of the Sunshine State.

The courthouse seemed to bear its bleak facade with a stoic dignity; it had played host to more than its share of human misery. Murderers, rapists, robbers, and their victims had passed through its portals.

Walking along the sidewalk, I passed a series of metal posts connected by a chain draped almost casually along the way. A large, moderately well-manicured lawn behind the chains was trampled only by squirrels that ran from one of the few large trees to another on the block-long complex.

I had thought we would see large protests outside the courthouse, but on this first morning I only saw two lone protesters holding signs with antichoice slogans: a short, dark-haired man held a sign that read, "Dr. Gunn Killed Children," and a taller blond man held a sign that read, "Disobey Unjust Laws."

They shouted at passersby, "God's law, not man's law!" and "Defend the innocent, not the butchers!" Their voices pierced the morning calm at the corner of Government and Baylon Streets. They acted like angry prophets of some ancient time as their faces twisted in rage with warnings of woe. The press people nearby ignored them, but suddenly someone was shouting back at them. An elderly man hollered, "I hope you people go to jail where you belong!"

For a brief moment, all of us who were within earshot began to move toward the potential conflict, but the old man had kept going toward the courthouse, so there would be no further confrontation, at least for the time being. I walked up to the two men and asked, "So, I guess he's not one of your fans?"

"He's one of the deathscorts; we've seen him at the Gates of Hell," said the dark-haired man, who introduced himself as Andrew Cabot, with a New England accent. "Deathscorts" was the derogatory tag that pro-life advocates assigned to the volunteers who escorted women through the lines of protesters into clinics that provided abortion services.

I knew this because I had been outside the clinics both as a reporter and as a friend of many "rescuers," the people who violated trespass laws to block access to clinics and hospitals that provided legal abortion services. The scene was always tense as the pro-choice and pro-life sides opposed each other like two armies at the front lines of a national confrontation.

"I know all about deathscorts and I've been at the Gates of Hell many times," I replied.

19

"You must be one of the few liberal media people who knows what we're talking about," said his friend, Paul Hill. I knew Hill's name already because he had gained national notoriety shortly after Dr. Gunn was killed by circulating a national petition calling the shooting of the doctor "justifiable homicide."

Twenty-nine "pro-life" leaders from all over America, many of them pastors, had signed Hill's so-called Defensive Action petition in praise of the shooter, and calling for his release. Hill had singlehandedly turned what most pro-life leaders considered the tragic and misguided action of a "lone, crazed killer" into a cause célèbre for the radical fringe of the pro-life movement.

I felt that he was someone I had to get to open up, because if anyone might know about coming violence, Hill had to top the list of suspects.

Reaching out my hand to shake his, I said, "My name's Jerry Reiter, and although I'm a member of the media, I don't think anyone would call me liberal. As a matter of fact, two years ago I put my reporting career on the line to help Operation Rescue in the national protest they brought to Buffalo, New York. You may have heard of my pastors there, the twin ministers Rob and Paul Schenck."

Both Hill's and Cabot's faces suddenly lost all traces of the anger that had contorted their features just moments before, replacing their hostility with surprise and then delight. Hill lit up as he said, "Yeah, I'm familiar with the Schencks. Those are some great pastors you've got! Great men of God!"

We talked for a little bit, and I gave the two men a copy of an article in the Christian Coalition's newspaper that covered my job woes related to my church affiliation and role in helping Operation Rescue. Before excusing myself to go inside the courthouse, I asked them if we could get together to talk some more. We agreed to meet at the same spot as soon as the trial broke for lunch that day.

Normally, I would not have told potential interview subjects about my personal background, but I wanted to find out about that "something big," and my hunch that these two men could give me some information would pay off far more than I could have expected. I had no way of knowing at the time, but at that moment I was addressing the next "pro-life" killer.

As I hurried on, I saw TV reporters in their own little turfs under shimmering lights doing stand-up reports for networks all over North America, while radio reporters like myself carried equipment toward the building. I approached a T in the sidewalk, so I turned and headed toward the glass doors at the side of the building. There was a sense of anticipation in the air as I stood among those who were waiting to get inside.

Stepping into the entranceway, I had to wait to navigate the metal detectors that had become an everyday part of security in American halls of justice. When my turn came to enter, a buzzer went off and a large African American woman with a plastic wand told me to stand still while she did what seemed an extra slow sweep of my arms, body, and legs. I could understand why she seemed to be taking more time than usual with security, given the nature of the trial.

Radicals from both "armies" in the culture war would be here to invade the media encampment in order to broadcast their message of fear and impending disaster to a waiting world, where their somber sobriquets would be delivered in digestible and spicy sound bites.

After clearing the security check, I collected my notebook; my soft-shelled black bag of pens, pads, tapes, batteries and tape recorders, one a small, voice-activated job I could carry in my pocket if need be; and a larger Marantz professional recorder for the court proceedings, complete with black vinyl-covered cables to plug into the electronic sound system of the court.

Heading down the shiny, imitation-stone floors, I turned to the right and pressed the button for the steel-doored elevators. The waiting area was filled with people and, as the doors opened, only a few people got off while more passengers than could fit aboard nudged into place to try to secure their spots. I was one of the lucky ones who got inside the first elevator, and I rode up to the fifth floor for the proceedings.

As we lurched to a stop, the doors parted to reveal a sea of people in the hallway leading to the courtroom. A game of stop and go, two steps forward and one step back, proceeded in slow motion. Women with generous amounts of perfume mingled with impatient men and stern-looking, armed law enforcement personnel as we approached the oak doors leading into courtroom 508. The chatter was hushed, yet near fever pitch as we finally neared the entranceway. Then, after a wait, we lurched forward and in a sudden move, I was inside the courtroom. I quickly found a seat in the second row of churchlike pews facing the judge's bench.

Just a moment after my behind hit the seat, the defendant was brought silently and without fanfare to sit at the table to our left. Thirty-two-year-old Michael Griffin looked so different from the person I'd seen in newspaper clippings. The hefty chemical worker had lost fifty pounds since the day he allegedly unloaded three bullets into the back of a diminutive doctor. At the time of his arrest, Griffin had been in a very defiant mood, waving his Bible in the air and saying that the holy book was the only defense he needed. His strident tone shocked his own family, who were accustomed to their vision of Michael as a quiet young man. A year of pleading by the family, combined with severe brutalization by fellow inmates, had together taken the wind out of the sails of the once-proud prisoner. He sat now, as he would through all the coming proceedings, as silently and nervously as a lamb.

Lawyers for the prosecution sat to our right, led by balding, dark-haired Assistant State's Attorney James Murray, who seemed to be a bundle of energy while he waited for things to begin. Whispers among the seated and those scurrying for seats continued right up until the large and imposing frame of Judge John Parnham entered briskly in black robes and took his elevated seat at the oak table in the center of the oak-paneled room.

The attorneys and the defendant were separated from the rest of us by a wooden railing. The courtroom seemed to have a certain simple elegance in its design; a crisp, modern efficiency suitable for the proceedings underway.

The proceedings moved briskly as each side made its opening presentations. There would be no Perry Mason–style cries of "I object, your honor!" on this first morning, because of a deal that had been struck ahead of time. A little horse trading had been going on behind the scenes. My fellow reporters in the know about the local scene filled me in on the particulars. During the prior week, speculation about the deal had been the only big story coming out of the days of jury selection.

There was a great deal of discussion, but the bottom line was that Griffin's attorneys had agreed to withhold their objection to testimony that would come from a prison guard in exchange for the prosecutor's agreement not to seek the death penalty.

When the first phase of the proceeding was settled, at around 10:30, the court took a short recess. Out poured the sea of bodies once again in waves rushing to the elevators. I stayed on the fifth floor and worked my way down to courtroom 506, where I got my media credentials and press packet, a thick pile of papers on various legal matters and procedural rules.

Then I headed back into the still-massive sea of people until my turn came to ride in the shiny silver sardine box down to the first floor. But I didn't leave the building, because an informal press conference was about to be hastily assembled by David Gunn Jr., the son of the slain doctor.

THREE

Young Gunn was an interesting character with a flower child appearance, complete with extremely long, poker-straight brown hair and bare feet showing through brown sandals, and he would prove to be every bit as articulate as you might expect a graduate student in English literature to be. But, more importantly, what David Gunn Jr. would say seemed to confirm my worst fears about what was going on in Pensacola.

Gunn was in complete command of the situation as the klieg lights came on and reporters snapped to attention. He read part of his statement about his father's tragic assassination by religious extremists as smoothly and conversationally as possible, but then he added a dire statement: "I do not believe that the man who killed my father acted alone. . . . He was part of a national conspiracy which will lead to the murder of more doctors and health-care workers in this country who offer women the right to safe and legal abortions." Gunn went on to demand that federal authorities look into the conspiracy "before it's too late."

What Gunn didn't know—what no one else at that press conference knew—was that the tip I'd secretly been given two weeks earlier sounded like it might confirm young Gunn's conspiracy theory, and it had given me an ominous hint about the direction of the next phase of the Religious Right's battle plans in its culture war. I was certain that the action would somehow come right there to Pensacola, already ground zero in the war over abortion, and one of the more battle-scarred places for the nation's conflict of wills, with the bombings of gay bars and abortion clinics, in addition to the shooting.

I wanted to tell David what I knew; I was worried about him and his family. They'd been through so much already, and now I feared they might all be in danger, though I had no solid evidence to offer them at least not yet.

As the lights were turned off and reporters drifted away, I stayed to talk to the young man, hoping I could find a way to warn him without scaring him off. I knew he'd want to know why one of the most radical men in the country had taken me into his exclusive confidence, and the answer to that question would have completely destroyed my credibility.

So I approached him gingerly, expressing my condolences for his loss, and then asking him a few carefully worded questions about his conspiracy theory. I told him that I had been writing about the abortion controversy and that I thought he was probably right, even though it was going to be difficult to prove.

He gave me his full attention, so undividedly and with so much openness that I felt that maybe I should go ahead and tell him everything right there, but I hesitated. And you know what they say about he who hesitates? Yes, in this case, I would be lost. Soon he would find out from someone else about my background, blowing my cover before I could explain to this earnest young man why I had once served the allies of the men who had called for his father's demise.

But, for the one brief moment when I spoke with him, David Gunn Jr. seemed to be the perfect emblem of his side of the culture war; he was bright, articulate, sensitive, and pro-choice. He was a living reminder that activists in the antichoice movement had been moving down the wrong track on a slippery slope of ends-justify-the-means morality that had taken the hard-edged street groups from minor illegal offenses to killing in the name of Christ.

Suddenly, I became aware that one of the cameramen had not left.

He had been shooting the conversation I'd been having with Gunn and even now, as David walked away, his camera was still rolling. "Have you been taping us the whole time?" I asked as it dawned on me that he was there.

"Yes, yes, it vas great, intense, vhat a moment!" he said with an obviously German accent.

"I didn't even see you there," I said, expressing my genuine surprise.

"Yah, I try to alvays be invisible, let the camera just capture de story as it happens; I'm vorking on a documentary about de whole abortion thing. Ve got over five hundred hours of footage from all around America, great stuff, ya know—street protests, clinic fights, people shouting these outrageous slogans, one-on-ones with some of the leaders of Operation Rescue and those kind of groups," he said in a burst of gleeful enthusiasm.

He stuck out his hand and introduced himself, "My name ees Hans Schmidt, vhat's yours?"

I responded, "I'm Jerry Reiter, nice to meet you."

He said, "Oh, your name, like mine, is German, isn't it?" Confirming that it was, I spelled it for him, and he said, "Oh, your name means cavalryman, a horse rider."

We talked in the hallway for a while. He explained that he had been hired within the past six months to work for independent filmmaker, Tony Kaye, in a growing Hollywood office. Kaye was known at the time for his TV commercials, but his passion was filmmaking. Kaye had been working on a massive documentary on the American abortion battles for over a year, and would arrive in Pensacola before the week was out.

I told Schmidt that we'd better get back upstairs because the trial would soon be underway. As we rode up on the elevator, he asked if I was working from the press room or the courtroom. "I've been in the courtroom, but I think I'll go into the press room now. I want to meet some of my colleagues."

Schmidt said that he had been in the press room that morning. "It's kind of veird in there," he said.

I laughed and replied, "You're probably just not used to American journalists; we're a pretty irreverent group."

"Maybe that's it, but it was even noisy sometimes," he concluded.

When we arrived in the press room, it was jam-packed with print and broadcast reporters from virtually everywhere. I went to the back of the room because I noticed an opening along the planklike bench just below the windows.

As I put my bag down on the bench, I noticed I was now looking down on the trees that had seemed so towering that morning as I arrived at the courthouse. I could still see the squirrels I'd observed on the way, too, only now they looked incredibly tiny, almost microscopic.

I said hello to the woman next to me, who turned out to be a reporter for the local PBS affiliate in Pensacola. She would occasionally give me helpful hints during the week of the trial, starting with, "You can plug in here," which she said matter-of-factly as she pointed to the makeshift board of outlets connected to the wires that had been strung around the room.

I thanked her and plugged my microphone cable into the board. I was now ready to record the criminal proceedings in the next room, where the lawyers were setting up and waiting for the judge to return. I checked my audio levels and corrected the trouble I was having with clarity, tinkering with the controls until I got it right.

In the room with me were some much better known reporters. CNN's Charles Jaco, who'd made his fame in the Persian Gulf War a few years earlier, stood off to my left, engaged in a conversation with a cameraman. Court TV's Kristen Jeanette Myers, who would later be a major legal commentator for the O. J. Simpson trial, was standing next to the unused judge's bench in the front of the room, talking to a couple of technicians.

Suddenly the forty or so reporters came to attention as Judge Parnham came back to his bench. We could see him on the monitors that were on some of the desks around the room. It seemed strange, having come all this way for the trial, to be now looking at it on TV. Folks all over the country who were watching Court TV could see everything that we could at exactly the same time.

For a moment, I thought, I could've stayed home and phoned this one in. Not only was that an unrealistic thought, but I immediately remembered my ultimate purpose in wanting to cover the trial. I was here to find out about the mysterious "something big" that I'd been warned about.

FOUR

The first day of the trial offered stunning revelations from prosecution witnesses and the assistant state's attorney, Jim Murray, who laid out the state's case against Griffin in simple, concrete terms during his opening remarks, making it sound like an open-and-shut case.

Murray read part of his statement and gave the rest from memory, careful all the while to make eye contact with jury members at the most important moments. He took his narrow reading glasses off and put them back on at different points, and purposefully strode about the room. He said in a loud and deliberate voice that witnesses would place Griffin near the scene, then at the scene carrying a large "Thirst Buster" cup from a nearby convenience store.

"Who ya gonna call? Thirst Busters," quipped one of the reporters in front of me, eliciting laughter from those in earshot on the left side of the press room. Schmidt suddenly shot me a look as if to say, "See, I told you so," about the rowdy reporters. He seemed surprised that I was among those laughing.

Our attention was immediately drawn back to the trial on the screens in front of us as Murray continued outlining the evidence against Griffin. Murray said that witnesses would describe seeing the husky Irishman concealing himself between a car and a truck in the parking lot of the clinic, and that another witness came out and told Griffin he was making the women inside nervous with his hanging around. He said all this happened right before the shooting of Dr. Gunn in that same parking lot. And Murray said that after the fatal attack, Griffin himself confessed to the deed, "Not once, but twice."

The assistant state's attorney said that just moments after the shooting took place, Griffin confessed to police officers on the other side of the building; and then, while in custody, he confessed again. In the pièce de résistance, Murray said that Griffin was overheard by a correctional officer telling his wife that he had shot Gunn because of his own newfound religious beliefs.

By the time Murray concluded, he had made a very powerful case. It sounded like it might be an airtight, slam-dunk situation for the jury. But I had been to enough trials to know that the defense often has very powerful evidence and observations of its own. This case would be no exception, with powerful allegations of conspiracy and double-cross, but first we would break for lunch.

FIVE

Flowing out with the sea of bodies to the elevators once more, I rode down to the ground floor and went out the same door I had come in four hours earlier. Very visible from the moment I was outside were Paul Hill and Andrew Cabot, the two protesters with whom I had a lunch date. They were back at their antics, waving their signs and shouting at all the passersby. They seemed to enjoy the shocked looks they engendered.

I had to wait for the pair to finish accosting the crowd before they turned to me. Hill then introduced me to a petite brunette named Donna Bray. He told her that I was a radio reporter and that I used to go to the Schencks' church. She smiled nicely and said, "Radio, huh? You're a good-looking guy, how come you're not on television?"

I said, "Well, I guess most people think I have the face for radio." Guffaws followed from the trio of radicals, and we started walking away from the building.

"Ya know, the feds are targeting us," Hill said suddenly.

"What do you mean?' I tentatively inquired. Hill said not a word, but took his finger and pointed up. At first I thought he was just pointing at the sky, but then I saw the marksmen atop the courthouse, and they were literally targeting us. Men at each of the corners were pointing their high-powered weapons directly at us.

A chill rushed over me and I stopped dead in my tracks. "What the heck?" I said, and I started to raise my hands in surrender.

Hill put his hands atop my arms and brought them down to my side. "It's all right," he said. "It's me they're after, not you. They're tryna intimidate us, that's all."

I felt like I was on pins and needles as we walked along, wondering if we were going to be shot. I could almost feel the bullets piercing my back. Hill saw how uncomfortable I was and tried to reassure me, but I was glad when we were out of bullet range and walking among the downtown lunch crowd that was unaware of the notorious few in their company.

We found a little café with brick walls and soft, dim lighting, a cozy spot to sit and talk, though this was hardly going to be the usual midday conversation. We selected sandwiches and drinks; three of the four of us picked some kind of iced tea. We grabbed a table that was off to the side of the restaurant where there were few people around.

At first we talked about the trial, but then I got right to the point. "I heard from Don Treshman that something really big is gonna happen at the end of this trial, and I'm wondering what it is."

Hill glanced at Cabot and they seemed to be fighting back grins. With a smug smirk fixed firmly in place, Hill said rather nonchalantly as we munched on our sandwiches and sipped our iced teas, "Well, what you're gonna see next now, brother, is an IRA-type reign of terror."

My jaw literally dropped and I sputtered out, "What do you mean?"

Turning stone-cold serious, Hill said, "There's too much pressure on all of us, too many people watching us to do anything major under direct orders from the national level, so what you're gonna see is individuals or small groups of people takin' action in their own hands to do what the leaders want to see done, but since there won't be any direct orders given, no one can prove conspiracy."

I felt myself going numb as I fought the urge to jump up and run from the room. I tried not to show how I was feeling as the three radicals stared at me, studying my every gesture and move to try to read what I was thinking about the plans they had shared with almost no one else. I was being given a special sneak preview into a strange new world, one I was not at all ready for.

So many things raced through my mind all at once. I wanted to say, "How the hell did you read the same Bible I did and come out at a vicious place like this? Are you nuts?" But instead I forced myself to remain as calm as I could. "You are quite serious about this, aren't you?" I asked.

"Deadly," Hill tersely replied.

"What do you think about this, Donna?" I asked, trying to divert attention away from myself and buy some time to gather my thoughts.

Donna said, "I know it sounds harsh, but you have to remember we're only trying to protect the unborn. The problem with most pro-lifers is that they say they believe that abortion is murder, but they don't act like it. It's time that we start defending innocent children. We can't let them keep killing four thousand babies each and every day and not try to stop it. We've tried all the legal means — the marches, the protests, the letters to the politicians — but now it's time to defend the babies, even if that means some people will have to use whatever force is necessary."

I said, "I don't mean to sound condescending, but I can't believe that a soft-spoken woman with your gentle demeanor is calling for such a militant use of force."

Suddenly Hill burst out loud laughing, and said, "You don't know her family, do you? Her brother-in-law, Michael Bray, is the author of the new book, *A Time to Kill*. He is our main spokesman for justifiable homicide."

Suddenly the name rang a bell, "Oh, is he the same guy who wrote *When Bricks Bleed, I'll Cry*?" I asked, referring to the rambling self-published diatribe that used Bible passages to justify blowing up abortion clinics and using every other violent tactic short of murder. Hill said that indeed he was the very same.

"I was given that book two years ago when I was in the secret communication and command center of Operation Rescue National during the Spring of Life protest in Buffalo, the one that got me into trouble with my career," I explained. "He wrote that book while he was in prison for conspiring to bomb clinics, didn't he?"

"Well, that's what they say," Hill said, apparently trying to be coy or clever.

Andrew Cabot, who'd been silent up to this point, asked me, "Where do you stand on all this?"

I tried to choose my words carefully, "I'm just as opposed to abortion as any of you, but I have to admit I don't understand how you can justify bombings or shootings based on the Bible. I know there's a lot of violence in the Old Testament, like in the Book of Joshua, but Jesus was totally committed to nonviolence. How do you explain that?"

Hill scrunched up his face with a sneer, saying in the kind of condescending manner that some adults use with a not-too-bright child, "Don't you read any good theology? Haven't you ever read R. J. Rushdoony or Gary North or any of the Reconstructionists?"

I was totally flabbergasted, "No, I'll be honest. I haven't read anything by those guys. I haven't even heard their names before."

Hill said, "You were a member of the Schencks' church and you never heard of those great men? You must've been asleep in some of the Schencks' sermons." The other two giggled briefly as I was left feeling more and more uncomfortable.

I asked Hill again for the names, and he explained impatiently. Rushdoony and his son-in-law, Gary North, had written theology books that called for Christians to stop ignoring the biggest part of their Bibles, the Old Testament. They and the other Reconstructionists had called for the church to take back its "rightful position" as supreme authority over all civil governments. Their agenda was not so much about opposing abortion as it was in converting America, and eventually the whole world, into a theocratic state in which God would tell the holy men what to do, and they in turn would give his commandments to the people. There would be no compromise, no dialogue, no debate. The choice for citizens would be a simple matter of "do or die" when God's holy men expressed the word of God for today.

Those who thought for themselves would be just as guilty of sin as the idolators Moses found when he brought God's Ten Commandments down from Mt. Sinai. To me the whole thing sounded incredible. To clarify, I asked Hill, "Does that mean that people could be arrested and possibly even executed for refusing to obey the men who would be in charge of communicating God's will?"

Hill said yes, and explained that we Christians were under an obligation to bring back the practices of the Old Testament law, including stoning people to death, and he said that abortionists would qualify for this kind of primitive punishment.

"Wouldn't there be others then, who also deserved this stoning?" I asked.

Cabot interjected, "Yeah, the sodomites for sure!"

Hill agreed that the "sodomites" (gay people) should surely be stoned to death, and he cited chapters and verses from the Bible condemning homosexuality. I couldn't believe what I was hearing, but I decided to continue with this line of reasoning to see how far it would go.

"Well, then, how about adulterers?" I said.

Hill and Cabot temporarily paused, and Cabot stayed quiet this time. Hill said, "In some situations, extreme situations, yes, adulterers would also have to be stoned."

I immediately noticed how much less enthusiastic the two were at the thought of adulterers being executed barbarically. There was none of the gleeful lustiness now; perhaps I'd struck too close to home.

Even though my head was spinning because of their outrageous theology, I asked one more question. "What other sinners' actions might warrant execution?"

Hill said nonchalantly that many other sins were worthy of the death penalty. "As the Bible says, children who curse their parents are worthy of the death penalty. And, of course, when people take the name of the Lord in vain, that's also clearly a capital offense according to the Scriptures. Just look at Leviticus and the rest of the Pentateuch [the first five books of the Bible]."

I could see that Hill knew his casual tone would make the provocative statements even more shocking, and I wondered for a moment if he really believed what he was telling me. Yet it wasn't as far-fetched as it seemed on the surface, because his thinking was only the extreme fulfillment of the Biblical literalism that was the theological and philosophical base of the entire born-again community. I'm not saying that anyone else was calling for the literal reinstitution of stoning or other Old Testament legal practices, but that all of us in the Religious Right did think that the key to our problems was to return to biblical teachings and values. Hill and the Reconstructionists merely took the concept to the nth degree.

I would find out later that even though Rushdoony and North were not familiar names known to the average born-again Christian, their writings had apparently influenced many popular televangelists.

According to the Reconstructionists, Christians were called by God to take dominion over the world and reestablish the one true church so that Jesus could return to the earth in his glorious second coming. Their task was to make the ancient prophecies a modern-day reality. Like the Blues Brothers, they were on a mission from God.

Cabot said, "You're like so many of the other pro-lifers [referring to the rescuers]. You don't get it. Man, this isn't the time to be sitting down outside o' clinics and gettin' your butt dragged off to jail, especially with the way they're usin' the FACE [Freedom of Access to Clinics Entrance] laws and the Rico laws; it's too much overkill. This is the time to take action that'll stop those doctors dead in their tracks."

"The way Griffin did last year?" I said, referring to the assassination.

"That was a start, but it's gonna seem like small potatoes after you see what's comin'," Hill predicted.

I could sense that Hill wanted to tell me more, but I couldn't get myself to play along well enough to earn his full trust. Even a poker face wasn't enough to get him to talk; he wanted me to show signs of being a full-fledged "Christian soldier," but I wasn't up to the task. My lack of knowledge about the Reconstructionists had been a clear sign that I was not fully one of them. They would have to keep their guards up with me to a certain extent.

Throughout the conversation that day, it seemed that Hill had a great deal of contempt for nearly everyone. He and his friends made it clear that they thought the pro-choice people were "baby-killing scum"; that the authorities in our police departments, courts, and legislatures

were "accomplices to murder"; and that the people who called themselves pro-life were a bunch of buffoons who didn't know how to get
the job done.

They seemed to hold almost as low a regard for people who were pro-
life activists, but who didn't understand or agree with their views on the
necessity of using force to stop abortions. In their view I was in that category at the moment, but my persistence would eventually pay off.

Yet they seemed to like me in spite of my ignorance. That's why Hill
was willing to lower himself to explain his lofty theological views to an
obviously slow-witted semi-Christian like me (even though I was in
good company, since 99.9 percent of all Christians were in that same
category in Hill's book).

Hill told me that Gary North was the writer he admired most, and
said that North was challenging Christians to recognize how far they
had come from following the Bible in their approach to law, government, and the church. He said that the church needed to get back to the
unified body that Jesus had always intended it to be, and that it had
been until its leaders grew so corrupt that the Reformation had to be
launched.

Hill asked me if I realized how many of my own views were from the
teachings of secular people and institutions rather than from the Bible.
When I asked him to explain, he said that my obvious revulsion to the
idea of shooting an abortionist revealed that I had adopted the "namby-
pamby" Christianity that had been popularized by the secular influence
in the church. He said that the whole notion that the church was just supposed to be kind and compassionate was foisted upon us by liberals who
failed to understand that God's people had always been committed to the
use of force and that the Bible said, "God is a man of war."

"But didn't Jesus take us past all that?" I asked.

Hill was ready with his answer. "Jesus himself said he did not want
to abolish one jot or tittle of the ancient law, but to fulfill the Old Testament covenant with the new covenant of his own blood. He was on a
specific mission to come and shed his blood for us, but he never said
that we were to be pacifist. He knocked the tables of the money
changers over, and his church has always been ready to fight just wars

and to take whatever action is necessary, not precluding the use of force, to bring justice and righteousness to this sinful world."

He could see I was surprised at his answer and the intensity with which he delivered it. He went on to point out that the church had never been pacifistic, except in a few small denominations, like the Quakers. Otherwise, the church had always been willing to fight, whether it was in the Crusades or in the wars of this century.

"Would you have been a pacifist in World War II when Hitler was marching across Europe?" he asked.

I admitted that I would have served, and indeed had been a commissioned Air Force and New York Air National Guard officer for four years in the 1980s and would have gone to war if called upon.

I pointed out that there was a huge difference between obeying orders as a military officer trying to protect my country and becoming a vigilante.

Hill challenged my assumptions with a little parable. "If you were walking through a park and you saw a sniper shooting little children, you'd want to stop him. But if you called the cops and they said that the sniper was simply exercising his 'right to choose' and that they couldn't possibly interfere because of the sniper's right to privacy, you wouldn't accept that, would you," he said rhetorically.

I shook my head, and he continued, "If there were no other way to stop that sniper and he clearly told you he was just going to keep pickin' off those kids one by one, and you watched him do it over and over again, and you had a gun in your hands, you know you would eventually shoot him, wouldn't you?"

"It seems so far-fetched," I said.

Hill admitted that of course it did, but it was exactly what was going on with the little children who were caught in the crosshairs of the abortionists whom the police refused to stop. "The only difference between the children being murdered in my hypothetical story, and the little ones being murdered by the abortionists in real life is the fact that the unborn aren't seen as human even by pro-lifers who claim to believe that they are, but act as though the abortionist is not as bad as the sniper."

Hill's analogy obviously had holes in it, and I certainly wasn't buying it all the way, but he had deeply touched a very sensitive nerve within me. I had been calling abortion murder as every other pro-lifer did, from the controversial activists of Operation Rescue to the more "respectable" National Right to Life Committee. At one point, I had even been one of the people who had an "Abortion Kills Children" bumper sticker on the back of my car.

Hill, Cabot, and Bray talked with me for over an hour, and pleaded with me with such great intensity that I could really feel what they were feeling. I knew they were wrong, but I wasn't sure what to say to convince them, and I knew I had to keep them talking to me if I was eventually going to get more information from them about the mysterious event that was to take place later that week. It was a very tight rope I was walking on, and one false move could kill the dialogue.

Hill, for all his intensity, seemed more balanced than Cabot. When he spoke of the coming IRA-type reign of terror Hill had mentioned, Cabot seemed to drift off into some kind of euphoric state. I had never met anyone like him before, and he unnerved me. I got the impression that Cabot was just itching to pull a trigger for Christ.

Hill, however, had a way of somehow reaching out to me at just the times I was ready to call it quits. He had a strain of natural compassion mixed in with his extreme views that made him a little more appealing and human. His appearance and manners seemed to belie his bold brand of extremist theology.

He looked so average, so harmless. I strongly suspected at the time that it would be Cabot rather than Hill who would be the trigger man for the cause if what I suspected came to pass. Only later would I realize that a mild-mannered, blond man with a next-door-neighbor quality could be a monster; that is exactly how Jeffrey Dahmer was described before people knew he was a psychopathic killer. And Hill, who fit the same outward description before he made his move, would prove to be as cool as any murderer could be after he crossed the line into his own killing spree.

But for the moment it was Cabot, with his jittery movements and lusty talk of guns and his bitterness toward the government and the media, who scared me the most. Hill seemed like the one who might pull back if given the chance. I decided I would try to gain Hill's trust and carefully try to steer him away from the course he was following.

Hill must have been feeling that he also had an obligation to try to steer me away from the course I was following; I noticed that he was trying hard to take me under his wing. I felt like he was trying to be a big brother to me, and there was something strangely touching about that because, as the oldest of seven kids, it was the one thing I'd never had.

Hill had a clear sense of his vision and purpose, and he was very articulate in outlining it. His zealous commitment to his cause was vaguely appealing in some way I didn't fully understand.

As we walked back from lunch that day, Hill agreed to meet with me again and to further explain the Reconstructionist theology that would make clear to me why it was necessary to kill in the name of life, and I would get much more in the bargain. Hill's brand of theology would shock me to my core and force me to reexamine everything I held near and dear, everything I had based my faith upon up until that moment.

But in the meantime, I had to go back to the press room. As I set up my equipment once again, I found myself so distracted and rattled that I couldn't seem to stay focused. I felt as though I'd just been in the presence of the most disturbed minds I had ever encountered, and yet I had to admit to myself that there was something strangely compelling about Hill.

The thought revolted me, but he and I were beginning to make an unexpected connection. I could feel the power of his commitment to his cause. I could feel the great energy that he was experiencing in his fanatically single-minded focus on fighting for the cause. I was suddenly getting a powerful insight into why men of good conscience could slip into such horrific groups as the IRA or the Ku Klux Klan. There was an intoxicating rush of righteous wrath that seemed capable of lifting a person higher than all of humanity, higher than mere mortality. It was a strange sensation, but an eerily haunting and darkly appealing one.

I couldn't fully admit it to myself yet, but I felt drawn to the intensity I'd experienced in Hill's company. I suddenly felt a little like a moth drawn to a flame. I knew it could destroy me, yet it was so mesmerizing

I wanted it the way an addict wants to get just one more taste of his chosen poison.

Shakespeare said, "Tomorrow and tomorrow and tomorrow; life creeps on at this petty pace," but Hill was offering a chance to rise above all that. He was urging us to tap into our most primal urges by giving into the immediacy of a cobralike strike with complete disregard for everything else. In exchange we would get a rush of adrenaline and power that would come from taking the kind of violent revenge most men only dream about taking when they feel an injustice has been done.

Hill was offering a chance to be a revolutionary, a radical, a warrior. He might have been Christian, but he was offering me a chance to join him in raw savagery against those who were not of our tribe. He had tapped into some ancient crevice in my own mind that I didn't even know existed. I knew that if I joined him, for one precious moment I would be free of the tedium of this life, transcending the plodding pace of living.

At that point I only sensed these things; I was not yet ready to articulate it. But I knew I would have to pretend to go along with Hill and company, and that was going to be tricky. I had heard of undercover cops who had been trapped inside the role they were playing in their efforts to snare the bad guys. They could get to a critical point where they saw the false identity as their true one, and their true identity was lost as their inability to hold steadfast to reality made them cross the line into some wicked deed that would separate them from their families and all of civilized society.

I thought of the infamous Patty Hearst case, in which she started out pretending to be on the side of her captors and ended up joining them in an armed bank robbery, a mistake that cost her many years in prison.

I had always thought that that kind of thing could only happen to unbalanced people, but now I was beginning to understand. My German ancestors had fallen prey to the power of their charismatic chancellor, Adolf Hitler, and throughout history, zealots and revolutionaries held a magnetic pull over large numbers of people.

Zealots and criminals got something out of their misdeeds that the rest of the world simply did not understand. They were tapping into their most primitive urges, ones our ancestors felt back in the warlike atmosphere of ancient times, and men who played the part sometimes got hooked on it.

I felt it instinctively, but I also felt certain that I must resist it, that I could resist it because I was neither unbalanced nor a bloodthirsty savage. I was not going to join Hill on the ramparts of the revolution he was launching in his own mind. I would allow myself to draw near and play make-believe with him, but then I would find out what he was up to with his talk of IRA-type terror, and I would find a way to stop him. Surely, this was America, and there would have to be a way to stop him, right?

My blithe certainty would not prove correct, but it was for the best that I didn't know on that day in Pensacola what I know now. If I had, I might not have taken the risks necessary to be faithful to my determination to stop the "something big" that was coming.

How lucky I was that I'd been tipped off by Donald Treshman, or else I would have simply gotten away from Hill and friends as quickly as possible. If it hadn't been for Treshman, the plans that Hill and company were making would have been too repulsive for me to stay with long enough to find out what they could tell me.

But the information I would need was still not available to me, and I wasn't certain how I could get it. I had to find others who could help me, because I could not count on Hill and company opening up enough to give me the details I would need to have in order to go the cops. I was becoming obsessed with unlocking the mysteries that now seemed to be confirmed just a little bit more at each turn of events.

Meanwhile, back in the press room, another antic by a colleague brought me back down to earth. One of my fellow reporters came walking in with a huge "Thirst Buster" cup, took a loud slurp, and said, "Ah, there's nothing like a good Thirst Buster!" The whole room cracked up with raucous laughter at the spoof on the day's earlier testimony about Griffin carrying a Thirst Buster to the scene of the crime.

I looked over at my new filmmaking friend, Hans, and was pleasantly surprised to see that even he was laughing. The room stayed noisy after the brief touch of comedy, and the mood seemed almost festive right up until the murder trial resumed.

We were drawn back to the proceedings when Griffin's lead defense attorney, white-haired Bob Kerrigan, rose to offer the opening statements on behalf of his client. My fellow reporters quickly quieted their rambunctious chatter in order to hear what Kerrigan could possibly have to say to defend someone who had sounded so guilty when the DA's office laid out its case.

What he said was a bombshell. Kerrigan suggested that not only was his client innocent, but that he had been framed in a conspiracy led by two other men, John Burt, a well-known antiabortion protest leader, and his faithful sidekick, Donnie Gratton. Kerrigan said an abortion clinic worker would testify that she saw Donnie Gratton walking back and forth in front of the clinic, and thought that he had been the one who shot the doctor.

Suddenly it seemed I was in the middle of a real spider's web. I had been tipped off to the possible coming violence by Burt's superior in Rescue America; now the defense was implying Burt might have masterminded the first murder. I immediately realized that if the defense's allegations were true, I might have stumbled right into the middle of a murderous group of men who had been involved in the original murder, and whatever was coming that would "make it look like small potatoes," as Paul Hill had put it.

I wondered if it were possible that Griffin had been a mere patsy to take the fall for Burt and Gratton. It seemed like a long shot, but it was worth checking out. And perhaps, in the process, I would find out more about the "something big" that Burt's boss had mentioned.

In the meantime, Judge Parnham told Jim Murray he could begin to introduce his witnesses that day, and the assistant state's attorney called the wife of the defendant to the stand as the very first witness for the prosecution. Patricia Griffin came forward slowly, seeming reluctant. As she put her hand on the Bible to be sworn in, she looked like she was in serious pain. No doubt the tension and trauma of the year-long ordeal was taking a heavy toll.

She sat down in the witness chair to the left of the judge and brushed her wreath of thick, wavy brunette hair from her moon-shaped face. Her features were small and round, her clothes humble and modest. She looked like the typical thirtyish wife and mother she had been until that fateful day one year earlier.

Two microphones secured on the outer edges of the witness stand pointed in toward her mouth to record her every word; one microphone was for the trial's court reporter and the other for the media feed for the press room.

She spoke softly and tentatively as Murray shot a rapid-fire string of questions at her in his staccato style. She was asked about samples of his handwriting and other issues that seemed to be of secondary relevance, but then the state's spokesman picked up a gun.

Holding the revolver high enough in the air that everyone could see it, Murray approached the witness after asking Judge Parnham for permission and announcing the state's first exhibit to be placed in evidence. The murder weapon had obviously been brought up first because of its powerful symbolism as well as its factual worth in the case.

Seeing Murray wave the gun around drew the attention of the jury and everyone else in the courtroom. Its shiny steel muzzle glinted with the light as he moved it around. It was the most potent visual symbol possible of the murder. It made the murder more real than anything else could have, short of the victim's corpse being dragged in and dropped lifeless in front of the jury.

Murray was a master of the moment as he shifted the gun around from hand to hand. We could feel the weight of the weapon, see its unusual crisscross handle, the barrel where the bullets had been lodged until they exploded out of the muzzle, and the trigger that had been squeezed three times in rapid succession.

Reluctantly, Patricia Griffin admitted to Murray that she recognized the gun. Murray pressed on to get more concrete concessions from Mrs. Michael Griffin. She admitted that she had seen her husband with the gun the very night before the murder, and that he took the gun with him as he went to work the graveyard shift.

Patricia Griffin looked like she might collapse as she slowly stepped down from the witness box, steadying herself with her left hand upon the oak rail atop the side of the stand. Her head hanging low, she slunk away from the scene looking as though she wished she could just die right then and there.

Murray chose as his second witness the person who was second in closeness to Michael Griffin, his own father. Dr. Thomas Griffin, a local dentist with salt-and-pepper hair and large-framed glasses that gave him a serious, studious look, came forward. His step was quicker than his daughter-in-law's had been, and his movements were snappier as he raised his right hand and took his oath.

Dressed in more expensive attire, a gray suit and subdued multicolored tie, the dentist appeared the picture of propriety, the reliable resident of Pensacola that he had always been. He, too, was visibly uncomfortable at times, but didn't seem as devastated as his daughter-in-law had been.

Again Murray flashed the gun, asking the witness if he recognized the weapon. Dr. Griffin admitted that he did. When Murray asked him to elaborate, he said that he had purchased the gun, but gave it to his son to use for a gun safety class in January of 1993, just two months before the murder.

Murray made a point of telling the jury that the serial number on the gun receipt that Dr. Griffin had provided to his office, and which he now submitted as his second piece of physical evidence, was an exact match for the gun found at the scene of the crime.

When Murray finished with the witness and Kerrigan declined to cross-examine, Dr. Griffin got up and walked away. Briefly, he glanced at his son with a look that revealed his concern over what he had just said, and the damage that he obviously had not wanted to cause his child. I suddenly thought of my own young sons and hoped I'd never have to be in the kind of position Dr. Griffin had just been in.

I found myself wondering whether their family had been dysfunctional in some way, which might have sown the seeds for the violent act of which the younger Griffin now stood accused, but from what I would learn during my week in Pensacola the Griffin family was pretty average. There were no warning signs that had been obviously overlooked before the fatal shooting.

But I thought to myself, I'll bet that Griffin's father wishes now that he had never given his son a gun. I couldn't help wondering: If Dr. Griffin had gotten rid of the weapon instead of giving it to his son, would the only thing the younger man stand accused of shooting off be his mouth? I told myself then and there that I would never give my own sons a firearm.

SEVEN

J u d g e Parnham announced a brief recess so that the prosecution could bring in models of the crime scene. I darted into the hall to look for someone whom I had not yet met, but whose photos I had seen. Standing at the far end of the hallway was the now notorious John Burt, answering questions from some people I did not recognize. I could see that there were a few members of the press standing close enough to hear his whiskey rasp.

He was a man who obviously had some hard miles on him, with deep lines cutting through his face and a pair of sagging jowls beneath his gray beard. There was something cruel in his expression, too, but it seemed to be burned into his face permanently.

The weather-beaten, craggy-faced, fifty-three-year-old Burt looked tired, but he seemed perfectly at home under the full-court press by the media. He was a man who thrived on, and some say lived for, the publicity that accompanied his radical activities.

Burt had learned that the way to get quoted in the press, especially broadcast media, was to say outrageous things. It was a tactic he'd picked up in his days with the Ku Klux Klan. The more he shocked, the more coverage he got.

As I got closer to where he was standing, I heard him loudly saying that the accusations against him were completely false. "I been slandered by that no-account Kerrigan, a dirty lawyer's trick to try ta win a case when he ain't got the fac's on his side. [pause] Ya'll should know better than ta take the word of a lawyer as gospel. Me an' Donnie Gratton ain't got nuthin' to do with this here crime. And we don't support killin' whether it's babies that are gettin' aborted or a doctor gettin' shot. [pause] The really important thing about this whole trial is that folks need ta get their focus back on the fact that there are four thousand babies gettin' killed ev'ry day in Uh-merica, thirty million in all since *Roe* v. *Wade*, but only one abortionist got killed. Thirty million ta one; that's what the score is!"

I realized that Burt was under the judge's gag order, but that what he was saying was being recorded by the reporters nearby. He just wasn't talking directly to them. No one could say he was disobeying the judge's orders.

It would've been obvious to me that this was far from his first time in the media limelight even if I hadn't seen some of his previous clippings. At least this time he wasn't dressed in battle fatigues, like he was in a photo in a 1993 issue of *Time* magazine. And he wasn't carrying a pickled fetus in a jar. That had been one of his favorite tactics, because it always got a huge reaction from passersby. According to one man I'd interviewed on the phone before going to Pensacola, Burt's delight with the horror expressed by onlookers at the display of a dead fetus was not unlike that of a child who shocks adults with the sight of a dead mouse or a living snake.

Burt had clearly perfected the art of the sound bite; he even knew when to pause between sentences so that the media could make their cut in the tape at just the right length. It was something that required practice, as I knew from my own previous work as a media coordinator for Operation Rescue.

I had my tape deck with me and let it run while Burt talked, but the frustrating thing about my deal with the people at the BBC was that they only wanted my tape cuts; I wasn't doing any reports. Sometimes that was what ABC wanted from me, too. But this time it was incredibly ironic since I had what looked like a fantastic story.

I couldn't tell the story yet, because I didn't want to tip my hand and, frankly, at this point I was having trouble believing this whole strange cast of characters myself. Still, I knew that these horrifying people were also incredibly fascinating in the darkest way possible. Little did I know the best (and worst) was yet to come.

The reporters and others soon drifted away, and I was alone with Burt and his associate, Donnie Gratton. I walked up and said, "Rev. Burt [he was an ordained minister], I'm Jerry Reiter; you don't know me, but you might know my pastors, Rob and Paul Schenck."

"Oh, yeah, sure. They're good guys, good young men o' God, and they been writin' some good things about me. I just seen their newsletter where they tole' about the good things me and Donnie are doin' with 'Our Father's House' [the home for unwed mothers the two men ran with the help of their wives]."

I had also seen the Schenck brothers' ministry newsletter before arriving. They had said that John Burt was a much-maligned minister who was unjustly attacked by the "liberal media." They said that his actions on behalf of the unborn were heroic and that he should be praised, not condemned.

I would find the Schencks' assessment of Burt just as far off base as I had found their earlier assessment of Operation Rescue. They had told me about the peaceful protesters, but ignored the more militant factions altogether. Their accounts of Burt's intentions and tactics were selectively chosen, to say the least.

Burt could be warm and even solicitous—he was that way to me this day—but later I would see other sides. He asked what brought me to the trial. I told him that I had risked my career in Buffalo for the pro-life cause, and was now working for a news organization in Houston, Texas. I explained that I was doing freelance work covering the trial, but I neglected to mention that I was trying to find out if he had masterminded the murder of Dr. Gunn, and what the "big thing" was that Treshman had forewarned me about.

Instead, we talked briefly about the way the pro-life movement was being portrayed in the press, then he introduced me to Donnie Gratton. I couldn't help but wonder if I was shaking the hand of the man who had pulled the trigger to kill Dr. Gunn, as Griffin's defense attorney had implied.

Gratton was a bear of a man, with wild, dark hair and a big, bushy beard flecked with a little gray. His grip was powerful, a man who had obviously done a lot of physical work in his day. According to a *Pensacola News Journal* story Gratton had, by his own admission, been a drug addict and alcoholic who was on the road to a life of crime before he met John Burt, the man who had gotten him "saved" and eventually ordained, though neither man was employed by a church.

Burt was Gratton's "father in the Lord," a term used to describe the person who had told you how to become a born-again Christian and who guided you in your days as a "baby Christian," the time when you were new to the concepts and lifestyle of fundamentalism.

It was striking that Burt, a former KKK member and a man who still carried great anger within his heart over various perceived injustices, was anyone's spiritual father. But it was beginning to appear that this was a case where the nut had not fallen far from the tree, at least if Kerrigan's accusations held up or if Treshman's tip and Hill's hints pointed to anything nearly as ominous as they implied.

I knew that my time in the hall with Burt and Gratton would be brief, so I pressed for a time when I could sit down with the two of them and interview them. Burt said, "Well, ah'm under a gag order from the judge not to talk about the trial to the press, but if ya just wanna come by an' talk a bit, I guess ya could do that."

He seemed to have a twinkle in his eye as he suggested that we "talk a bit." It struck me that he was probably enjoying skirting the judge's order with his fellow Christian brother. He and Donnie would do what they wanted, court orders be damned.

I was willing to play the game, too, because I wanted to see if I could get to the bottom of all this. And I continued to feel a sense that the clock was ticking as we moved closer to whatever was coming.

Burt told me to call him at home the next night, "and we'll see what we can work out. Ya'll keep this on the QT now," he said in a hushed drawl. He shook my hand once again and was gone off in a hurry back into the courtroom. He didn't want to miss a minute of the action.

EIGHT

As I turned and headed back toward the press room, I bumped into Hans Schmidt again. "Oh, I see you got to talk to John Burt. Vas he as scary as the lawyer made him out to be?"

"I can tell you better after I get back from visiting with him at his house."

"You are joking vith me, no?" Hans said.

I replied, "No," and started to walk back to the press room.

Hans followed me and tugged at the back of my shirt sleeve, "Hey, vait, you've gotta talk to me. Tell me about this thing."

Realizing I had his interest, I was enjoying the tease of pulling away, and I knew he really wanted the info I had, so I said half-jokingly, "I'll tell you all about it if you buy me dinner tonight."

"You got a deal," he said with earnest enthusiasm.

Hans followed me back into the press room and, just a few moments after I sat back down in my usual spot, he joined me.

It dawned on me that Hans didn't look like the rest of the reporters there. He had a bohemian style of dress, unkempt brown hair, and an obvious and innocent fascination with the whole trial.

"You have never been to a murder trial before, have you?" I whispered.

"No, usually I'm making films of make-believe stories or sometimes industrial movies; boring compared with this."

I told him that since he was going to buy me dinner that night I'd tell him my war stories about murder trials, the radical Right, and John Burt. He looked as excited as a little child on Christmas Eve. I had to fight back a laugh because I was used to my jaded colleagues, and the wide-eyed response of this make-believe moviemaker, so new to America, struck me as amusing and endearing.

As the trial was gaveled back into order, the prosecution took a different tack, moving to the more remote testimony first and then moving in toward the most relevant, saving the most powerful testimony for the time when it would be most effective. The witnesses were brought forward in rapid succession.

First, Larry Bailey, a grizzled veteran of the Pensacola police department, testified that he saw the blue Chevy belonging to Michael Griffin parked in a lot west of the Cordova Square plaza where the shooting took place. Then came dark-haired Debbie Slack, an office worker who testified that Griffin came into her neurology office near the scene of the crime to pay a bill the Griffin family owed; it was around 8:40 A.M., about an hour before the shooting.

Marsha Ray, a Northwest Florida Home Health Agency nurse, looked like she had a case of stage fright as she took the stand and told how she saw Michael Griffin apparently trying to conceal himself between a high-rise truck and a car. She thought it was suspicious at the time, and sent her coworker Mike Jenkins out to ask Griffin what he was doing there.

Jenkins, a muscular but baby-faced file clerk, talked to Griffin and told him that he was making some of the women in the health agency uncomfortable. He testified that Griffin claimed to be waiting for his wife, but pliantly said that he would move along.

To continue placing Griffin closer and closer to the scene, Murray called Lisa Plotter to the stand. The health agency worker watched as

Griffin did indeed move on after her coworker Jenkins spoke to him. She saw him head to an office near the abortion clinic, and then saw him walk briskly toward the parking lot. Moments later she heard shots being fired—*blam, blam, blam!*

Prosecutor Murray used three-dimensional models of Cordova Square, where the clinic was located, as a visual aid during each person's testimony to show the jury where Griffin was in relation to the shooting. He had a full-color, cardboard scale model, about a foot high and four feet long, of the entire area.

Christina Holland, a beautiful brunette coworker of the three previous witnesses, added that she also saw Griffin acting suspiciously between the truck and the car, and then he walked briskly toward the clinic.

Steve Powell, a lawn maintenance worker who was nearby when he heard the shots being fired, turned in time to see Michael Griffin dropping a gun from his hand. At Murray's request, Powell pointed toward the defendant to verify that this was indeed the man he had seen at the shooting.

It was the most powerful moment thus far, but then defense attorney Bob Kerrigan jumped to his feet for a cross-examination, and asked Powell about the description of the shooter he originally gave to police. As Kerrigan read the police report aloud, it was obvious that Powell was describing someone substantially different than Michael Griffin. It was a strong point for the defense.

The prosecution's most devastating testimony of the day immediately followed. Husky jail guard Brenda Fuqua took the stand. In her matter-of-fact, almost masculine style, she told the court that she was in the room with Griffin and his wife, Patricia, when they held a very intimate and emotional conversation about the murder on the day after the shooting. She had been assigned to guard the high-visibility prisoner, and she clearly heard Griffin tell his wife that his religious convictions had led him to shoot the doctor.

Kerrigan strongly objected, and told the judge that he believed Fuqua was lying. He called for her to be investigated for perjury. He also raised objections about her prior testimony at a hearing the month before, and the fact that she had not come forward for almost a year. He said that because she had waited so long to come forward, they should be suspicious of her credibility.

Kerrigan also had Patricia Griffin recalled to the stand to tell the court that the guard had promised her three times that anything she and her husband discussed would be kept in the room, and not reported to anyone.

Murray battled back. He reminded the judge that Fuqua had already explained that she had been under the impression that the conversation was privileged information, but that once she realized she had an obligation to come forward, she did. He also reassured the jury that the guard was a very credible witness.

He again asked simple, clear questions of the guard. "Why don't you just tell me what you claim you heard Mr. Griffin say?"

"He didn't do it for notoriety and he didn't do it to get any public kind of response or recognition."

"That's everything you heard him say?"

"No, sir," she answered.

"Okay, well, tell me what else," Kerrigan pressed.

Fuqua concluded with the devastating words she had heard Griffin say, "I killed him because of my beliefs and convictions, and if I spend the rest of my life in jail it will be worth it to save one baby."

NINE

There was a moment of silence in the courtroom as everyone was hit by the power of the guard's words. It was clear to everyone that the testimony was damning. One of my colleagues in the press room put it best: "Well, that about does it for this trial. Point, game, set, match—it's all over, baby! Time for the fat lady to sing!"

Peals of laughter poured out of the press room. Even Hans laughed, but he said, "I can't believe ve're laughing at such a serious time."

I asked him, "Did you ever read Superman comics, by any chance?"

"Yah, I'm a huge Superman fan, but vhy are you asking me dat?"

I asked, "You remember how there was a 'bizarro' world where everything was similar, but strangely twisted around?"

He said that he loved that part of the Superman series.

"Well, look around. You're in the bizarro version of the courtroom. This room is an exact mirror image of the one where the trial is set, but you see that technician from Court TV up there on the judge's seat? He's got a Burger

King crown on that he brought back from lunch today instead of a judge's robe. His feet are sprawled across the desk while he tweaks the knobs, and those guys around him working on the technical stuff for TV look like his bizarro courtroom assistants, with their frumpy flannel shirts and jeans instead of the stuffy suits and ties out there in the real courtroom.

"Out there in the real courtroom, everyone is deadly serious as the lawyers face off in a game with life-and-death consequences, while here in the bizarro courtroom you can see two of our colleagues over there totally engrossed in a totally meaningless game of checkers."

Hans laughed.

"And out there in the real courtroom they observe the real trial, while in here we watch TV, and everyone knows TV is all a part of entertainment, and just turns everything, even matters of life and death, into a commodity to hold the public's attention long enough to sell them deodorant and beer and mouthwash."

"Oh, my gosh, you're right, that's brilliant!" Hans replied, with great relish. He slapped his knee in delight.

"You pointed out that we're not a serious bunch in the media, but you're wrong," I said. "We are when we have to be, but we see the absurdity of life, too. We are the working women and men who bring the world the information it craves in this information age, and we see more tragedy than most people ever do, but that's why we need our comedy; it keeps us balanced. It keeps us sane in a sometimes insane world. So, you see, sometimes it's we who are in the bizarro world, and sometimes it's the so-called real world out there that is truly strange and twisted."

Hans was so delighted with my impromptu observations that he gave me a private standing ovation. I laughed and then said, "Let's go to dinner. If you like my little commentary, you're gonna love my war stories over a drink."

"I can't wait to hear vhat else you vill tell me. I'm beginning to think you might have a future in Hollywood even more dan me. You're just vhat they're looking for: a clever, comic mad genius!"

TEN

Hans and I went to dinner that night at a seafood house not far from the courthouse. We looked like comic strip characters Mutt and Jeff as we entered the restaurant. Hans Schmidt was short and frail looking, while I towered over him with my six-foot-four, 210-pound frame.

Hans asked me, "Did you ever play basketball or football?"

I laughed and said, "I get the basketball question all the time, but I played soccer in the fall and downhill skiing in the winter. I worked at a ski resort all through college, and eventually became a ski instructor."

Hans said that he was surprised I played soccer because he didn't think of it as an American sport. He said that he played it a little back in Germany.

We were happy to see that the restaurant wasn't very crowded, and we were seated right away. Our very attractive blonde waitress joked with us as she served dinner. Hans said, "I think she likes you."

I quipped, "What's not to like?"

"You are a very confident person, aren't you?"

"Yes," I said. "But that's just part of the picture. See, although I got the German name from my father's father,

I'm three quarters Irish. I grew up in south Buffalo, New York, in a little Irish Catholic ghetto where everyone asks you what parish you're from, and we Irish people spend half our time bragging about ourselves and the other half putting ourselves down with a self-deprecating humor that can be quite disarming."

"Irish people are usually good storytellers, too, yes?"

I said, "That definitely holds up for me. I can remember almost every story, joke, or song I've ever heard, but don't ask me where I put my keys a few minutes ago."

The waitress returned with our drinks and took our food orders. She talked to us for a moment and asked if we were from the area.

Hans said, "He's from Houston, and I'm from Los Angeles. Ve're here to cover the murder trial."

When the waitress left, Hans said, "She seemed impressed about our vork and ev'rything."

"Yeah, thanks for impressing her so much, she'll think we're gettin' the big bucks at the network and now we'll have to leave her a big tip."

The levity stopped abruptly as soon as Hans inquired, "So tell me some of these var stories you mentioned. I vant to hear."

I wasn't sure how much to tell him about the "something big" or the key players I suspected to be involved, so I decided to start with my own background. "Believe it or not, I once worked for an antiabortion group, a radical one. Have you ever heard of Operation Rescue?"

"Of course, they're the men who block the doors for the vomen that vant to have abortions. I have been traveling around the country because my boss, Tony Kaye, wants to make this major documentary I vas telling you about. Ve have over five hundred hours of footage."

"Well, you're gonna love this, then. I was working as a news reporter for the ABC affiliate station in Buffalo. I was also a member of a local charismatic church. You know, the kind where they talk in tongues and have those huge healing services and lots and lots of singing."

"I have been to such services. They sometimes sing for an hour before they do the rest of the service."

I nodded and confirmed, "My local church was pastored by these twin brothers, Rob and Paul Schenck. They were close friends of the man who started the whole Operation Rescue thing, this really outrageous guy named Randall Terry."

"I have him on tape from the big protest in Vichita, Kansas, back in the summer of 1991," Hans told me.

I said, "You're kidding! Wichita was such a huge protest, over two thousand arrests, and it lasted for several weeks. How long were you there?"

Hans explained that he was out there twice for a total of three weeks. "Some of those protests are so crazy. The people got on their hands and knees like dogs and crawled up to the clinics, but most of 'em got arrested vhile they were trying to get to the clinic. Then you've got the whole scene of cops grabbing little old ladies and slappin' the handcuffs on 'em, and carrying them, and sometimes these big husky men would get arrested and it would take two or three cops."

"Yeah, the rescuers never go willingly," I said. "They just go limp. They make the cops carry them 'cause it takes more time that way, and that gives the other protesters time to get to the clinic doors, and block access."

"Do you know who started that technique?" Hans asked.

I said, "Yeah, Randall Terry back in around 1986 when he formed Operation Rescue."

Hans disagreed. "That's vhat ev'rybody thinks, but that is not so. I interviewed this guy down in Florida, Ed Martin, who told me the real story. He said that before Randall Terry came along there was a bunch of Catholic women who were liberals and college-educated ladies who used to protest the Vietnam War with sit-ins and protests and stuff. Well, anyway, because they were Catholic, they wanted to protest abortions. So this Catholic lady named Joan Andrews started these little groups of ladies who would use the peaceful protest form of passive civil disobedience from the 1960s to try to stop abortion.

"Andrews told them that they vould imitate the fetuses when the police tried to arrest them by taking up the fetal position and being passive like the fetus vould. They started to get some press coverage for their tactics, and some fundamentalists began to join the Catholics. The fundamentalists vere starting to vork with the Catholics until Randall Terry came along. He stole the concept and changed it all around. The emphasis had been on peaceful civil disobedience, but he created the military sounding name Operation Rescue, and put only fundamentalist preachers in power."

"And they're all men in this supposedly women's issue," I said.

Hans asked why that was the case: "Don't they know that makes them look bad?"

"I asked the same thing myself in Buffalo when Operation Rescue was planning the big protest there. We had a local spokeswoman who was excellent, a Ph.D. candidate from the State University of New York at Buffalo who was very articulate, but when I asked about having her take a more prominent national role during the protest in Buffalo, the national leaders brushed my suggestions aside intentionally. It wasn't until I spent some time in the Operation Rescue headquarters that I realized what was going on. Operation Rescue isn't just about stopping abortion. It's run by a group of men who want to turn America into a theocratic state."

Hans scrunched up his face. "Vhat is this theocratic?"

"It means a nation run by God. The model is from the Old Testament, where God would pick a king, and the people had to obey."

"Ah, the divine right of kings, and all that; ve in Europe know all about the horrible things that come from such a teaching."

"Yeah, but the ironic thing is that even in the Old Testament writings it's very clear that the theocratic state led by a king was what the people wanted, even though God kept telling them they did not need a king. And even when Jesus came, they wanted him to be a king of military power, but he did everything he could to show them he was not involved in that kind of warlike power. But now, even today, with two thousand years of hindsight in their favor, there are still people who want this ironclad king to tell them what to do so they can follow along in blind faith as he leads them into battle against all the 'devils' out there. And it has a strangely appealing quality to it."

Hans offered an understanding nod. "Dictators, many of them cloaking themselves in religion, have always been appealing to many people in Europe, from the old militant popes who led the Crusades back in the days of the Holy Roman Empire to Hitler and Mussolini in this century."

"And today I just met someone who I think would like very much to become the next dictator, the next king."

"Are you talking about that John Burt guy?" Hans asked.

"No," I replied. "Though he's creepy; I met someone who has far more ambitious goals. His name is Paul Hill."

Hans was definitely intrigued, so once again I milked the situation. "I'm not sure how much I should tell you. It's some pretty wild stuff."

Hans took the bait. "Oh, come on, you've gotta tell me this now. I must know."

"I'll tell you only if you promise not to tell anyone else until I say it's all right."

Hans vowed right away to keep the confidence.

I told him, "You are the only person I am going to tell this to because I want your help."

"How?"

I told him that I wanted him to keep his eyes open for any potential extremists, and to pretend to go along with them if he did any interviews. "I strongly suspect that we are going to see more radicals coming to town to help Paul Hill with his plans," I said.

"Vhat plans?" asked Hans urgently.

"That's the part I haven't told anyone about. Although I'm here to cover this story, the truth is that my freelance work is simply allowing me to cover my expenses for a chance to check out a lead I was given."

"Vhat lead?" Hans was intrigued.

"I'm getting to that. Two weeks before this trial, I called a guy named Donald Treshman on the phone. Treshman happens to be John Burt's boss in Rescue America, an ally of Operation Rescue. When Treshman found out who my old pastors were, and that I'd risked my career to help Operation Rescue, he mentioned that the National Coalition of Abortion Providers was going to gather here in Pensacola on the one-year anniversary of the death of Dr. Gunn, which is probably going to come right after this trial ends. And in this really ominous tone of voice, Treshman warned me that 'somethin' big, somethin' *really* big, is coming.'"

Hans asked if I knew what the warning meant. I explained about meeting Paul Hill and the conversation we'd had at lunch. When I told him about Hill's calm prediction that "you're about to see a coming IRA-type reign of terror," my moviemaking friend's eyes grew wide once again.

"Holy shit! That sounds so creepy that it's givin' me the villies. Maybe I shouldn't be hanging out vith you. You might get us both killed! These people sound nuts!"

I laughed and said, "It is a little dangerous, but I'm sort of used to that. I've covered all kinds of dangerous situations from chemical explosions to walking all by myself onto the scene of a homicide in the worst part of town to ask if anyone knew anything about the murder."

Hans asked if anything bad had ever happened to me in my work.

"I've been chased away a couple of times by family members of the person who got shot because they didn't want the press around at that horrible time. The closest I ever came to death was one time when I was supposed to sub for our traffic reporter. He had been out sick and the woman who had filled in for him couldn't make it one day, so she asked me to fly. I agreed, but then on my way home from church my car broke down. When I called into the station, they called the main traffic guy and he went into work instead of me the next morning. There was a terrible thick fog so they took the helicopter up that day instead of the plane.

"Unfortunately, the pilot failed to see the high-power lines over the Niagara River, and they ran right into them, and then crashed into the icy waters below. They must've been instantaneously killed, because when the divers found them at the bottom of the river they were still strapped into their seats."

Hans said, "That vould've been you if you didn't have the car trouble at church. It's like it vas meant to be."

"That's definitely how I felt at the time. I felt horrible for my colleague, of course, but I was grateful to be alive."

"You are von of the most interesting storytellers I've ever met. Your life is filled vith real-life adventure."

I laughed and said, "I guess I purposely picked the media field because it was interesting, and the rest has just happened, but this stuff about the radicals came about because of my involvement with the Religious Right."

Hans then told me that he'd like to get my story down on film. He wanted me to sit down and talk into the camera about my experiences. I said I'd consider it as long as he would hold the story until I said it was okay to release it, and that he couldn't tell anyone else about it until then. Hans said he'd have to tell his boss because his boss would want to come out and meet me in person. "You know, having a successful Hollywood director like Tony Kaye meet you could lead to something big."

I laughed and said, "What a choice of words. Now when I hear someone say 'something big' my mind immediately goes back to the prediction by these militants."

Hans chuckled, and we discussed things a little further, but soon we called it a night.

ELEVEN

I didn't tell Hans that I had one more important interview that very night right at midnight. The strange time was because my subject was working the 3:00-to-11:00 P.M. shift. I had set up the interview before I got to Pensacola, and I had high hopes that it would be helpful to all I was trying to accomplish.

The young man I was going to see, Barry Mann, was a former roommate of a "Christian" bomber. The darkness of the hour as I drove to meet him would turn out to match the mood and content of the conversation I was about to have.

I pulled up to the condos where Mann lived and found a spot to park. As I got out of my car I could hear a dog barking in the background. No one was around the parking lot and very few lights were turned on inside the condos at this late hour on a Monday night, which made it easier to find Mann's place.

I walked up the winding sidewalk, noticing the lush tropical flowers along the way. I stepped inside the hallway of the security building and found the buzzer for Mann's condo. He buzzed me in and I walked over to his door, where he stood waiting.

We made our intros and he offered me some coffee,

which I accepted. He began to fumble around the stark white kitchen to find what he needed to get the pot going. His dark-bearded face looked tired and he told me he'd been working a lot of overtime the past couple of weeks.

I sat at his kitchen counter; there was no table in the room, and I could see out into the living room. The place looked like a typical bachelor's pad, with no sign of a woman's touch anywhere. He told me he had come to the trial that morning and stayed as long as he could until he had to go get ready for work.

I set up my tape deck and asked him what he thought of the trial.

"It gave me goose bumps when I heard Kerrigan say right out loud in front of everybody that he thought Griffin didn't shoot Gunn, but Gratton did as part of a master plan by John Burt."

"Do you think he was right?" I asked.

"Yer damn right I do, but I can't prove it. All I can do is tell you what I know. My old roommate, Matt Goldsby, was just like Michael Griffin in the sense that he had never been involved in anything violent in his life, and never involved in the antiabortion movement. But then he meets John Burt and within a few months he turns into a terrorist."

"Really?"

"And Matt's not the only one. The pattern always seems to be the same. I know of at least six people now, all total, who have come to meet John Burt and within weeks or months turn into a terrorist for Jesus. It's absolutely creepy, and I don't think it's gonna change because every time it happens, the young person goes to jail and John Burt gets immunity. Plus, he reaps a whirlwind of publicity!"

I pressed him to continue. Mann explained that John Burt had received immunity in the shooting of Gunn even though the defense implied that the former KKK activist was the mastermind of the murder. "How is that possible?" I asked.

"I don't know. Pensacola's a small enough city to operate like a podunk town sometimes. Maybe he's payin' somebody off or has the goods on somebody. I don't know, but he always gets away with it."

I asked Mann for the specifics.

"Well, from what I've heard, Burt learned how to use people as pawns for the cause back in his days with the KKK. I think he was some kind of wizard with them, and the Klan was famous for gettin' these expendable young men to do the dirty work while the leaders always kept their hands clean. Somehow . . . I don't know how they did it, if they brainwashed 'em or jes' found these impressionable people and got 'em all riled up, but, anyway, these young rubes would go off and do some dastardly deed and when they got caught the Klan would publicly say they didn't foster the violence, but they would always get their leaders quoted in the press, and they'd always get to make their points to the public. It was a win-win situation for the Klan 'cause they got the nasty stuff done by some innocent doofus and some free publicity thrown in with the deal."

Mann brought me the coffee and continued, "Really, though, that's before I got acquainted with John Burt. All I know for sure is that when my old roommate, Matt Goldsby, and his friend Jimmy Simmons met up with Burt, they went from being model citizens to makin' pipe bombs in their spare time. The first thing that happened was that John Burt showed 'em these really sick videos about all these dead fetuses floatin' in a sea of blood while Christian music played.

"I remember the night Matt first saw the videos. He came home all agitated and said he had puked his guts out when he saw what they were doin' to babies that got aborted. After that he started hangin' out with Burt more, and he got majorly obsessed with stoppin' abortions. Him and Jimmy used ta tell me all the time about how many abortions happened and how horrible these doctors were, etc., but I jes' told 'em to keep it in perspective. Of course, that was the last thing they wanted to hear."

Mann finally sat down, straddling his chair, which he had turned around backward. "It was scary watchin' him change over the months, but there wasn't nothin' I could do about it. And at the time, I didn't even know Matt and Jimmy had started buildin' bombs together. We ended up splittin' up as roommates, and I was awful glad we did when I found out later about the bombings. I coulda been arrested like they were."

"Tell me about the bombings."

"They planted bombs in all three of the abortion clinics in town and set their timers to go off right about the same time in hopes of confusing the 911 operators about which clinic had been hit. It was an effective tactic 'cause it worked when the time came, but I highly doubt they came up with it on their own."

I agreed with Mann that the knowledge of how to create a sophisticated diversionary tactic like that did not sound like it would be the MO for two brand-new terrorists unless they had been given guidance by more seasoned veterans.

"Ya wanna know the kicker to all this?" Mann asked. "They bombed the clinics on, of all the strangest times to pick, Christmas Day. And believe it or not, they called it a 'gift for baby Jesus.' "

I was stunned. I was literally struck speechless. My mind started to swim and spin. Between the weirdness of the words I'd heard that day and the fact that I'd gone without sleep the night before, I was beginning to feel like I'd entered some religious version of *The Twilight Zone*. At that point, I wouldn't have been surprised to hear the voice of Rod Serling behind me, saying, "He was an average news reporter, just trying to make a living grinding out stories day after day, until he entered *The Christian Terrorist Zone*."

Mann saw the look on my face, and asked if I was all right. I pulled myself back together and said that I'd just been so shocked about what he was telling me, "Christmas Day?" I stammered out.

Mann said he wasn't surprised at my reaction. "Matt and Jimmy got busted by the feds, and the worst part of it was they dragged their old ladies into it as well. Matt's fiancée, Kaye Wiggins, and Jimmy's wife, Kathy Simmons, had known what their men were up to, so all four of them had to stand trial.

"The friggin' trial was a circus, like the B.S. that went on today with all the press all over the damn place. And guess who got the lion's share of publicity?"

"John Burt?"

"You got it. He gobbled up the limelight like the turkey he is, and he prob'ly got a ton of money for that phony home for unwed mothers he runs out there in Milton. You oughta check it out; it's a scam and a half. It's no charity, it's a friggin' terrorist training camp."

Once again he had shocked me, and I don't shock easily. I told him

I was planning to go there and would see what I could uncover. At that moment I felt my first real sensation of impending danger.

"Anyway, Matt and the others all got hard time, the girls got five years each in prison just for bein' accessories to the crime, and Matt and Jimmy got ten years each. It was brutal. From what I heard, Matt didn't get abused as much as Jimmy did because of his muscles and weight lifting, but bad stuff happened. Neither one of 'em will ever talk to anybody about it even though they're out of there now. Matt moved outta state, and started over. I can give you his number, but he won't talk to you.

"He and Kaye broke up long ago, so he's on his own. Jimmy came back and is tryna make a go of it here, but he's pretty wrecked up emotionally, not that I blame him. People don't know the cost these poor suckers have had to pay for the likes of John Burt. I wish somebody would bring him down."

Then he added, "By the way, after Matt and his friends went to jail, Burt found another poor sucker, a guy named John Broeckhoft. This poor sap went to John Burt's house, and Burt actually went with him in his car down to one of the clinics. They scoped out the place together, no doubt Burt was giving him the inside skinny on the joint 'cause then they went back to Burt's house and this guy Broeckhoft drops Burt off and starts to back outta the driveway, the feds stop him and make him open his trunk. Inside is a shitload of explosives. Once again, the guy gets busted and goes to trial and eventually to jail for four years, but Burt walks scot-free. All that happens to Burt is that he gets another windfall of free publicity."

"Sure sounds like a pattern developing," I said. "But it won't be the kind of thing you can either prove or disprove. You'd have to show intent, and so on."

Mann agreed, and said, "Anyway, after that comes the number-six sucker that I know of, our biggest pigeon of all, Michael Griffin. And it's possible that Griffin was just supposed to blow up Gunn's clinic like the other guys, but decided on his own to shoot the doctor. It's hard to tell. This case gets a little more complicated than the other ones because this time Burt is at the scene of the crime personally when the violence goes down. Of course he 'just happens' to be on the other side of the building from Griffin, which 'just happens' to keep him free of any possible legal entanglement, but he's on a walkie-talkie the whole time with his stooge, Donnie Gratton, who is right near the scene of the crime.

"Now it looks like the defense will be going after Gratton, but I don't know if they can prove that Gratton did the actual shooting or not. And if he did, why did Griffin go up to the cops and confess?"

I told Mann that that was a good question, and asked if he could think of any possible answers.

He said, "I have thought about the possibility that Griffin had agreed ahead of time to say he did it, and to play the part until the court case came up at which time he would somehow be proven innocent without getting Gratton in trouble. Burt would have pulled off his greatest coup ever. Of course, this is only speculation on my part. I don't think anyone really knows what happened except Burt, Gratton, and Griffin. And, so far, Griffin may be the only one who's willing to talk at all, and I think he's more afraid of Burt than he is of prison 'cause the legal system can't go after his wife and kids."

I acknowledged his point, but wondered if there was any evidence to back up his speculation.

"Well, let's look at the facts about the murder. Michael Griffin kills this doctor even though he had never met the man and had no reason to personally want him dead. But John Burt had faced off against Gunn many times and absolutely hated his guts."

I asked how long Burt had been picketing Gunn's clinic.

"Ten long years, and things had gotten worse right before the shooting than ever before. On January 22, the *Roe* v. *Wade* anniversary, Dr. Gunn spoke back to Burt in front of his antiabortion troops for the first time ever. He'd been quietly taking Burt's bullying for a decade, but he just got to the point where he couldn't take it any more. I guess maybe he figured that by being so quiet he was only making Burt bolder."

"I know that the dynamics between a bully and his victim can turn ugly when the victim tries to break free. It's the same thing in domestic violence, for instance, when a woman tries to finally break free of her abusive husband for the first time, that's when things turn most dangerous."

"That's right," Mann said. "And Dr. Gunn looked like the classic target for an abusive bully because he had been sick as a child with some serious disease that had left him with a really noticeable limp, and he was a tiny, frail-looking guy who was also very intelligent, sensitive, and educated, just the kind of guy you'd expect to get bullied by a boorish brute like Burt."

I jotted down "boorish brute like Burt," then asked Mann to continue.

"The funny thing in this situation is that what Dr. Gunn did when he finally fought back was so relatively innocent, sort of childlike. He brought out a big boom box, put it on top of his car, sang 'Happy Birthday *Roe* v. *Wade*,' and then cranked out a song from Tom Petty and the Heartbreakers called 'At the Gates of Hell.' It went something like: 'At the gates of hell, I'll stand my ground. I won't back down. I won't back down.' Gunn sang along with it, then did a little jig and danced his way into the clinic."

"I bet that didn't go over too big with Burt and his buddies."

Mann said, "Are you kidding? They went absolutely apoplectic! It was like a major meltdown, and I think Burt decided that he was gonna get Gunn somehow, some way. The shooting 'just happened' to take place on the ten-year anniversary of Burt's protests against Gunn and the other abortion doctors in town. It was a date that had a great deal of significance to Burt, but none for Griffin."

"But you still don't know if Burt ordered a hit, like a mafia mobster, or if it was just coincidence that Griffin decided to do what he did when he did it."

Mann acknowledged that he couldn't prove anything, certainly nothing that would stand up in court. And then he cursed himself for getting involved with the whole matter as far as even talking to me about it. He called Burt "The Tar Baby" because he said that anyone who got near him ended up getting smeared while each ugly encounter only made Burt look better, at least to his disciples.

"On the day the shooting happened," Mann continued, "you had Burt on one side of the clinic with a group of protesters loudly marching around and shouting, which 'just happened' to create a classic diversion to draw people's attention out front while the shooting was taking place in the back, literally—the back of the clinic and the back of the doctor."

I told Mann that he was painting a word-picture for me that was very helpful.

"And the gall of this guy Burt is just un-friggin'-believable! He had the nerve to show up at Gunn's funeral right in the cemetery with his bullhorn and his sheep in tow, and start screamin' at the top of his lungs that Gunn was a baby killer who was burnin' in hell! This happens right while the family is trying to deal with their most intimate moments of mourning, and he won't stop no matter what. It was like he was dancin' on the guy's grave or, more accurately, pissin' on it!"

"Did anybody try to stop him?" I interjected.

"Of course. Family members, including David Gunn Jr., told him to stop and leave them alone. The kid wanted to kill Burt at that point, and he mighta too, if his family didn't hold him back. Who could blame him? It was the craziest thing you ever heard of, way over the top. Finally, the cops came and made Burt leave, but nothing happened to him. The guy can get away with murder in this town, at least figuratively, and we may find out if he can get away with it literally by the time this trial ends."

"It sounds like the defense is gonna go after him big time."

"Yeah, well, I wouldn't hold your breath. John Burt seems to be the untouchable in Pensacola. God only knows why. He's a real sonnuva'bitch asshole, pardon my language, but he's the worst damn thing that ever happened to this city. I'm thinkin' of movin' just to get away from his stench."

TWELVE

I left Barry Mann's condo at close to 3:00 A.M., after getting the phone numbers for Matt Goldsby and Jimmy Simmons from him. Both would later prove to be dead ends because neither man would talk, just as Mann predicted. In the meantime, I had to find a place to crash for the night. I was exhausted.

Around 3:25 I pulled up to a Motel 6, just off I-10 near route 110, which led from the city. I dragged my suitcase up to the second-floor bedroom I'd been assigned, opened the door, tossed in the suitcase, and went directly to bed, too tired to even brush my teeth after being up for nearly forty-eight hours.

But as I lay in bed, I had that uncomfortable feeling that told me I wasn't going to be able to get to sleep. Mann's words had hit me with great force, suddenly I felt as though I could see the whole murder scene in my mind's eye for the first time.

Burt marching around on the sidewalk out in front of the clinic with his bullhorn and his "sheep" following behind, their homemade signs with fierce warnings of woe and photos of bloody fetuses. I imagined Burt surreptitiously whispering orders or questions to Gratton on the walkie-talkie from time to time before the doctor arrived.

In back of the clinic, Michael Griffin and Donnie Gratton, the only two from the protest group, were drifting around. Griffin had been spotted at the scene, but Gratton seemed to have been far less visible. Had he been better at concealing himself, or was it part of a plan, or just another one of a million coincidences in the case?

One thing I hadn't admitted to Mann was that I'd had a brief conversation with Michael Griffin on the phone before I came up to cover the trial, and Griffin had claimed that he was innocent and that Gratton had shot the doctor under orders from Burt.

I started to ask Griffin why he confessed, but he said he had to go. At the time, I just took it as a typical "I'm innocent" kind of jailhouse talk, but now I wasn't so sure. Would the defense attorney have raised those very points if he didn't have some hard evidence, at least enough to possibly create some reasonable doubt in the jurors' minds?

There were so many unanswered questions: Why were Gratton and Griffin both in the same spot if Burt didn't know anything about Griffin's plans, as Burt continued to maintain? And was it really possible that Gratton could have been the one who took Griffin's gun to shoot the doctor, as Griffin had claimed and as his defense attorney was now claiming?

I thought about one of the last things that Mann told me as I was about to leave his condo. He mentioned that on the morning of the shooting, Burt, Gratton, and Griffin were all wearing similar suits and ties. He said it could have just been a coincidence, but it was strange because anyone who knew the three men knew that they almost never dressed that way. These were three blue-collar guys who were far more likely to be in T-shirts and jeans.

I suddenly realized that the fact that they were dressed so much alike could have been designed to create possible confusion by eyewitnesses. Police reports made after crimes are committed always describe what the suspected perpetrator was wearing. If they had wanted to confuse the public so that Griffin would be indistinguishable from Gratton, the similar suits would have been a big help.

Also, Gratton's and Griffin's frames looked somewhat alike from a distance (even though Griffin was smaller when they stood side by side), especially when they both wore beards, as they did in 1993. If the wearing of the suits and all the other coincidences weren't planned, it certainly was an unusually high number of similar events. But, then again, I knew as a reporter not to jump to any conclusions without the full facts.

However, the way it appeared to me that night, there were three main possible explanations for what had happened on the fateful day:

1. Griffin acted alone to kill a man he'd never met, who just happened to be hated by John Burt, at a place and time John Burt just happened to be talking to his most trusted aide on a walkie-talkie.
2. Griffin acted under guidance from Burt, probably in some kind of indirect series of manipulations rather than direct control. As Paul Hill had put it, the leaders didn't want to give direct orders so they couldn't be arrested for conspiracy. This was the "doofus used as a pawn" idea that Barry Mann had talked about. It would also allow for the possibility that Burt was genuinely surprised at the shooting, but only because he may have expected a bombing, like in the cases of his other protégés.
3. Gratton killed Dr. Gunn with Griffin's gun, and had Griffin confess as part of a prearranged plan to throw police off the real trail. If this was true, then Griffin was right when he claimed he'd been used and abused by Burt and Gratton. It certainly sounded like this is what the defense was planning to try to prove, but they would have to provide facts to back it up.

I knew I'd have to wait until all the evidence came in to know what really happened. Surely, I thought—overly optimistic once again?—it would be finally settled by the end of the trial. In the meantime, I could only wonder what kind of men I was going to be meeting when I went to Burt's house, possibly that very next night.

I thought, I've gotta get to sleep, but after an hour of tossing and turning, I got up, went to the bathroom, took a shower, and brushed my teeth. I lay down again, but to no avail.

I looked at the clock; it was 4:47 A.M.. I looked at least ten minutes later, but the clock said it was only 4:48. I couldn't believe it. I tried all my usual tricks for relaxing and falling asleep, from picturing myself in a relaxing cabin in the mountains to saying repetitive prayers. Nothing helped.

The weird words and frenzied faces I had encountered over the last twenty-four hours were running circles in my mind. I wanted to get up and go home. This was all way too crazy. How had things ever gotten like this? Most of my memories of Christian events back in the good old days before the Christian Coalition and Operation Rescue and the whole street theater in the culture war were happy and upbeat.

I had grown up in a very devout Roman Catholic family, but had become a born-again Christian at the age of fourteen after some "Jesus freaks" gave me a gospel tract that said to ensure that I got to heaven I just had to say these special prayers, and I would instantly be "saved" from my sins and guaranteed a place forever in heaven. The only cost to me was to pray the prayers that they enclosed in their little pamphlet with sincerity in my heart. I was perfectly willing to do that.

After I did, I felt nothing at all, but the pamphlet had that contingency covered, warning that we were not to rely on our feelings, but on our faith and the fact that Jesus is real, and that all I had to do now was to get a Bible and start going to church so that I could get support in my new Christian life.

When I was fifteen, I got involved in the Catholic charismatic renewal, which brought the "holy roller" healing services and the "gift of tongues" (the ability to speak in unintelligible sounds believed to be a mysterious prayer language) into the oldest and largest denomination in Christianity from the relatively new Pentecostal or charismatic churches.

The charismatic services were admittedly a little eccentric at times, but filled with effervescent happiness and lively music. I belonged to a charismatic prayer group at my home church and another one in a nearby town just for teens.

I was "baptized in the Spirit" in the teen group, which meant making the same kind of prayers as the born-again people had asked me to pray, but adding a request for special, charismatic gifts (healing, prophecy, miracles, tongues-speaking, and so on). Some of the people who went through this experience before me shared amazingly dramatic stories of having their lives completely changed in one moment or of feeling a great rush of holy energy and power. I was disappointed the night I was baptized in the Spirit because I felt nothing except a sort of quiet peacefulness.

I didn't even get the gift of tongues, which charismatics always called "the least of the gifts" (quoting St. Paul) even though they inexplicably acted like it was the most important. The many groups and charismatic churches I would see over the years always seemed to press people to try to "help" God give them that gift.

In my case, for instance, an older man told me that it was a little like driving a car, which I was not quite old enough to do. He said that if I would open my mouth and start to make some sounds myself, that it would make it easier for the Holy Spirit to guide me. "Just like driving a car 'cause it's a whole lot easier to steer once you have the car moving," he said (in what would be an often-used analogy in charismatic circles).

So I took my first "Holy Spirit driving lesson" that night, and after a few more sessions, I was able to help the Holy Spirit enough that I could speak in tongues with the best of them. Later, I would also add "interpretation of tongues" and "prophecy," the former being the interpretation of what I or the other person who spoke aloud was saying in the gibberish-sounding tongue, while prophecy was a message that came from God, which I would speak aloud in the first person (for example, "My dear children, I, the Lord your God, have not called you to live in fear, but in love"). The messages were usually generically encouraging and—remarkably—often touched on things that we were already concerned about.

But, though much of it sounds strange now, especially to those who never went through it, one thing I can say for it is that ever since those days when I was a teenager in the Catholic charismatic renewal I had always been known for my positive approach to people and my willingness to give of myself to a great degree. For instance, on a couple of Christmases when I was in high school, I made my parents send all the money they would have spent on Christmas gifts for me to a missionary who helped the poor in South America. And I was always doing nice things for people. My family and friends all noticed the changes and appreciated them even if they didn't understand why I was so religious.

So I wondered that night in the hotel room: If I became more tenderhearted and giving after accepting the fundamentalist born-again experience combined with the charismatics' baptism in the Spirit, how could these people I was meeting, who were also fundamentalists and/or charismatics, have read the same Bible and had the same experiences I had, and then come to justify terrorism?

And then, suddenly, a thought came out of the blue about a fact that hadn't fully registered about the murder of Dr. Gunn. Every single pro-life group in America had distanced itself from the shooting when it happened—with one notable exception. I had read in the *Pensacola News Journal* the first day I arrived in town that Rescue America, the group that John Burt and Don Treshman were leading, had immediately begun raising money for Griffin's family after the shooting.

Treshman, the same man who had warned me of the "something big" to come had also said that they were raising money for the self-confessed murderer's family as a chance to minister to a family in need. When asked if he was going to raise money for the victim's family, Treshman said the Gunn family didn't need it because they had all that money from his "baby killing."

Talk about another huge coincidence! What were the chances that the one and only organization to see the shooting as a chance to "minister" would be the same one that John Burt was a major leader in? But surely, it must've been a coincidence, since the Rev. John Burt himself had clearly declared that he was not involved at all with the "pro-life" killing.

There was one troubling comment Burt made right after the shooting, when he tried to explain away any claims of culpability on his part. His defense, as quoted in the *Pensacola News Journal*, was, "If I am a general with troops under me and give them a game plan and send them out, I can't be responsible for every soldier in that army."

And a nurse who was on the jury in Griffin's trial said of Burt, "He seems to be a very controlling person. I don't want to say cult [leader], but he has a group of people who think they have to follow his commands."

Burt later corrected his public position about what he meant when he called himself the general who had sent out troops, saying that he had meant to inspire people like Griffin to join him in protest, but he said that he was surprised at the slaying by Griffin, adding that he himself was innocent.

Poor John Burt. As a totally innocent person, he sure was having a lot of bad luck as far as public perception went because of all these pesky coincidences. While people like Barry Mann thought that Burt could get away with anything, clearly they failed to realize that a misunderstood minister like Burt had a particularly heavy cross to bear as people unjustly looked at him as a mastermind in a murder case. Obviously he was a man of God. And, if we didn't believe it, all we had to do was read his fund-raising newsletters; they told all about the good work he was doing at Our Father's House.

I thought of the Bible verse that says, "In my Father's house there are many rooms." I wondered if some of those "rooms" in Our Father's House were filled with cobwebs and dark, dank crevices where spiders might live and weave wicked webs for their unsuspecting prey.

But even my most twisted late-night thoughts, darkly colored by my exhaustion and the overstimulation of all the outrageous things I'd heard, could not have prepared me for the surreal experience I was going to have when I finally met John Burt at Our Father's House.

THIRTEEN

As it turned out, I didn't go to Burt's house the next night. Instead, he asked me to come two nights later. That was to be on Thursday, March 3, the night before he would testify in court. I guess if you're going to trample on the edges of the judge's gag order, you might as well do it right before you're scheduled to take the stand.

Anyway, the trial started to drag. Tuesday, Wednesday, and Thursday seemed interminably long after the powerful start on Monday—not to mention my lack of ability to sleep all week long. I thought, Who wouldn't have trouble sleeping with the kind of things I've got on my mind?

I interviewed Paul Hill again, this time on a park bench on the far side of the courthouse during the morning break. It was a better location since we were not in the line of sight of the federal snipers still atop the courthouse.

Hill went into great detail on why it was important to establish God's rule over all humanity. He mocked the concept of pluralism, saying, "Why should there be a church on one corner, a mosque on another, and a temple on another? There can't be multiple truths, so those of us who know the truth have to stop those spreaders of lies from dragging other people to hell with them."

I asked what he would do to stop these other religions. Was he going to outlaw them? Hill said he was in favor of exactly that. I asked how the government could pick which religion was the true one. He said I failed to understand that the civil government should be subservient to the church's rule.

"Like in the days of the Holy Roman Empire?" I said, trying to hold back the sarcasm welling up inside me. Hill said that the goal of his theology of Reconstructionism was to get the world back to the time when there was only one true church, not the thousands of splinter groups that "broke the body of Christ" into the mess it is in today.

"So you want to more or less turn the hands of time back to before the Renaissance brought in civil government and pluralism, and before the Reformation brought multiple denominations to Christianity?"

"Yes, it's extremely important that we reinstate church discipline the way it used to be. When the church had the authority to truly punish people who got out of line, there was no splintering. For all its faults, the church stayed together. That's what we need today.

"In the past, when the church excommunicated a person, it was incredibly powerful. A person could not only be banned from receiving the sacraments of the church, but was entirely shunned by family, friends, and the entire community, including the church. He was thus forced to repent to get his life back. We need to get that kind of discipline back into the church today. Instead, we have these goofy church hoppers who shop for a church the way they shop for underwear. It's absurd. Everyone is just doing whatever they want, but if church discipline was reinvigorated then those kinds of behaviors would come to a screeching halt."

"I can see that a practice like that would be very controlling, but let me ask you about your personal situation. I don't mean any disrespect here, but let me ask you about something I heard about you."

He fixed his smug smirk, which I would realize later he did to hide his true feelings or fears, and he told me to go ahead and ask my question.

"I heard that you used to be a conservative Bible Presbyterian minister, but that your church defrocked you because you refused to follow the church's authority in your activities advancing the shooting of doctors with your 'Defensive Action' petition. If it's true that you personally refused to obey church authorities even though you were a licensed and ordained minister, how do you justify your belief that church authority should be absolute?"

Hill looked extremely uncomfortable for a brief moment, then regained his smirk and said, "That's easy. My church failed to understand true biblical law and theology. It failed to be faithful to what the Bible teaches. It didn't have the right to disobey when the Bible teachings make members uncomfortable. They were afraid of my courageous actions, afraid that donations would drop off if they spoke the truth, afraid that their friends and others in the community wouldn't like them if they took such an unpopular stance."

His answer did not surprise me as much as it would have surprised many other people, because I had heard many radicals in the antiabortion movement express such feelings of superiority toward their own church's leadership. To me, though, it seemed to be incredible hypocrisy on Hill's part for him to call upon other people to give absolute submission to the one true church while he mocked the authority of the church in which he had been ordained.

I tried to choose my words carefully. "Okay, you don't think that your denomination was faithful to the Bible in this disagreement they had with you regarding the shooting of doctors, but you still believe that we are called to follow the teachings of the one true church. Let me ask you, where is this one true church? Are you a member of it now, or are you going to launch a new church?"

Hill harrumphed and said, "I don't have to launch anything. God is in complete control of everything. The one true church is being raised up by divine authority. It's as simple as that."

"Well, that's good," I said, "but I want to be in the one true church. I don't want to waste my time in the wrong church, and as you said, drag others to hell with me. So, please tell me where I can find the one true church. This is extremely important. Let's not waste any more time."

Hill squirmed around on the bench, uncrossing his legs and leaning forward. "Well, you know it's not like I can just point my finger and say go over there or over here, but if you are faithful, you will find yourself in the one true church."

I told him I thought he was being awfully vague and that I was just a simple son of a firefighter from a blue-collar family. I needed him to tell me where the right church was. We went around and around, and finally he admitted that there would probably always be different denominations in Christianity, but that he still favored outlawing other religions.

"After all, this was a Christian nation until the ACLU led the liberal charge in the 1960s," explained Hill. He then launched into a tirade against secularism, pluralism, feminism, and all other schools of thought in modern times.

Hill, like all fundamentalists, longs for a bygone era that never actually existed. His message, like that of televangelists and Bible thumpers everywhere, is that there was a time when the world was right, but that this current generation is sliding into sin worse than ever before and that society won't get better unless people accept the message of fundamentalism.

Ironically, in Hill's case, I felt certain that had he lived in the era of the one true church he would have been just as much a dissident from that church's authority as he had been to his own church's authority today. He was willing to break with the church over just one issue — even though at the time he did there was only one practitioner of "justifiable homicide" in the entire nation. And even though that alleged practitioner was deeply regretting his own action in whatever form it had taken leading up to the death of Dr. Gunn.

After the interview I stayed outside for a while by myself. I wondered why Pensacola was such a hotbed of radicalism. From what I had learned about the small Florida city above the Gulf of Mexico, it had a skeleton or two in its closet. Pirates, known for their violent law-breaking and reckless ways, had made Pensacola home a couple of hundred years earlier, because it was a natural port and a good stopping-off point between New Orleans to the west and Miami to the south. I mused only half-seriously, "Maybe Paul Hill and John Burt are just the heirs of long-lost pirates."

But Pensacola had been having more recent troubles, and had been "ground zero" for not only the abortion war, but the culture war as a whole. The city on the Emerald Coast seemed to be a crossroads between the old south and the new, a microcosm of the larger society of which it was a part. Racial tensions had flared there when the civil rights struggles had gone on in the 1950s and 1960s, but not anything as major as what had happened in the neighboring city of Mobile, Alabama, where cops released dogs on the crowd, an act that would remain forever in the nation's collective memory.

However, during the rise of the gay rights movement around the country in the 1970s, there were multiple incidents of violence against gays and their business establishments. Bombs had exploded in gay bars in Pensacola during the same period when fundamentalist preachers warned their flocks that homosexuals were going to usher in Satan's kingdom and bring down the traditional family and launch unprecedented pedophilia against their children if the gay rights movement wasn't stopped.

The women's movement also was under attack when the Equal Rights Amendment was making the rounds of states in the mid-1970s. Pensacola tended to come down on the conservative side of all the social issues. Morality was shaped by the Sunday schools more than the public schools. Obedience to God was more highly valued than free thinking was, and most people were churchgoing in spite of the growing influence of secularism.

The Ku Klux Klan had once had a powerful hold on the area, as it did throughout much of the South, but by the 1970s it was on the decline. The election of Ronald Reagan in 1980 and his highly visible support from Jerry Falwell and his "Moral Majority" did coincide with a new wave of conservative radicalism, this time in the form of abortion clinic bombings.

This is when John Burt coincidentally appeared publicly, in 1983, the first time he decided to picket a clinic that offered abortion services.

It was the very same clinic that would witness the slaying of Dr. Gunn ten years later.

The model of Pensacola Women's Medical Services in the Cordova Square shopping and office complex would be featured prominently throughout Tuesday's trial testimony. Prosecutor Murray called a string of witnesses who placed Michael Griffin nearby just minutes before the shooting. Most devastating to the defense's explanation of a frame-up was the testimony of the one and only witness who claimed to see Michael Griffin actually firing the shots. Della Lindsay, a middle-aged African American salesperson, testified that she saw Griffin shoot Dr. Gunn and then walk over to two police officers on the other side of the building.

Her testimony came out in simple, direct words that seemed to ring with integrity, but that is not how Michael Griffin perceived it. The defendant approached the judge in a hallway during a break in the trial and made some startling accusations.

Justice Parnham asked him to repeat those accusations in court. With the jury out of the room, a tearful Griffin whined, "It's not right, all I want is a fair trial, and it's not right." Then Griffin went on to accuse the prosecutor of using his eyeglasses to direct the witness. He claimed that Murray would look over his lawyerly reading glasses when he wanted a yes to a question, and look down when he wanted a no.

Griffin's attorney admitted he had not noticed such a pattern, and Murray said that he just looked over the top of his "granny glasses" to see. "I can assure you that I'm not communicating with the witnesses directly or indirectly," Murray told the court.

Parnham assured Griffin he wanted him to have a fair trial, then advised the lawyers to be careful not to do anything that a witness could inadvertently take as a sign. Seeing Griffin cry as he spoke with a cracking voice was a startling development. He had shown no emotion up to that point, even when a witness testified eloquently to how fine a man the doctor was and how much pain his death caused her. And he didn't even look concerned when Kim Dodd, a coworker of Gunn, described finding him face down and unconscious in a pool of his own blood.

Overall, it was a very bad day for the defense, as Murray brought more than ten witnesses, including the two police officers that Griffin had walked up to. Blond police officer Bernard Jablonski testified that Griffin came up to him, and confessed to shooting the doctor. Murray extracted every possible detail about the moment to nail down in the jury's minds that this had actually happened and that there was no way to misinterpret the testimony Jablonski gave.

Up next came Sergeant Ken Franks, with darker hair and a darker demeanor than Jablonski. He bore the crispness of a Secret Service agent and his gravity of tone seemed to add weight to his testimony. He told the court that he was standing next to the officer when Griffin came up. He heard every word and repeated exactly what Jablonski had said about the defendant's brief confession.

The frosting on the cake was an insurance salesman, Chip Frost, who happened to be standing close enough to the officers to also over-hear Griffin confess. The white-haired, bespectacled citizen seemed to verify the policemen's testimony, but on cross-examination by defense attorney Kerrigan, Frost admitted a little bit of uncertainty over whether Griffin actually said the word "shot" or not.

Though Kerrigan had tried to cast doubts on the testimony, so far it was obvious that the jury had not been given enough evidence to dis-believe the police and the salesman. But one of the haunting parts of the testimony that stayed with all who heard it was how calm and collected Griffin seemed at the moment he confessed, just as earlier witnesses had described him in the hour before the shooting took place.

FOURTEEN

During the afternoon break, Hans Schmidt came over and asked me if he could interview me. I laughed about the unusual turn of events, the reporter who asks questions being the one who has to give the answers, but I agreed to do it because Hans was not in the news business, and no competition to me. I was also anticipating the chance to meet his boss, Tony Kaye. I figured it couldn't hurt to get on the good side of a successful Hollywood director.

We went out to the park bench where I had interviewed Hill in the morning, and Hans took his film camera in hand and told me to just speak naturally into the camera, and not to pay any attention if he moved around while I was talking.

I felt slightly self-conscious with all the cars and occasional pedestrians passing by. But I'm not one to be shy, so I plunged into the interview. Hans asked, "Tell me about your background, who you are, and about the stuff you told me about the Christian Coalition and all that."

Here's what I said into the camera as Hans moved around to film me:

"My name is Jerry Reiter; I'm a broadcast news reporter now, but I was invited into some of the earliest formative meetings of the Christian Coalition because of my pastors' ties to televangelist Pat Robertson. I used to attend a church called New Covenant Tabernacle in the Buffalo area that was pastored by twin ministers, Rob and Paul Schenck.

"The Schenck brothers were right-wing versions of the Berrigan brothers, the Catholic priests who became infamous for their left-wing tactics in the Vietnam War era. The Schencks were good friends of Randall Terry, the fiery founder of Operation Rescue, the group that gets arrested for blocking access to abortion clinic doors.

"Anyway, because I had been politically active in the Republican Party, my pastors' attorney invited me to talk to a then-unknown young man named Ralph Reed who was going to launch some kind of new political organization for televangelist Pat Robertson, using the mailing lists from his unsuccessful 1988 presidential campaign.

"In the attorney's office, I spoke to Reed on a private phone call about the pros and cons of using the name he had in mind for the group. He was going to call the organization the Christian Coalition, but I suggested that he pick something more inclusive, like the Family Values Coalition. Reed would have none of it, saying, 'Born-again Christians are nearly one-quarter of the voters out there. It's time we show our power.'

"Reed took the time to share some of his story with me. He was a former Republican Party political operative who had most recently been an aide to a Georgia state representative, but then he had approached Pat Robertson after his campaign was over, and made the case that born-agains needed to have some presence in the political arena.

"Robertson was so impressed that he wedded himself to the concept that Reed proposed. With Robertson's seed money, Reed was able to launch the new organization. On the day that I talked to Reed, he *was* the Christian Coalition. He was working out of a tiny office on a shoestring budget. He joked that actually the budget was so small that he couldn't even afford the shoestring.

"However, even then he had big plans. He was certain that he could create a tidal wave that would change the course of American politics, starting not at the top, where conservative Christians had been focusing, but on the bottom. His plan was to build a grassroots organization that would train and equip born-agains to get educated on political issues and run for election to local school boards and town boards. He said that by getting established on the bottom rungs of elective office they would be poised to climb higher and higher.

"Having made his pitch, the call soon ended and the Schenck brothers' attorney asked me for my assessment of the concept, because they were thinking of merging the local activist groups into the Christian Coalition. I told him I didn't see any objections, but that he might want to wait and see if it was going to catch on in the rest of the country.

"The attorney said that there was going to be a teleconference call that very afternoon with all the potential new leaders of the Christian Coalition, and he invited me to stick around to hear it so that I could help them decide whether or not to launch the New York State chapter.

"Looking back on it now, I realize how amazing it was that I was there at a time when the Christian Coalition was so small that virtually all of its leaders could gather together on one teleconference call. That afternoon there was only a relative handful of people from around the United States who were anxious to launch the new state chapters that would form the national network that would be the Christian Coalition.

"As Ralph Reed talked to the activists and prospective leaders, we could hear him shuffling papers. He admitted he was occasionally having trouble reading his own handwritten notes on the legal pad he had on his desk.

"He wasn't nearly as smooth as he would later be on such national political news programs as *Meet the Press* or *This Week with David Brinkley*. But he was just as enthusiastic. He came across with a boyish sound to his voice. Later, when I would meet him in person, I would see it matched his baby face. He looked about twelve years old and I towered over him.

"Reed came to the Buffalo area in February 1991 to personally train me and the other volunteers, many from the Schenck brothers' church, who were the nucleus of the then-embryonic New York State chapter of the Christian Coalition, or CCNY as it was tagged by insiders.

"I was approached about becoming a state chairman myself, because of my background as an elected town committeeman and editor of the county Republican Party newspaper, as well as my media work as a TV host and radio announcer. But I turned it down because I didn't want to move to Idaho or someplace, and I liked my current work.

"I did help the new organization get started, creating their first literature and helping them promote the Christian Coalition throughout New York. Eventually, I became a regional leader, taking a tiny group to ten times its size in a few months, in part because of my dynamic speaking style and because I was somewhat well known in the local community around Buffalo.

"One of the things that surprised me about the Christian Coalition was that even though it publicly denounced the illegal tactics of groups like Operation Rescue, when the big national antiabortion protest came to Buffalo in 1992, Operation Rescue National housed its secret command and communication offices in the basement suite of offices that the Christian Coalition of New York had as its state headquarters. And the state chairman assured me that they had received permission from the national headquarters to do so.

"The point is that publicly the Christian Coalition was telling the world it denounced the intimidating, extremist tactics of Operation Rescue but, unknown to even its own membership, the Christian Coalition was offering its offices to the extremists for their secret sessions of plotting attacks on clinics and disseminating the purple prose of their inflammatory propaganda."

I stopped and said, "I'll have to call it quits for now because we've gotta get back inside for court."

"I hate to stop," Hans said. "This is great stuff!"

FIFTEEN

The prosecutor had spent Tuesday on testimony that:

1. Michael Griffin was in the area of the shooting minutes before the act;
2. Griffin was seen by an eyewitness shooting the doctor and going to the cops;
3. had two police officers relay Griffin's confession; and
4. had a civilian confirm the cops' story.

Wednesday was spent proving that the fatal bullets were fired by Griffin's gun. Many of the details were technical in nature, pertaining to the make, caliber, and unique features of the gun Griffin owned. Murray made sure that the jury knew that the gun he had shown them over and over again was both the same weapon Michael Griffin had been given and the same weapon that took the life of Dr. Gunn.

On Thursday, March 3, a clinic office manager testified that more than three years earlier, John Burt had forced his way into the clinic where she worked. She said he assaulted her and some of the other employees and had to be removed and arrested by police. The physical encounter in which she was pinned down by Burt had been a traumatic event and she felt she was in a very dire situation.

The description of the assault startled me because it seemed out of character for Burt to be involved himself rather than letting his protégés act on whatever suggestions of his they chose to fulfill. But later there would be other testimony that showed Burt himself was capable of using physical intimidation, though in the case of the next witness it would be in using his van as the instrument of intimidation. In both cases, his victims were women. There was no instance of Burt personally going face-to-face against a man. That part kept in step with the bullying role he'd been accused of by the defense, not to mention his many enemies in town.

Late Thursday afternoon, shortly after the break in the trial had ended, Hans came over to me all agitated, but trying not to show it. "Jerry, you're not gonna believe this, but you see that big, husky guy over there? He told me he's got two duffel bags filled with automatic veapons, and also, he's a friend of Paul Hill's. I mean, I saw them together and they vere talking in a group that Hill was part of, like they vere all vaiting for this guy. He might be the key to vhat you were telling me about. This is damned scary shit!"

I shushed him and then said I would go over to talk to the man. I looked his way again and he was heading out the door. I asked Hans to stay with my tape deck because one of the tapes was going to need to be flipped over in a few minutes. Then I dashed toward the door, trying not to look panicked that the man was going to get away.

As I stepped through the doorway to the hall, John Burt was standing with a cup in his hand, and said, "Jerry, where ya goin' in such a big hurry?" It stunned me for a moment, but I blurted out, "To the bathroom." As I race-walked away, I could hear Burt saying aloud, "Geez, ya must have to go awful bad!"

I could see the husky man heading toward the elevators, but I headed down the side corridor toward the bathroom to try not to tip off Burt that I was after someone who might be a key player in the suspected "something big" to come. My heart was pounding as I ducked around the corner to gather my thoughts. I couldn't think of any way to get out of there without Burt seeing me, so all I could do was wait a minute and then head to the stairs on the far end of the floor.

I looked at my watch and the second hand seemed to be moving in slow motion. I forced myself to wait for sixty seconds, and then as casually as I could I walked back out into the hall and turned away from Burt without even looking to see if he was there. I was afraid my eyes would give me away, so I just went down the hall wondering if I was being watched, feeling like his eyes must've been burning into my back.

As I reached the stairwell I glanced back but could see no one. I pushed the big fire door open and started down the stairs. I was on the fifth floor, so I figured I'd just go down to the fourth floor and catch the elevators, but then I realized I'd have to find a way to make up lost time or I'd never catch the mystery man.

Running an all-out sprint down flight after flight of stairs, I nearly lost my balance but I kept going. When I finally got to the ground floor I pushed open the door as fast as I could without looking like I was in a hurry.

I walked briskly out and around the corner to the area near the elevators. An elderly man was talking loudly to a younger woman about the trial, and a security guard was waiting to catch a ride up, but otherwise there was no one in front of the elevators.

People were walking nearby and I blended in with the flow of traffic heading to the outer doors. I walked out onto the sidewalk and looked around. No sign of the husky stranger. He was gone.

I bent over for a moment to catch my breath, sucking wind and upset over the way things had gone. Was Burt standing watch over the man? I wondered. But by this time I was beginning to feel like the sleepless nights I was still having were making me paranoid.

When I finally got back upstairs to the press room, I told Hans I wanted to hear all about the husky man who got away from me.

"Let's get together as soon as the trial breaks," he said. "I'll tell you about the man, but I vant you to let me interview you again."

As soon as the proceedings wrapped for the day, I rushed to gather up my radio equipment and Hans, hurrying him toward the elevators.

Once we were alone outside, I asked him to tell me about the man, but he said it was time for dinner, anyway, so we might as well go somewhere. "Besides, that vay ve don't have to vorry about someone lis'ning in on us," he said.

We went to a quaint little French restaurant downtown, but once we got inside I told Hans we could never talk there because it was too quiet. Instead we went to a local steakhouse that was filled with people.

As soon as we had our grisly steaks and assorted veggies, we sat down in an out-of-the-way table. "All right, now tell me all about this guy," I said.

"This flannel-shirted mountain man kinda guy vith that scraggly black beard and kinda grungy all over was talkin' with Hill and a gang of guys I did not know. Like I said before, they seemed all excited to see him, and I got the impression he was going to do something very important for de men.

"I mixed in as much as I could, you know, blend in, and vithout turning my camera on. Hill noticed I vas there, he recognized me from the interviews I did vith him. And he told the men that I was a Hollywood documentary maker and the bearded guy was all like, 'Hey, ya oughta stick around here, pal. This is gonna be a great place to shoot movies, action movies. But these ain't gonna be no stories, they gonna be real.'

"Hill told him to stay away from me, but I pretended like I vas leaving and vatched until the group broke up. The bearded man vent to get a hot dog so I followed him. "Vhen I catch up vith him, he tells me he is a big fan of the Second Amendment. He loves guns. He vants to have sex vith guns, it sounds like."

I knew what Hans meant. I'd met so many pro-gun people in the Christian Coalition, and some of them seemed to care about their weapons more than anything else. I asked Hans what else happened.

"The guy is like really talking to me a lot, even though he says a couple times he's not supposed to talk vith me. I tell him all this bullshit about how I vant to put him in the film I'm making and he is really into it. He must think he looks like a movie star, but I'm thinking he looks more like a homeless bag lady, bag man. Vell, anyway, he tells me he has two duffel bags—big ones—filled vith these powerful, fast-shooting guns, like automatic-type guns."

"Holy shit, this guy could be the bag man for Hill's whole operation. Did you get his name?" I asked.

"Yah, I think it vas Dan or Dave; damn, I can't remember for sure."

I asked if he got the guy on film. He said, "No, but he's gonna meet me at the hot dog stand tonight around 7:00."

"That's great!" I said, but then I remembered something. "I'm gonna be with John Burt at 7:00 tonight, dammit! Maybe I should cancel."

"No, you go to Burt's and I'll get this guy on film. I'll make sure to get his name, and he'll prob'ly talk more if I am the only vun vith him."

I agreed to the plan, and we ate our cheap meals, marveling at the madness at this murder trial. Then, Hans asked me to suggest a place where we should go to tape his next filmed interview with me.

"I know exactly where we should go—Cordova Square, right to the very spot of the shooting."

He loved the idea and away we went. Driving up to the scene of the crime was eerie because we knew exactly where to go, even though we'd never been there before. The scale model of the area we'd been looking at for days in the courthouse had indelibly printed the directions in our minds. Seeing the actual site seemed surreal because it was so much like what we'd seen in court, yet it felt so different.

I pointed this out to Hans and started to describe the way I saw the differences. "The model was lifeless, but Cordova Square has people passing through or milling around. The model was tiny and bright, but the real place now seems huge in comparison and it's cloaked in darkness."

"The difference is night and day!" Hans quipped.

We laughed, but then Hans said he felt the spookiness of being there, too. He added, "But this is the perfect place for you to tell me your stories about all the antiabortion people."

We stood in the general area where the shooting had taken place, and I began to tell my story as Hans crouched down to get the shot he wanted. I started my soliloquy to the camera once again:

"Here I stand in the very spot where Dr. David Gunn became the nation's first casualty of America's 'culture war,' as Pat Buchanan kept calling it at the Republican Convention in 1992. It's now officially a shooting war.

"I personally have a unique perspective on the culture war, having been a sort of junior officer in two very important brigades on the front lines of the action. First, I was a founding father, or at least a friendly uncle, as the Christian Coalition was born. However, while it was still in its infancy, I had to go away for a while because of my work.

"I was offered a job as a broadcast news reporter for the ABC affiliate in Buffalo, and I also worked as a regional radio news stringer for ABC National News, covering events of national interest that happened in the area. During my first summer at the station, 1991, there was a far-off protest going on over abortion. It was way out in Wichita, Kansas, and although my pastors, Rob and Paul Schenck, were among the more than two thousand arrested during the seven-week protest, I didn't think it was going to affect me.

"But, just a few weeks after the all-time biggest Operation Rescue protest in the nation ended, the founder of Operation Rescue, Randall Terry, came clear across the country, right into the studios of the radio station I was working in, and announced that the next major national protest would be held right there in Buffalo. And he promised that it would be bigger than Wichita.

"That phrase, 'bigger than Wichita,' frightened the entire community. Howls of protest against the protest poured forth on the airwaves and around water coolers and coffee shops throughout the region. And for me, the concern went much deeper. I knew that my twin pastors were going to coordinate the event that they would call the Spring of Life. That meant I would have to go to my news director before the protest started and offer to recuse myself from covering the event.

Unfortunately for me, my boss overreacted, telling me I was going to be taken off of all on-air duties for as long as the Spring of Life protest lasted. I was terribly upset because I didn't see why I couldn't cover a fire or baseball game or town hall meeting, things that had nothing to do with the protest.

"When one of my pastors found out, he told me that it may have been God's way of making me a nonjournalist so I could serve the cause as a media coordinator, writing press releases and doing radio interviews everywhere in the country except Buffalo, so that I could return to my job after the Spring of Life protest ended.

"Concern for the cause mixed with anger at my boss, and I agreed to go into the secret communication and command center of Operation Rescue. Its national protest operation was housed in the headquarters of the New York State Christian Coalition, in a basement suite of offices the rescue people dubbed 'The Bunker.'

"That phrase turned out to be very revealing of the mindset of the men I was about to meet, and they were all male leaders in this women's issue. While I had been told by my pastors that the rescue people were committed to peaceful civil disobedience in the tradition of Gandhi and Martin Luther King Jr., I found a very different reality.

"During my first week in the bunker, I was given literature that advocated violence. First, there was a book called *99 Ways to Close an Abortion Clinic*, written by Joe Scheidler, one of the grand old crotchety men of the pro-life movement. It advocated all kinds of crazy things, from spraying noxious chemicals inside to locking yourself to the outside door with chains and Crazy Glue. The other really outrageous book was *When Bricks Bleed, I'll Cry*, which advocated the bombing of clinics, and had been written by minister Michael Bray, who was in jail for doing just that.

"While I was in the bunker I heard a national rescue leader lie on the phone to a church employee. He pretended to be the local United Methodist bishop so he could dig up dirt on a liberal minister who had helped the pro-choice side shuttle women through the picket lines outside the clinics. When the man was done with the call, I asked him why he would deceive someone like that. He said to me, 'Truth is the first casualty of war, and this is war, brother!'

"I knew something was wrong right then and there, but I thought the solution was to get people out of the illegal groups and into the Christian Coalition. I used to go right into the Operation Rescue rallies held weekly after the protest ended, and give pitches for people to get involved in the county chapter of the Christian Coalition, which I had recently been elected to head. I tried to stay friendly with the local Operation Rescue leaders while I tried to rescue the rescuers from the clutches of their own shepherds.

"I realized that Operation Rescue National had too many men in power who had adopted an ends-justify-the-means morality that put them on a very slippery slope. I realized that most of the leaders wanted to avoid violence, but those who had broken the law to block clinics no longer had the moral authority to stop those who wanted to go to the next step, and the next step, and so on.

"But even I was shocked when the Spring of Life protest was followed just one year later by what I now refer to as the Spring of Death, as bullets flew in the name of Christ to make diminutive Dr. David Gunn the target of the nation's first 'pro-life' killing. And that is how we got to where we are right here, right now . . . the scene of the crime."

SIXTEEN

The fog was as heavy as I'd ever seen it later that evening as I drove the half-hour trip east from Pensacola to Milton, where Rev. Burt pastored his flock of unwed mothers, the wayward women who had faced the choice between having an abortion or "keeping their babies."

The Our Father's House ministry, in which Burt both lived and worked, was in an isolated area nowhere near sight of the townspeople who gathered gregariously in the town named after the author of the classic work, *Paradise Lost*. But this Milton's paradise was going to be very different from anything I could possibly have foreseen.

As I got close to the house, a very dark thought entered my head. What if somehow Burt knew I was there to uncover his secrets and he was waiting to get his revenge? I brushed the thought aside, chalking it up to residual weariness from the lack of sleep I'd been getting. I told myself that although Burt had been the man who happened to "inspire" those young bombers before they went out and dropped off their "birthday gifts for baby Jesus," Burt had never taken it upon himself to do any violence to anyone. I had no way of knowing as I drove out to meet him that there were some surprises in store for me.

My first visual clue of things to come came as I finally pulled into the driveway of the house I hoped was his. There, on the back of a blue van, was a bumper sticker that read "Execute Murderers/Abortionists." I knew I was in the right place.

As I got out of my car and closed the door, I realized that there was perfect silence. I didn't hear a dog, a car, or even a cricket. I felt that if I stood really still, I might have been able to hear my heartbeat.

I looked at the driveway I was standing in and imagined the scene when the bomber "wanna-be," John Broeckhoft, dropped Burt off here and backed up a bit only to have federal agents find the explosives he had stashed in his trunk, bombs that had likely been there when he and Burt had taken their little drive-by around a local clinic moments earlier, unless he loaded them up right before he pulled out of Burt's driveway.

I walked toward the back door, feeling the dampness of the dewy, soupy fog, and knocked on the white outside door. Dogs started barking loudly from a kennel fifteen or twenty feet off to my right. They must've been some kind of hunting dogs for tracking prey. They howled in their hound dog blasts like fog horns, that elongated moan so distinct from other dogs.

One of the beasts threw itself at the chain link fence that I could barely see in the blanket of darkness that seemed to smother everything around me. I'd called Burt right before coming over, and now I was glad I had. Burt had locked the hounds from hell in their cages before I arrived, but I could only imagine the reception I'd have received otherwise.

A light came on over my head suddenly and the bigger, heavier inside door slowly opened. Through the glass on the top half of the outside door, I could see Burt's bearded countenance breaking into a smile, a big smarmy welcoming smile. Whether it was sincere or phony was not certain, but I'd sure take it over some of the other looks I'd seen him give at the courthouse earlier that week.

I opened the outside door and stepped up toward Burt. He said, "Come in, come in," and in my mind I added, "Said the spider to the fly." Burt stuck his hand out to shake mine and said, "So you made it out here on this horrible night, huh?"

We exchanged some pleasantries as we stood there on his back porch, which it looked like he was using for some kind of patriotic memorial to the Old South. There was a Stars and Bars battle flag of the Confederate forces, and there were huge prints of "Johnny Reb" soldiers, including one with a gray-uniformed young man whose head was bowed as he stood somberly above the slogan, "The South will rise again."

I said, "So, I see you're a fan of the Civil War?"

"The War Between the States; that's what we call it here, ya know? Once a Southerner, always a Southerner, I guess."

I couldn't help but wonder if Burt had collected some of these confederate souvenirs when he was in the Ku Klux Klan. His hooded friends from the group he said he was no longer part of certainly would have approved of his décor.

And, speaking of décor, I suddenly noticed the strangest lamp I had ever seen, and I dare say the strangest lamp that anyone anywhere had ever seen. Sitting atop a tiny desk across the room from me, the base of the lamp was what appeared to be four sticks of dynamite with wire lashed around the outside to hold them together with an alarm clock lashed in front. Above this bizarre contraption was a regular little white lampshade and an illuminated light bulb underneath.

"That's kind of different, isn't it?" I said as I pointed to the lamp (aka the bomb).

Burt chuckled, "Oh, yeah, it surely is. Walk over and get a closer look, ya'll will be surprised at how real it looks."

I took a few steps over there to stand right in front of the lamp. It really did look like dynamite. I thought of the five young bombers who had also been befriended by Burt. Had they stood in this very room before they just happened to decide to take action on their own? The lamp seemed to be Burt's way of showing the world that he was a part of the militant army of resistance to abortion, at least symbolically.

"Pick it up."

I snapped my head in his direction as I said, "No, thanks."

"C'mon, pick it up. Whaddya think, it's gonna bite ya?"

"Oh, that's all right, I can see it just fine from here."

"C'mon, pick it up."

To this day, I don't know why I did it, but I ever so slowly reached my hands out to the lamp. It looked heavy, and I wasn't sure what to think. Was he putting me on because it was so heavy I'd never be able to lift it?

I put my hands on the base, where the sticks of dynamite were and gave it a good pull up. Just as it lifted up off the desk, I heard this incredibly loud, "Tick! Tick! Tick! Tick!"

I immediately dropped it back down the few inches to the desk and jumped back reflexively, my heart racing from the sound that made it seem like it was getting ready to explode. But there was nothing but a brief second of silence.

It never blew up, but Burt exploded with laughter, a hearty chortle. It was the same "dirty joke" kind of laugh that Don Treshman had made back a couple weeks earlier on the call that started me down this path.

I thought to myself, This guy is nuts! Why else would he have this lamp here? It's the weirdest "practical joke" I've ever seen! But I knew I couldn't let on if I was going to get any helpful information from Burt, so I said, "Ya sure got me with that one."

"It scares everybody. Don't know why they're all so jumpy around little old me." Burt turned and walked into the next room as he said over his shoulder, "C'mon, I'll give you the grand tour. Ya'll are gonna be impressed."

I was already "impressed"; now I just had to get my heart restarted and I'd be fine.

The room we were stepping into turned out to be Burt's private study. There was a huge, dark cherry desk dominating the space in front of me, with bookcases behind the desk and smaller ones off to both sides. Most of the wood was dark cherry and it was nicer looking than I'd expected.

I followed Burt out into the large open area where I could see a living room, dining room, and part of the kitchen serving area. The place was cavernous, with cathedral ceilings above and casual colonial furnishings around the room. It was very homey and even cozy in spite of its size.

Burt introduced me to his wife, Linda, a pleasant-looking matron who greeted me with a smile. Then he introduced me to a couple of young women who were obviously pregnant and twenty-some years younger than the Burts. We barely said hello when Burt led me off to some of the rooms where the babies were.

In the separate boys' and girls' baby rooms, there were multiple cribs with mobiles twirling overhead. Every corner of the place seemed immaculately clean, and the décor was simple but warm, colorful, and inviting for this large, extended family. Burt was right after all; I was impressed, at least for the moment.

Burt had one of the women fix me a cup of coffee and then us men went back into his study while the women worked in the kitchen. Ah, divine order is good. Women are supposed to be "submissive" to men after all, aren't they? I thought to myself; of course, I didn't say anything out loud right then.

As we walked to the study, Burt started spouting facts and figures about the place, and I tried to pay attention but my mind drifted, "Rifles, guns, ammo," flashed through my mind. Where were they? Surely, a guy like Burt would have weapons. The lack of them was almost as disturbing as the sight of them would have been. But I couldn't find a way to work guns and ammo into the conversation in a way that wouldn't wreck the mood I was trying to create.

My goal was to get Burt talking as freely as possible. I wanted him to ease back a bit, drop his guard, and spill his guts. My interview would be the biggest soft-soap I'd ever sold. I found things to admire about the house, praised the cleanliness, the country setting, and so on.

Then I started talking about my pastors and my role in helping Operation Rescue when the big protest came to Buffalo. I was purposely looking for as much common ground as possible before beginning talk about anything even remotely related to the Griffin trial or the mysterious things to come. After all, I had come here on the premise to "just talk a bit."

Suddenly, the phone rang. Burt made no attempt to answer it, but someone elsewhere in the house did. One of the younger pregnant women came into the study, and said, "I'm sorry to interrupt, Rev. Burt, but you've got a call I think you should take in the living room."

"Oh, yeah, okay, I'll be out there in jes' a sec," he said. "'Scuse me."

I got the impression that he was going to take the call in the other room because I was not supposed to hear what was going on.

Being a nosy reporter, I stood up and started to walk toward the door to try to hear what he was saying. The young mother-to-be who'd called Burt away popped up in the doorway below my face so suddenly it startled me. "Rev. Burt will be with you when he can, Mr. Reiter. Why don't I take his place for a while, if you don't mind?"

There was something in her style of speaking that suddenly reminded me of the creepy automatons in the movie *The Stepford Wives*. But all I said to her was, "Sure, I don't mind. You could give me the point of view of a woman, a resident. Tell me your name, how long you've been here, and what you think of the place?"

She introduced herself as Michelle Andrews from Michigan. She'd been at Burt's facility for three months, and though she was young, only nineteen, she was a leader among the women. I asked her about that, and she was quite talkative. Her answers would prove to be more profuse than I could have ever used in my radio sound bites, but her observations would give me insights I'm sure John Burt never would have.

At first she gave me the usual spiel: wonderful place, great people, outstanding ministry, and so on. It was obvious that Our Father's House was helping some of the women who came there. That was good to hear, but nothing extraordinary. Then she happened to mention that all the women there were required to be born-again believers and to abide by the rules of the house and the ministry. As I inquired further into the difference between the house rules and the ministry rules she began to paint a portrait of women who were gung-ho about Jesus and John Burt or given the heave-ho to the door. She said nonchalantly, "A lot of the women don't make it. It's not easy, but it is right."

Then she began to get the glazed, euphoric look I'd seen on Andrew Cabot's face as she launched into an apocalyptic prediction, "The end times are upon us, and we have to be ready to put on the whole armor of God, to be ready to do battle with the powers and principalities of darkness. The devil and all his demons will not prevail against us, though, we already know we have the victory in Jesus, amen."

I knew what was expected, and said, "Amen!" I recognized that she was quoting from the Epistles of St. Paul and making reference to the final victory of Jesus over the devil promised in the Bible's Book of Revelation, the world's most famous piece of apocalyptic literature, the colorful work that has inspired poets and master manipulating cult leaders like deathbound David Koresh in Waco, Texas, or Jim Jones and his mass suicide in Guyana.

I asked Michelle how they were getting ready for the end times, and she said that they were storing food and water, and going on maneuvers. "Military maneuvers?" I asked.

"Well, not really," she laughed. "We're just a bunch of women, but we wanna be ready. Some of us are learnin' to shoot at least."

"Really? Are you any good at that?" I inquired as casually as I could.

"I'm gettin' there. I can shoot a pistol pretty good, and I like shooting semiautomatic rifles, but some of the women don't want anything to do with it."

I asked if shooting was part of the required house rules, and she said that it wasn't, but some of the women were really enthused about Rev. Burt's "encouragement" to take the end times seriously. Later, I would realize that I had failed to ask if the gun shooting that was not required under the house rules was required under the ministry rules.

Michelle told me she'd been told who my old pastors were. She didn't know the Schenck brothers, but she mentioned that Rev. Burt had been singing their praises and told her about how I risked my reporting career for the cause. She said, "You must be a brave man."

I got the feeling she wanted to impress me. She brought out some press clippings about the ministry, including one that showed her and two other young women dressed partly in paramilitary gear. The article made it sound like the young women were proud to be part of a militant extremist group, and I began to wonder if I'd stumbled into a "terrorist training camp," as Mann had put it.

Michelle was so young, a teen mother-to-be, and it was so obvious that she wanted to please, she wanted to be liked. How vulnerable she must have been to Burt's methods, I thought. I wondered if she would end up in jail in some future act of violence, "inspired" in the way that the six other young people had been to be part of either a bombing or a shooting.

There was something poignant about her situation. I realized that she would not have been talking about the end times and firing weapons if she had not met John Burt. She was a good kid at heart, but somehow she wanted to be accepted into this ministry so much she was willing to go gung-ho for God and get herself ready for guerrilla warfare in the coming end times.

Although the end times focus was unique to religious groups, Burt's ministry was beginning to appear to have much the same kind of effect on young people like Michelle as an inner-city gang. Michelle wanted to be accepted into the extended family they were offering, so she had to be ready to go to war for the group.

Like a street gang, Burt's ministry offered gun training and required a willingness to use weaponry when the leader said to. Blind faith to the group was going to be the number one priority of life. In both cases, it was a matter of survival. Gangs had to protect themselves from the bad guys in other gangs. Burt's followers had to protect themselves from the bad guys in Satan's gang.

Gangs had no problem using an ends-justify-the-means morality when they felt they were threatened or had to take action against their enemies, and Burt's protégés had shown some of the same willingness to do evil in order to protect their good cause.

In gangs the leader has a right to take a cut of the money the young people bring in. And, according to Michelle, John Burt took half of the welfare checks from the mothers-to-be in his "ministry."

In addition to whatever Burt took in from the women themselves, he also solicited donations from around the country for the young, needy mothers-to-be who were keeping their babies because of the dedicated staff who gave them a place to stay in Our Father's House.

Gauzy mother-and-child photos tugged at the heartstrings of pro-life donors from across America, but there was no mention of militancy in Burt's mainstream efforts. That was saved for the "true believers."

Since Burt was not on the staff of any church, there was no

accountability to any pastoral management authority. This was not uncommon in fundamentalist ministries, including many of the big televangelists on TV and radio who were raking in millions. But that meant that the bottom line at Our Father's House was that the only one who really seemed to know how much money he was bringing in was John Burt himself.

He may have made general financial reports, but when the envelopes arrived in the mail from concerned citizens who coughed up their hard-earned bucks to improve the lives of unwed mothers, it was John Burt who was there to count and account for the money. There was no evidence that he was pocketing the money for himself; but then again, how could there be? Burt was the only one who would know if cash or checks were going where they should. Since he wasn't going to report on himself, it was a situation that put him in the path of temptation, at the very least.

And speaking of temptation, Michelle said that she was going to have to excuse herself after talking with me for twenty minutes because it wasn't good that a man and woman were alone together for too long. As she got up to her feet, her stomach protruding outward as she approached her seventh month of pregnancy, I thought, Does she really think she's tempting me in this situation?

Then it occurred to me that maybe the thought was the other way around. Not that I, a person more than fifteen years her senior, would normally have been a temptation for her, but I got the impression that I was with someone who was ultimately very lonely, and I could see she was enjoying my visit. She never had male company herself there, and the only male company around on a regular basis was John Burt and Donnie Gratton, "eons older" in her mind, overweight, unattractive, and with their wives living under the same roof.

In some ways Michelle was just a normal nineteen-year-old girl who wanted to be with other youthful people and who enjoyed having a decent-looking guy listen to her as she shared her struggles and hopes and fears. In spite of her radical talk, she wanted to have some fun and socialize. Looking at her pregnant condition, she must have been having some fun in the past, but because of it there was hell to pay, so now she was leery of letting go anymore. She excused herself and left the room. I though about how different her life would have been if she had used birth control and stayed with her old crowd of friends. She said they were a good group, but she did some things she shouldn't have done. She became a sinner, John Burt had said when she told him about her past.

Unfortunately, as I would see time and again, the power of extreme ideas could steer people down an irreversible path in spite of all the good they could have accomplished had they been in an environment where others encouraged their higher potential instead of pandering to their worst fears.

It was ironic that people like Michelle, who had such a great fear of hell and damnation, were creating their own private hells where they were damned to live in fear of fellow humans who happened to be outside their chosen tribe or gang or ministry. The apocalyptic terror that bound them together gave them a heightened sense of community, which made them feel more closeness than they had ever experienced with any other group they'd been a part of in their lives.

These groups make their members feel like they are more alive than other people because of the energy that comes from the sense of mission they offer. Their theme is always some variation of "We, the faithful few, can change the world for our god." This was the carrot to keep them moving forward when they were weary.

And the stick that got their butts in gear when they were distracted was the darker side of the message, "The devil, like a lion, is lying in wait for you," giving them a sense that they were there to protect each other spiritually and physically in a hostile environment where no one but their fellow hardcore faithful brothers and sisters could be trusted. "It's us against the world."

That approach has been around since at least the days of the Old Testament, when one of the groups of ancient Israel declared itself "the faithful remnant of God" during a time they considered to be in a state of growing moral decay, when the world they saw around them had drifted into serious sin, sliding deeper and deeper toward the great spiritual abyss that threatened to swallow them whole.

The word "sin" had come from the time of Moses when he came down from his beautiful mountaintop experience carrying God's commands, and saw the people misbehaving in the Desert of Sin. From then on, sin became synonymous with people who were far from the high elevation where God lived and spoke. The Desert of Sin was where people were trapped in the harsh, arid conditions of life without the streams of living water that flowed from the mountains where God made his home.

Mountains were recognized in all religions throughout the world as a place where a truly devout person can go to commune with the Almighty. The mountain "high" is a physical reality that comes from the reduction of oxygen to the brain and the rush of sensory delights as one lifts his gaze off in great distances to see beauty all around. Going to the mountaintop also gives one a chance to look down on others, both literally and figuratively.

The sense of superiority was a trademark not only for the most radical people like Burt's young protégés, but for all groups that claim to have the "one true message" for the world. And, remarkably, these kinds of groups do very well in terms of growth and survival. Religious groups that are narrowly defined this way seem to flourish more than their open-minded counterparts, perhaps because it's so much easier and less complicated to be a "sheep" than an independent thinker.

People who have never been inside such a group scratch their heads in bewilderment at the apparent insanity of it all, but for those who are in it, that kind of absolute certainty can make a person feel like there is something solid under their feet in an ever changing world. It offers absolutes on an ever spinning planet where change is otherwise the only constant.

And, in spite of speculation that only unbalanced or uneducated people are drawn to absolutist groups, the facts and figures simply don't bear that out. Those lost to cults and dogmatic religions are just as likely to have been of sound mind and well educated as the population at large, but there are myriad complex reasons why some people find an absolutist solution to satisfy the various voids they feel within themselves. I know from my own experience how powerful the draw is.

What the outside world doesn't understand about these tiny extremist groups was that they give their members the same kind of comradery that members of the military feel when they are together in war or preparing for battle on the front lines. These apocalyptic apostles have a more intense bond with one another than they have with their own families, but the terror that brings them together and keeps them together also leads them to prepare for the worst possible scenario.

When the talk about fiery flames and final showdowns of Armageddon becomes too intensely real in the subconscious minds of the disciples, their visions can be indistinguishable from reality. As we see from time to time in cults and militia groups who arm themselves to the teeth, sometimes preparing for the bitter end becomes a self-fulfilling prophecy. When the "evil" empire of federal authorities comes knocking on their door, the disciples have to shoot first and ask questions later—because if they don't, they may be casualties in the culture war that is leading to the inevitable, divinely ordained Armageddon.

As I sat alone with my thoughts, I started to look around the room more carefully. On a small end table in the corner near my chair was a small statue. I reached over and picked it up. It was only about seven inches tall, so I hadn't noticed it before. It appeared to be handcrafted with great attention to detail in the paint strokes of the animal it depicted. As I looked at it, I couldn't believe my eyes. It was a wolf in sheep's clothing.

I had no idea why or how it had gotten there, but I was tempted to take it with me to show the world the only statue John Burt has in his home, the perfect symbol of what every one of his enemies had been saying about him. By hook or by crook, John Burt had been working hard to do what he believed had to be done.

He had been telling the faithful who sent him money that he was the shepherd of an innocent flock of sheep who had gone astray until he rescued them and gave them a place to stay until their little lambs were born, but his true intentions deep down may have inspired him to buy this small piece of art. Art imitates life.

Finally, Burt came rushing back into the room about twenty-five minutes after he had left. "Ah'm so sorry, but ah jes' hadda take that call," he explained. He sat behind his big desk facing me, looking a little rattled. I told him that the wait was fine, that I had been able to talk to Michelle for a while. He said, "Oh, really? That girl sure can talk, cain't she?"

I laughed and agreed, but said some positive things to soothe any possible concerns he might have had about what his young recruit might have said. He seemed to relax and get into our conversation. He smiled as he told me he had checked me out a bit, and I got good reviews.

We talked about the trial a little then, but mainly about the pro-life movement in general. Burt was concerned over the FACE bill becoming a big factor in the rescue movement, possibly destroying it altogether. Burt felt that that would only leave room for those who were willing to take more radical steps. He mentioned Paul Hill as an example.

I told him I'd had lunch with Hill, Andrew Cabot, and Donna Bray.

He chuckled and said, "Musta been a' interestin' talk."

I said, "That's for sure," and asked him how long Hill had been involved with the pro-life cause.

His answer surprised me. "Hill was never involved in the pro-life cause, not a rescue or a march or anything, far as ah can tell. Then, a coupla weeks after Dr. Gunn gets killed, Hill goes out and hires his self a publicist. Ya know, like a movie star or somethin'. First time ah ever laid eyes on the guy he's on the Phil Donahue show sayin' that what Mike [Griffin] done was justifiable homicide 'cause the doc was killin' babies. Then he showed off his Defensive Action Declaration paper, the petition."

I asked how Hill got the twenty-nine pro-life leaders from around the country to sign it, but Burt said he had no idea.

"But doesn't Hill live right in Pensacola here?"

Burt acknowledged that he did, but maintained that he didn't know Paul Hill prior to his public appearances in the media. I had no evidence to the contrary, but I thought that it was amazing how much John Burt "didn't know" about the people who were right around him in the cause.

He didn't know those five young people he shepherded into the pro-life movement would be advocates of bombing the nearby clinics within months of getting acquainted with him. He didn't know Michael

Griffin would shoot the doctor after spending time in a mentor-style relationship with him personally for several weeks. He didn't know Paul Hill before everyone else in the community did through the media, even though they were in the same small city.

Any or all of those positions were possible, after all. But one thing that would become clear as we spoke was that Burt didn't seem to lack any knowledge of Hill's future plans. First, though, he asked me to turn my tape recorder off so he could speak more freely.

I did and then told him about Hill's prediction of a coming reign of IRA-type terror. He laughed and said, "Paul's an enthusiastic guy who talks a good game so far; we'll see if he does more than talk."

I said that from what Paul Hill told me, it seemed like we were going to find out really soon. "I got a feelin' those abortionists aren't gonna know what hit 'em."

Burt smiled a knowing, Cheshire cat kind of grin, and said, "You could be right."

I said, "Well, I'm doin' a little more than guessing here. See, before I came down, our mutual friend, Don Treshman, told me that when I came down here I should stick around to cover the National Coalition of Abortion Providers pow-wow on the one year anniversary of Gunn's trip to heaven 'cause I'd see 'something big, something *really* big.' "

Burt smiled again, but said nothing. "What's the matter?" I said. "Don't you think I should cover that little get-together?"

"Oh, yeah, you should cover it . . . but not too closely." He laughed with the same kind of dirty chortle Don Treshman had when he talked to me about the coming event.

There was something creepy about the way Burt said not to cover it too closely. Obviously he wasn't talking about a picket or a prayer session. I told Burt I'd try to take his advice about not getting too close, and then I asked, "You're gonna be there, aren't you?"

"No way. Me and Don are gonna be somewhere far, far away."

"But this is gonna be really big," I said. "Why do you two want to miss it?"

Burt looked me hard in the eyes, and after a pause that was just long enough to drive the point home said, "'Cause we'd be the first suspects!"

Suspects, I thought to myself, sure sounds criminal to me. But I said aloud, "Oh, yeah, well I know I'm gonna stick around till next week, but I don't wanna get caught in the crossfire, if ya know what ah mean." Burt was now smiling like I was his long-lost son.

I took advantage of the feeling: "The trick for me is to find someplace close enough to the action to get a good look without getting myself in danger. But I don't even know exactly when I oughta be keepin' my eyes open the most. Guess I'll just have to stay on my toes the whole time."

"Yeah, just keep on your toes, that's good. But, did you know that them baby killers are gonna bring in a whole bunch of femi-Nazis from NOW and all those groups from around the country, and they're all gonna stand outside in the dark in a candlelight vigil together on the wide open grassy area near their meeting? Ain't that the dumbest thing they coulda thoughta doin'?"

Is he telling me the location and time of the "something big"? I thought. Are they going to toss bombs or open fire on the men, women, and children gathered on the grass? I managed to keep a poker face, and said, "You're kidding me! They're gonna stand outside together in the dark in a parklike area with candles in front of their faces, which'll be just bright enough to blind 'em to anybody standin' more than ten or twenty feet away?"

Burt laughed and said, "I don't know how anybody could be that dumb!"

"They're liberals," I said in agreement.

Burt loved it. "That's right. They think they know it all, and they'll be out there singing spiritual songs for the baby killer, and totally goin' along like they're a bunch o' good, God-fearin' Christians, and . . ."

I picked up the thought. "And like I said, they prob'ly won't know what hit 'em."

Burt laughed, but said nothing. He got up and started to walk away. Then from over his shoulder, he threw out a call for me to hang on for something special. He disappeared around the corner. I couldn't imagine what he was going to get, but I hoped it would be something about the plans. As I stood there feeling numb over the surreal conversation I'd just had, I felt the temptation to run out the door. But I knew I would have to wait. I wondered if he was going to give me a gun or a bomb or instructions to make a bomb. Instead, when he returned he was holding two T-shirts.

"These are special, and I want you to have them." The first T-shirt was black and done in the style of the POW shirts popular in the Vietnam War era, but instead of talking about the Vietnam War, it was dedicated to the "war on the unborn," and said, "25 million babies dead from abortion. More than all the casualties of all the wars America ever fought combined." It showed Jesus weeping with his head bowed, and the question, "How many more must die?"

I realized that this simple T-shirt was the summation of all that Burt believed about abortion. He wanted to share it with me as a token gesture to show that he was recognizing me as an ally in the cause. I myself had said words to the same effect as the T-shirt's message on many occasions when I was a leader in the Christian Coalition and later as a media coordinator for Operation Rescue. But now I felt I was inexorably tied to the murder of the doctor whose namesake I had recently met because I was one of the pushers of political rhetoric that was red-hot enough to have created a climate where some men felt they must take up arms in the "war" we told them about.

I felt a moment of compassion for Burt. He was trying to share something with me that he really valued. And maybe if I had come from his background, I would have ended up in the same spot he was.

After all, I had to admit to myself that the actions that he seemed to have at least inspired were the logical next steps to the groups I had worked for, which called abortion the genocide of the unborn, the holocaust of the womb.

The moment of connection and compassion I felt for Burt was immediately cut short by the second gift he gave me. On the front of this T-shirt was a drawing of the now-slain Dr. Gunn. It showed him holding a bloody fetus in his hands with the bright red blood running down his arms, and the caption, "Your doctor at the Murder Mill."

Then Burt flipped the T-shirt around and showed me the back. It had a picture of Dr. Gunn again, but this time there were big flames all around him, almost totally engulfing him. The caption said: "Your doctor in Hell!"

The impact of that T-shirt at that time felt like a right cross to the jaw, and Burt saw my surprise. He started to laugh his dirty chortle again, and said, "I wouldn't show that one to too many people."

Frankly, I don't remember where the conversation went after that, but somehow I found myself back in the car driving down the foggy roads. I didn't know what to do or who to call or how to stop this nightmare I seemed to be trapped in during this sleep-deprived week. I was so numb that I felt my mind was in as big a fog as the night air on the road to Pensacola.

SEVENTEEN

When the time came for the National Coalition of Abortion Providers to gather in Pensacola the following weekend, I still hadn't done anything. I guess I thought that since I couldn't prove anything, I would have to wait and hope for the best.

I went to the candlelight vigil for Dr. Gunn and was careful to stand a good, long distance away from the crowd. The crowd was predominantly made up of women, combined with smaller numbers of children and men. They were quietly singing "We Shall Overcome" as I approached on the sidewalk near the main entrance.

Suddenly, Paul Hill stepped forward with a bullhorn and a Bible. He began to read aloud, "To those who have ears, let them hear." The crowd started to sing louder in an attempt to drown him out. Hill just put that smug smirk that I'd seen earlier back onto his face, and then leaned forward and shouted, "This is the time to repent of the sin of baby killing! Is there one among you who will turn from your wicked ways? God says, 'If my people shall humble themselves and pray, and turn from their wicked ways, then will I hear their prayers!' "

A long-haired man stepped forward. Hill said, "Have you come to repent, brother?"

"Why don't you drop dead?" the man asked.

Hill replied, "I've got a better idea. Why don't you?" He reached into his knapsack and pulled out a grenade. The man stopped dead in his tracks. Hill pulled the pin and then tossed the grenade right near the man. There was a horrific explosion so loud it seemed to poke a hole in the night sky, but so bright it was day for the briefest fraction of a moment. Gasps, then screams followed.

"You were warned, now judgment day has come!" shouted Hill. Suddenly from behind the trees that surrounded the grassy area came a blaze of bullets screaming into the bodies of the women, men, and children who had nowhere to run.

I dropped to the sidewalk and crawled back behind a big Cadillac. I was terrified, but forced myself to look around. I could see a pay phone on the corner across the street, but it wasn't safe to get up and run over there. I wondered where the cops were. Then I saw two police officers starting to return fire, but one was shot in the head instantly, and the other was hit from behind and fell to the ground. As he lifted himself up on his elbow to take another shot, a grenade came from somewhere amidst the trees and—*kablow*—he was annihilated in a blast that left a bloody mess of tangled body parts, the remains of the cop and the people who were near him when the grenade went off.

A little girl was sitting near her fallen mother crying, "Get up, Mommy, get up!" The bullets just kept coming. The little girl took one in the head. I thought, This is insane. They're killin' babies and women and totally innocent people who have nothing to do with abortion.

A TV reporter and cameraman were crouched next to me. The reporter tried to do a stand up when a bullet hit her in the back of the head. She slumped down right next to me, and gurgled the most awful sound of pain and horror.

The TV cameraman was frozen but kept his camera rolling as he ducked for cover. I asked, "Are you broadcasting or taping?"

He replied, "Broadcasting."

I told him to put the camera on me so I could tell people what was going on. "This incredible scene of carnage is the result of a radical anti-abortion group led by a man named Paul Hill, a minister who was defrocked by his conservative church because of his work to garner national support for the idea that it was justifiable homicide to kill abortion doctors. Now Hill has taken his rhetoric and turned it to action right here in his hometown of Pensacola."

Just then Paul Hill himself came crawling around the corner of the car with a pistol in his hand, and said to me, "Did they at least give you thirty pieces of silver, Judas?"

I said, "Paul, this is your chance to tell the world why you are doing this."

He said, "The world will not understand for I am not of this world. But you will not be in this world much longer. Do you know you are standing at the Gates of Hell one last time, and this is your very last chance to repent?"

He pointed his pistol at my face, just inches away from me. I thought it was all over . . . over . . . over. . . .

Then I jumped up in a cold sweat, my heart racing wildly, realizing suddenly that I was in my motel room again. I was all alone in the dark. I trembled as I tried to come fully back to reality. It must have been a nightmare, but it had been so vivid, so real. Everyone has those kinds of dreams from time to time, but why did it have to be now, of all times?

I stumbled my way over to the light switch on the wall. Then I walked into the bathroom. The cold ceramic tiles beneath my feet felt real, and the cold water I splashed on my face brought me back into my body completely, but the fear I'd felt stayed close to the surface of my subconscious.

"I've gotta do something!" I said aloud. I dried my face and walked back to the bed. I would have to go to the cops, but I didn't want to go to just any cop. As a reporter, I'd had too many difficult or unpleasant experiences trying to get information from the police to want to just walk up to one and hope he'd take my information seriously.

I remembered a reporter from the local TV station who had befriended me at the beginning of the trial. I decided that I would go to her the next day and ask if she knew a cop who was trustworthy. The idea just seemed right. I turned off the light and lay back down on the bed. For the first time that week I fell into a deep and peaceful sleep.

EIGHTEEN

On Friday morning, March 4, while everyone was awaiting the testimony of John Burt, I went up to local TV reporter Lee Sinclair during the morning break in the trial. I asked her for the name of a trustworthy policeman in town and she suggested I talk to Detective Perry Knowles, a local SWAT team member. She assured me that he was a great guy and would help me if he could. She asked what was up, and I told her briefly what I suspected.

She asked to get me on tape that day for possible use the following week only if the suspected act of terrorism did occur. Out of gratitude for her help, I offered an interview where my face was covered and my voice altered. She said she would arrange it immediately. She asked me to go with her and her cameraman to the lawn outside so we could tape a segment.

As we got outside we saw Hans and I told him to come with us to tape the segment I was going to do. We found an isolated spot on the lawn and as soon as the cameraman waved his finger toward me, I began.

"As I tape this, the trial of Michael Griffin is nearing its end, but I have evidence which suggests the trouble in Pensacola is far from over. I have reason to believe that the same man who is accused of masterminding the murder of Dr. Gunn has knowledge of a mass-murder plot to be led by Pensacola's own Paul Hill, the former minister who was defrocked for advocating the use of force to stop abortions.

"During the week that the trial has been conducted, I have been told by Hill that we are all about to see what he calls "a coming reign of IRA-type terror," and Hill is not alone. He has been joined this week by a group of people from around the country who believe that he is a great visionary who is going to do for the antiabortion movement what John Brown did for the abolitionist movement as the nation moved toward civil war a century ago.

"Hill has told me that he believes America is once again heading toward a full-fledged civil war, but that this time it will be over the issue of abortion and the rest of the issues involved in the culture war. He has applauded the actions of the assassin who committed a 'pro-life' murder and approves of the culture war turning into a shooting one.

"Yesterday, I was given an uncomfirmed report that a man with two duffel bags said to be filled with automatic or semiautomatic weapons had arrived at the trial and had conferred with Hill's group. I have made arrangements to talk to the Pensacola police, and I hope that you never see this tape because if you do, it means that something has gone wrong for those of us who want a peaceful resolution to these controversial issues."

Lee thanked me and said that she also hoped that this would be one story we would not have to tell. With the help of the police, there should be some way to stop this. She thanked me for being brave enough to come forward in such a dangerous situation.

She and the cameraman went back inside while I talked to Hans. He said, "I've got bad news. De guy vith the guns never showed last night at the hot dog stand. I don't know vhere he is."

We were both upset, but I told Hans, "All we can do now is let the cops handle this."

He agreed and said he didn't want to ever deal with these people again. I couldn't say that I blamed him. I was very anxious to get the whole thing behind me, too. But it wasn't over yet.

As we entered the courthouse and got past the metal detector (which we were now glad was in place), we saw Paul Hill and his entourage. Donna Bray was missing, but Andrew Cabot was there along with a bunch of men I did not recognize. We said hello as we approached, and Hill called me over. He told the men about my work for Operation Rescue and who my old pastors were. Then he introduced me to them. I wish I could have remembered all the names, but some would stick out.

There was an older minister named Donald Spitz, who appeared to be one of those "powerful and controlling types" like John Burt. With him was a dark-haired young man who seemed rather disturbed. Later I would come to the conclusion that he was likely the man I saw on television shooting and killing health-care workers at abortion clinics. I strongly suspected, though I've never been able to verify, that the young dark-haired man's name was John Salvi. The rest of the names went by in a blur, though I wrote some of them down a moment later on inside the elevator.

When I got back upstairs it was hard to focus on the routine radio setups, throwing cable and connecting coaxials while my mind raced with thoughts of the approaching apocalyptic showdown. But I had to get refocused.

The day before, the prosecution had rested its case, and the defense had begun to present its own. Defense attorneys Bob Kerrigan and Bill Eddins had begun to look for the chinks in the armor of the state's case against Michael Griffin.

They didn't go after the fact that it was Griffin's gun that killed Gunn or that Griffin was at the scene. Instead, they tried to prove that John Burt had masterminded the whole scene and Donnie Gratton had shot the doctor. They stuck to their story that the defendant only turned himself in because he was under Burt's influence after having watched the gory antiabortion videos and having come under the mysterious spell of John Burt.

The defense attorneys had both Burt and Gratton on their list of witnesses, but first they called a string of other witnesses in to offer a different version of events than the prosecution had served up. Since the defense wanted to show that Burt was capable of doing something so horrible as masterminding a murder, they called the slain doctor's girlfriend, Paula Leonard, to the stand. Leonard, a striking blonde many years the doctor's junior, came across as a kind and caring woman who had been harassed horribly by one of Pensacola's most notorious characters, none other than John Burt.

The single mother told of terrifying incidents when a blue van she believed to be Burt's tailed her closely down rural roads, forcing her to drive faster and faster to get away. She described careening around corners wondering if she and her small daughter were going to be pushed off the road.

Leonard also said that Burt often followed her to her home, where Dr. Gunn also lived when he was not on the road driving the three-state, six-day-a-week trek he endured to provide abortion services at women's clinics in the region. Leonard said that Burt and Gratton would often picket outside the house as she and the kids would enter, and Burt would shout at her such greetings as, "Why don't you find a real man and a real daddy for your kids instead of a butcher?"

Leonard described her shock and horror when Burt showed up at the funeral with his bullhorn and Bible, saying, "Even after David died, he wouldn't leave us alone." The petite young mother was shaking and weeping at times as she told the stories. Everyone could feel the intensity of her fear and grief coming through, and when she said that she held Burt partially to blame for the slaying even the prosecutor didn't object.

Talk about a tough act to follow. By the time Paula Leonard left the witness stand, with hankie in hand, she had made everyone in the courtroom feel what she had endured from John Burt. Then Burt himself had to take the stand.

There would be no games of checkers or technicians wearing funny hats in the press room as Burt strode to the box. My colleagues all knew that this might be the main event in this weeklong, real-life drama.

Dressed in a dark suit and conservative tie, armed with a look of somber sincerity, the graybeard took the stand, which he saw as a potential bully pulpit for his views. To John Burt, this testimony was not so much about a dead doctor as it was about twenty-five million dead unborn babies. But Burt would also be careful to keep his guard up as he testified, so that he did not say anything that could get him into legal trouble.

Well aware that he had been accused of such heinous acts, Burt tried to soften his image by speaking in an uncharacteristically reserved way. But he couldn't completely cover the hard edge in his whiskey rasp of a voice; he could only lower the volume and modulate the tones to sound more moderate than he really was.

Obviously, Burt was no stranger to the limelight in court or in the media, and he drew on every trick he'd ever learned. He spoke respectfully to Bob Kerrigan, the defense attorney he had publicly accused of slandering his good name during the opening remarks. The reverend knew how to say the minimum required when it came to matters of substance, but he also used every opportunity he could to preach on the tragedy of abortion.

Burt admitted that he had shown two graphic antiabortion videos to Michael Griffin and his wife. They were called, *The Hard Truth* and *A Song for David* (which seemed to have a new, ironic meaning now that David Gunn was dead). "They show the truth," Burt said as he saw the opportunity to preach his message. He became more animated than he had been in his controlled moments as he said, "The abortionists say it's just a blob of tissue. But they lie. When you see these videos, you can see they're babies."

Burt claimed that Michael Griffin had shown no emotional reaction whatsoever to the "Christian" videos or to the jars of pickled fetuses he had been shown in Burt's home, even though the jars contained baby parts—arms and legs torn from torsos and tiny feet floating in formaldehyde.

Burt was making the point that Griffin was not emotionally distraught in order to try to refute the defense's claim that the videos and other propaganda Burt used had altered Griffin's emotional state to the point that he was willing to do anything for the cause. It was obviously something that had been well thought out ahead of time, and had Burt stopped there he might have squelched the defense's claims convincingly.

But Burt wanted to talk about the abortion war and the defense wanted to let him. Burt told the court about a "funeral" he had held for babies that had never been born. "It was a decent Christian burial, like them little babies deserved," Burt said.

Suddenly all eyes shifted away from John Burt because the defendant was bursting into tears, his face fully contorted with the pain inside himself at the recollection of the images that Burt's testimony so chillingly made alive once again. This wasn't a case of a tear running down the cheek, either. Michael Griffin was actually sobbing audibly and visibly. It was a shocking and visceral cue revealing to all of us the connection between the two men, and the power of the shocking imagery that Burt could muster even when he was just talking.

It felt to many of us that this moment was as real and genuine a statement as any testimony that had been spoken. Without any words, the high-school-educated chemical worker had articulated a stronger point than either of his better-educated attorneys had.

But as he settled down, Griffin's attorney helped him. He drove the point his client had made right home as powerfully as could be. Burt was asked about an effigy. He freely admitted and even seemed proud of the fact that at the chilling funereal scene he created for the fetuses, he had displayed an almost life-size effigy of Dr. Gunn with a noose around his neck, blood-colored paint on his hands, and a Bible verse scrawled on his chest.

We could feel the powerful connection between Burt's desire to have Gunn killed, as symbolized by the effigy, added to Griffin's obvious sense of symbiotic connection to his svengali-like mentor. Even though Burt was trying to hide his powerful personality, his controlling ways of thinking came through in the courtroom. Burt was on his best behavior, but his darker nature was still visible behind the mask from time to time.

Though we would never fully know the specifics of the words that had passed between the two men, the defendant and John Burt had together created the first palpable reasonable doubt that Griffin had really done what the prosecution said he had done—acted alone to commit a premeditated murder.

Had the defense stopped right there, the jury might have come down with a reduced verdict. But that was not the goal of the defense team. They were going to go all out, win it or lose it all based on where the chips fell in the final throw of the dice. Everything would ride on the outcome of the testimony of one last witness.

Burt was immediately followed to the stand by his faithful friend, Donnie Gratton, the man a clinic worker said received a handshake from Burt immediately after the shooting, what the worker described as the equivalent of a high five after a victory.

Gratton gave almost identical testimony to Burt's, almost word for word, but was more combative in tone. When asked about the handshake following the shooting (which Burt had denied), Gratton stated that he didn't recall shaking hands with Burt in the entire decade they were friends. That didn't ring true, and Kerrigan fired off question after question to try to rattle this critical witness.

Gratton answered in cold, clear tones. He said flatly that he had not shot the doctor, that he was not behind the clinic at the time of the shooting, but up in front with his pal Burt. He was bold and unapologetic in tone. His attitude seemed to say, "I didn't do the crime, and you ain't gonna make me do the time."

The verbal blows between Kerrigan and Gratton were so fierce at some points that Brian Wice, a commentator for Court TV, later said, "Gratton was punishing. If it had been a prize fight, the referee would have called it on cuts."

The bottom line after the smoke cleared was that the defense attorneys had presented no hard evidence to prove their contention that Gratton was the triggerman instead of Griffin. Gratton walked away from the witness chair completely confident that he had cleared himself. He had given no quarter in his effort to disprove the allegations against him. He publicly maintained his innocence and said the allegations had angered him because—plain and simple—they weren't true.

The feeling of momentum shift was palpable for all of us who had invested ourselves in the weeklong soap opera. It now seemed a foregone conclusion that Michael Griffin would be convicted, while John Burt and Donnie Gratton had cleared themselves of any possible criminal entanglements, though we did not yet know that the Gunn family would go after Burt in a civil trial.

The Griffin trial was not over yet. Both sides would offer up their closing arguments the following day, though it was not expected to take all day. Remembering how Hans loved comics and cartoons, I quipped to him that we would probably be out in time for him to watch Saturday morning cartoons.

Even though we had at least part of another day ahead, all my colleagues were feeling that it was all over, while I was worrying about what was to come. Lee had given me a note that indicated Detective Perry Knowles would be waiting for me outside the courthouse as soon as we broke for the day.

Sure enough, as soon as I stepped out the doors I saw a SWAT officer standing there scanning the crowd. He was wearing a black T-shirt, black fatigues, and black boots. He had a walkie-talkie on one hip and a gun on the other. His arms were semifolded across his chest, with one hand reaching toward his face and his fingers caressing his salt-and-pepper moustache.

With a macho swagger in his walk, he came up to me and nonchalantly said, "Hi, Jerry," as though we were casual acquaintances getting together for a cup of coffee.

"I guess Lee filled you in on who I am and why I wanted to talk to you."

He nodded in acknowledgment but said, "Go ahead and just start from the beginning, anyway."

I gave him all the relevant pieces of evidence and quickly outlined what I suspected was going to happen: "I believe it's possible they will open fire at the candlelight vigil during the National Coalition of Abortion Providers gathering on the one-year anniversary of the death of the slain doctor. And if they do, they may kill dozens or even a hundred or more people."

Knowles bit down on his lower lip, absorbing what I had just hit him with, and then said, "I'd like you to talk with Fred McFaul, a special agent with the FBI. Would you do that for me, Jerry?" His tone was so cordial it surprised me. As a reporter, I had dealt with a lot of rough-around-the-edges cops; I realized that this time I was dealing with a very smooth and professional officer.

I agreed and, being a good reporter, asked when and where.

Knowles said he would have to set something up with Agent McFaul. He took my number at the motel and asked me to meet him in the morning back in the same spot when the trial took a break.

Later that evening, Hans called me in my motel room and asked me to come over to meet his boss, Tony Kaye. The director had finally arrived in town and was very excited to hear the incredible string of events I had been telling Hans about.

He asked me to join them at 7:30 in the morning, before the trial started. "It's on us, and ve'll take you to your favorite restaurant for breakfast," Hans said to lure me. He knew that I always raved about the buffet they put out at Shoney's each morning. He had laughed at me for being so enthusiastic about a national chain restaurant known for its bargain prices rather than its gourmet cuisine, teasing, "You must be a cheap date."

That night I was feeling restless, so I went to a nightclub I'd heard was good. It had been such an incredibly stressful week that I wanted a chance to get a drink and let off some steam. *Thump, thump, thump* pounded the bass as I approached the club that I'd heard about from some of my colleagues. The place was big and dark and fairly crowded with Friday night revelers. I went to the bar, got some drinks and conversation, and the next thing I knew it was 2 A.M.

Not being much of a drinker, I was feeling it as I drove back to the motel. I thought how ironic it would be if I couldn't meet the police and the FBI in the morning because I had gotten busted for DWI on my way home that night.

Fortunately, I made it back fine, but when the alarm clock went off at 6:30, the four hours of sleep I'd had felt more like four minutes. Even the shower spray hitting me in the face didn't seem to wake me all the way. When I got down to Shoney's I had to wait for Hans and Tony. Being Hollywood types they must be planning to make a big arrival scene, I thought to myself, but they arrived shortly.

Hans was beaming as he said, "Tony Kaye, this is Jerry Reiter, the fabulous reporter, and Jerry, this is Tony Kaye, the fabulous director."

We each said, "Nice to meet you," and made a little small talk as we made our way to the buffet to load up on eggs and pancakes and fruit.

With his long leonine mane brushed back and a dark goatee and moustache above his Nehru jacket, Tony Kaye looked every bit the avant-garde artist he is, though the stylish filmmaker had made his mark not in the world of independent art films, but in the much more lucrative and cutthroat world of commercials.

He was a world-traveling jet-setter, originally from England, and though he's lived in California for many years, his British accent is one of the first things people notice about him. His worldliness is one of the other things that comes through in short order. He has a way of speaking that reveals an idealistic heart tinged with a world-weary cynicism.

He told me about the documentary that Hans was helping him produce. They were going to produce this huge compendium of interviews and action shots, and "let the story tell itself," he stated. I suggested that they consider giving the story a dramatic sense of build and story development. Tony asked, "What did you have in mind?"

I said that I thought my experience, having been a hardcore pro-lifer and then being horrified by the growing violence, would make a perfect thread to hold the footage together as a strong narrative. Tony said my story was fascinating and he would consider it, but he wasn't ready to ditch his original approach.

I was disappointed because it could have been a very interesting possibility for me, and could have opened up some other doors. Then Hans reminded me that he needed me to sign a permission waiver so they could use my interviews in their film, only he had no more with him, so he'd have to send me one.

When we arrived at the courthouse, the media room seemed unusually warm. As we listened to the closing arguments, I nearly dozed off, due in no small part to the night before. I remembered the old biblical quote my friend's mother had thrown at him on the nights he came home after drinking too much, "The wages of sin is death," and I thought it was appropriate because I felt like I was dying.

When the jury went out around lunchtime to begin the deliberations, a pro-choice group launched a "verdict vigil" to wait for the results. But both Paul Hill and John Burt had announced ahead of time that they would not do likewise. They had decided to keep a lower profile, at least for the time being.

Normally, in a murder trial, the wait for the verdict is a time when reporters get to visit with each other and unwind a bit from the long days or weeks of proceedings. But for me, it was time to meet with the FBI.

I'd seen Detective Knowles at the break and he told me that Agent McFaul would meet me around 1:00. While I was waiting for him outside the courthouse, Eleanor Smeal, president of the Feminist Majority, came out. I asked her for a brief interview. She agreed and was a charming, articulate spokesperson for her issues, not at all the ogre I had suspected feminists to be just a few years before when I was being fed the usual line by conservative Republicans, conservative Christians, and Rush Limbaugh. I had been a faithful dittohead listener to Rush and other conservative talk show hosts back then, but my world was rapidly changing.

At a few minutes to 1:00, Agent McFaul arrived. Fred was even taller than I, and he was pretty husky for a federal agent. I didn't know then that he was only months from retiring. He was a courtly old gent with a quick laugh when appropriate, and with a very detail-oriented approach to his questioning techniques.

As he started to pepper me with questions, McFaul realized there was a lot to my story. He said, "We need to go over to headquarters, and get this all down." I told him that I needed to stay at the trial until the verdict came down, and that the plot I suspected would take place there would not happen right away—we had time. He agreed to wait until I was done getting the verdict, and I explained I had to get the tape of the verdict to the BBC before I could leave.

Fortunately, we had a short wait, as jury deliberations go. Only two hours and forty minutes after they began the process, the jury was ready to render its verdict. It was an urgent rush back to the press room for all of us, and the sense of anticipation was electrifying.

Like a courtroom drama in the movies or on TV, the judge asked the foreman for the verdict. The twelve-member jury had to decide unanimously in order to convict. As prosecutor Murray put it, "The prosecution needs twelve jurors, the defense only needs one," referring to the possibility of a hung jury.

There would be no hung jury in this case, however. All twelve jurors unanimously agreed that Michael Griffin was guilty of first-degree, premeditated murder. A wave of cheers started up in the court-room, but was immediately squelched by Judge Parnham.

Smiles graced the faces of the surviving Gunn family members and their friends and supporters, while tears flowed quietly down the stricken face of Patricia Griffin at finding out that, for all practical intents and purposes, she had just lost her husband.

The judge thanked the jury for its service, praised the attorneys for their ethical and professional handling of the case, and immediately pronounced the mandatory sentence of life in prison, with no chance of parole for twenty-five years. Michael Griffin showed no emotion as he was taken away from his wife and his children; their childhood would be long gone if and when he was let out of prison.

I gathered my tapes together and phoned in the recording of the verdict. I was working with employees of the BBC in Washington, D.C., and they thanked me for my work. Then I took my black bag and left the courthouse for the last time.

An unmarked gray car was idling at the curb with Fred McFaul inside. I walked up and asked him to wait just a few more minutes. I wanted to get the family's reaction when they came down in a few moments. McFaul agreed and turned off the car to wait.

A hastily assembled podium with microphones was waiting on the walkway near the main doors as the family, led by David Gunn Jr., came out. The women were smiling, but young Gunn had a more serious look on his brow as he stepped up to the podium. He had become accustomed now, at the age of twenty-three, to being the father figure to his family in the year since his father's death.

He called for a federal investigation to determine whether Michael Griffin acted as part of a conspiracy. He mentioned the "Wanted— Dead or Alive" posters of his father that had been distributed at a rally led by Operation Rescue founder Randall Terry just weeks before his father was assassinated. He referred indirectly to the points made by the defense attorneys, "There have always been allusions to a con-spiracy and I have always thought that Michael Griffin did not act alone. . . . We will not rest until there is a complete investigation."

When asked, Gunn stopped short of saying who he thought the

conspirators could be. In response to a reporter's question, Gunn mentioned the shooting in Alabama of an abortion doctor the summer after his father was killed. Police had said robbery, rather than abortion beliefs, had been the motive. Gunn said he wasn't so sure.

He was followed to the podium by Eleanor Smeal, president of the Feminist Majority, who did not echo the talk of conspiracy directly, but complemented it, saying, "The questions raised by the defense about the climate of violence here must be addressed." I thought about going over and telling her that she and her friends might become victims of that "climate of violence" within the week, but I realized I would have to let the FBI handle it so that they might be able to arrest any possible perpetrators. If I told her what I suspected, I might spill the beans on the investigation. It was one of those tough calls where both options, telling or not telling, had very major downsides.

As Smeal and Gunn stood together for a moment to allow their photographs to be taken, a very unwelcome guest came to the microphone. Leaning over the podium was the tall, gangly body of Paul Hill. He immediately launched into his tirade calling the murder of Dr. Gunn justifiable homicide and warning that God was going to judge the nation for its murder of the unborn. He predicted that many righteous Christians were going to rise up and take to the streets, that the Gunn shooting was just the first of a new resistance that would culminate in a civil war.

"Are you the next shooter, Hill?" one of the reporters bluntly asked. Hill hesitated a moment and another reporter said, "Nah, he's all talk." A third reporter groused, "What a windbag!"

Hill was visibly upset and warned them, "You are going to see God's judgment." I wished my sarcastic colleagues would not have taunted him. I felt they were egging him on, and that his fragile ego might snap. And I did not want to see him feeling even more justified in his positions as he pondered how to proceed.

"Vengeance is mine." So said the God of the Old Testament. Hill was going to adopt that slogan with one minor variation; he was going to "help" God pass out that vengeful judgment. He was glad to live in a country that was wise enough to hold onto the Second Amendment to its constitution.

Hill put on his smug smirk and walked away; the next time I would see him covered in such a major way by the electronic media would be after he had taken up some serious firepower and launched a shooting spree that would end with multiple homicides as part of "helping" to promote God's grand and glorious plan to "purify" the nation and the church.

John Burt and Donnie Gratton did not wish to follow Hill to the podium after his ranting preachments, but they told the reporters present that they had been slandered by the defense attorneys during the trial, and that they were considering suing Kerrigan—that is, until they were made aware that witnesses or attorneys cannot be sued for statements made in a courtroom.

Gratton said, "Kerrigan should stick to ambulance chasing and leave criminal defense to a real attorney."

When told of the comments by the two men, Kerrigan replied, "If they don't like it, they should take it up with the witnesses. The best thing they could do is quit advocating violence, get rid of those bumper stickers and those effigies of abortion doctors with nooses around their necks."

Gratton's comments on David Gunn Jr. were the most surprising of all, and more telling than he himself realized. He was particularly impressed that young Gunn had come up to Burt to shake his hand during the trial, and Gratton said of the fatherless young man, "In some ways he outdid some of the Christians. I am sorry he will live without a father and Griffin's family will live without a father. It is a tragedy that should have been avoided."

Though his statement sounded reasonable on the surface, those who thought he had been more involved than he let on were chilled by the logic. It sounded like it might be constructed to say different things to different audiences, the way that Burt often seemed to.

Burt used the media's willingness to listen as a way to warn the public what might be ahead for them if pro-lifers did not get what they wanted. He said that the verdict against Griffin could "inspire even more extreme actions." He said that he and Gratton would not take part in any such tactics, and I recalled his earlier words, "Cause we'd be the first suspects."

Gratton bemoaned the growing buffer zones around clinics and the restrictions on people who protested. He ominously predicted, "Now all you're going to have left are the extremists, the shooters and the bombers." He warned that the future belonged to the Paul Hills and Michael Brays, who were calling the slaying of doctors "justifiable homicide."

One woman thought that Gratton's attempt to scare people by raising the specter of other extremists was missing the mark. K. B. Kohls, administrator of a women's center across the border in Alabama, said in response, "I think anyone who saw the testimony of Burt and Gratton would be truly scared, I don't care where you stand on the issue." She was not alone in putting Burt and Gratton in the same camp that day, not surprising in light of all that had been said during the week by the defense attorneys.

Burt and Gratton were less than happy about their new public image, to say the least. Outside the courtroom Gratton said, "I went from being looked upon as a loveable, funny character to a murderer packing a gun. I would walk around and people would say, 'There is the man that killed Dr. Gunn.'"

NINETEEN

I was whisked away by the FBI agent right after hearing Burt and Gratton's comments. I thought that they had either given a denial of their wrongdoing or a wrathful warning of woe to come, depending on which way you wanted to interpret it. I wondered, as we roared along in the nondescript cruiser following Detective Knowles and two other SWAT officers in another unmarked vehicle, if Burt had seen me get into the gray car.

I was pretty far from them and they were still talking to the press about their reactions to the whole thing while I was whizzing down Pensacola streets at speeds I thought were for life-and-death situations. Then again, that's exactly what this was—or at least it had the potential to be.

McFaul told me he was going to take me to a Pensacola police precinct station for questioning. I'm not sure why we didn't go to his office, though I didn't really care where we went as long as we got there soon. When we screeched to a stop outside the police department office, McFaul and I followed the three SWAT officers into the building.

When we entered the main area there was a long, high counter in front of us in the slightly shabby station. The place looked deserted other than the five of us who had just entered. McFaul told me to take a seat "while they fix up a place for us upstairs."

I sat on one of the green-seated, silver-framed chairs along the wall. Its back was made of three straight square silver bars and it was very uncomfortable, which matched my mood at the moment. McFaul and the officers went up in the elevator, leaving me all alone with my thoughts, which started racing: If John Burt finds out about this I could end up like Dr. Gunn, and my wife would go through a trial like Paula Leonard did. Suddenly, in my mind's eye, I envisioned the surreal scene. My grieving widow having to sit there in court while John Burt and Donnie Gratton told everyone how innocent they were in my murder, that some poor schmuck who had never even met me was the murderer.

It was so vivid because I had just come through the real-life experience that seemed so similar to it, and the thought of my own potential situation gave me a greater insight into what the Gunn family might've been going through at the trial.

Sitting there alone in that dreary place, I felt more fear than I had at any time up to this point. Part of me wanted to run out the door and head home. I found myself getting to my feet and pacing back and forth across the ancient-looking checkerboard tiles in the reception area.

I thought about the incredible irony of the moment. Here I was, a person who was vehemently against abortion to the point where I had risked my career only two years earlier by helping Operation Rescue, and now I was literally risking my life to protect the lives of abortionists. It was as if my world was turning inside out. For my whole life, right up until the first week I went to work inside the headquarters of Operation Rescue National, I was as certain as anyone could be that we in the pro-life movement had God on our side, and that the pro-choice people had sold their souls to the devil.

But since then, I had met so many twisted, angry men who seemed to be trying so hard to turn back the hands of time to some glorious era of perfect paradise in the past that they were ruining their own futures and their families' futures. Paul Hill lost his pastoral ordination because of his fanatical insistence on getting people to applaud Michael Griffin's actions, but didn't he see what had really happened?

Griffin hadn't saved any "babies," because the women who wanted to have abortions merely had to drive to another clinic to get them, and his actions were the nail in the coffin that essentially shut down the entire protest movement run by the various rescue groups. The net result was that after the shooting, clinics had better security and, without the blockaders in the way, women had easier access to clinics than before.

In the meantime, he had lost the babies who counted most, his own young children, and while he risked his very life to stop mothers from getting abortions, he could no longer be with either his own mother or the mother of his children, because his actions had put walls and bars and miles between them for life.

And to top it all off, this "hero," whom Paul Hill had thrown away his own livelihood to laud, had broken under the brutality of prison and would have gone back in time if he could have in order to undo the damage. He was fully ready to recant and would have pled insanity if it had been feasible.

This brave practitioner of the new theology that was going to conquer the world for Christ turned into a broken shadow of a man, reduced to tears and whining when the pressure mounted. The Bible he waved in the air as a symbol of his defiance was now a sad reminder of a life gone terribly wrong.

I thought about a lesson I'd learned many years earlier as a Boy Scout learning to read maps and follow compasses. We were told that sometimes people make a simple mistake when reading the compass, and then base their entire journey on that premise. No matter how carefully they plan the trip from there on out, though, they are going to be lost.

We were warned that when you take a reading with the compass, give it one more test, the test of simple common sense. If the compass tells you that west is over in that direction where the morning sun is rising, you'd better recheck it.

I thought of the parallel here. Michael Griffin and Paul Hill had misread their own inner compasses. It was obvious to everyone who knew them best, including their wives and pastors (and in Paul's case, his entire church ruling board), but they had mapped out a journey for themselves that would get them lost from their families and friends forever.

In Griffin's case, it was easier to understand because he did not get good guidance in that bad time, but Hill seemed hell-bent on going down the same path Griffin had just gone down, and he seemed to be able to blind himself to the consequences. I felt that I might be the only person who could stop him.

Still, I did not wish to become the flip side of the same coin. I did not want to be martyred by these seemingly mad messiahs for playing Judas to them. I did not want to have to go into hiding, like author Salman Rushdie when the Ayotollah issued the sacred *fatwah* death order against him.

But I couldn't focus too much on the danger right now. I had made up my mind that I was going to give this information to the authorities because it was the right thing to do, and I had come too far to turn back now. I began to wonder if the feeling of having come too far to turn back was what was motivating Paul Hill at this point.

He had lost his career as a pastor for his position on justifiable homicide, and he was spending his days working on broken-down cars for a used-car dealer. His family was hurting, and no doubt so was his pride at the stinging rebuke he received from his church board and the low to which he had fallen in his career.

Hill wanted to prove them all wrong. There may have been times when he questioned his course, but it was possible that he felt he couldn't turn back now because he'd come so far and given up so much already. I only hoped there was a way to stop him now, and maybe he could somehow find a positive way to rebuild his life.

That would be the best possible scenario for everyone. Without Paul Hill's leadership skills, the rest of the "kill 'em for Christ" crowd might fade into the woodwork from whence they came.

I thought of my family back home—my wife, Susan, and our two sons, Billy and Eric. Why was I out here involved in all of this? I vowed that as soon as I did my duty I would leave Pensacola and not return as long as Paul Hill or John Burt was still in town. And I would steer clear of any radicals in the future. Of course, the road to hell is usually paved with good intentions and, in spite of mine, this was not going to be the end of my involvement with radicals, though I could not have imagined it right then.

Agent McFaul returned with two of the three SWAT officers and all four of us walked down the hall together and got in the elevator. On the way up I noticed that these rugged men looked concerned over my well-being. It seemed unnecessary for them to come and escort me the way they did, but there was a reason for it. I would realize later that they were as fascinated as I was by these horrific characters I was coming to them to talk about.

They wanted to make sure that these radical types didn't get to do damage "in their house" again. And these boys meant business. It was easy to see that they had spent some serious time in the gym and no doubt on the weapons range as well. It was nice to have them on my side if push came to shove — or shooting.

McFaul brought me into a small conference room at first to talk one-on-one, but later the SWAT guys would all want to listen to my tapes and read my notes. One of the first things the FBI agent had done when we sat down was to request that I turn over all my materials so they could copy them and give them back.

Then, sitting under a small overhead light that made me feel like I was in some cheesy film noir detective flick from the black-and-white-movie era, he began to ask me to tell parts of my story over and over again while he took voluminous notes.

I told him right up front that what I had to offer would not likely hold up in court as far as proving criminal conspiracy for Hill and company, but that I had come to them because I thought there was enough evidence to launch an investigation.

I outlined the situation. My concerns came from the following series of events:

1. The "something big" prediction two weeks before the trial started, given to me by Don Treshman, national leader of Rescue America, and the mention of the National Coalition of Abortion Providers gathering on the first anniversary of the death of Dr. Gunn

2. Treshman's regional leader in Rescue America, John Burt, tacitly acknowledged Treshman's comments as I relayed them

regarding the coming event, adding the comment that I should "Cover it, but not too closely," and that he and Treshman would not be there because "we would be the first suspects." Burt laughed about the abortion providers and feminist leaders from around the country being so stupid as to gather in the open grassy part of the park for a candlelight vigil on the first anniversary of the doctor's death, implying they would be sitting ducks if attacked.

3. Paul Hill told me over sandwiches that "the next thing you are about to see is a coming reign of terror in which individuals or small groups" would take action. Hill had gathered a group of radical men from around the nation who looked up to him, and rejoiced when a man who bragged of having two duffel bags full of automatic weapons arrived. Hill and his followers had a theology similar to the kind that motivated Muslim extremists. They would be doing the will of God (Allah) if they killed his enemies. The killings would be part of a larger agenda that would advance their militant political goal of creating a theocratic state in which their soon-to-be-created "one true church" would rule over all. That very day, after the verdict came in, Hill had said to the assembled press that God's judgment was coming (with his "help").

McFaul acknowledged that the information would not be enough to go out and arrest Hill and his troops, but that they could launch an investigation that would at least bring pressure on them, hopefully enough to halt the potential plot. Also, they would do everything possible to go after the guy with the guns. McFaul said he could definitely see why I was worried about what might be coming, and that I did the right thing in coming forward.

He said that my stories about these guys would have been unbelievable to him except that he had been watching the trial and the statements that were made by all the radicals, and the thread he could see developing wove in neatly with what I was telling him. He thanked me for bringing the information to the police in the first place, and being willing to get involved.

He let the SWAT team join us because I said it was okay, and they had me tell them about all the characters in Pensacola and their various direct or indirect contacts throughout the country, from Donald Treshman, head of Rescue America, to Randall Terry, founder of Operation Rescue, and all the way up to the former Republican presidential candidate, televangelist Pat Robertson (I would later get a better understanding of his ties).

When I mentioned the information that Hans Schmidt had given me about the man named Dan or Dave who claimed to have two duffel bags filled with automatic weapons, the FBI agent immediately wanted to see his filmed interviews. I told him the address and phone number of the hotel where Hans and his boss, the Hollywood director, were staying, so he barked out, "Bring those guys in."

Two of the SWAT team officers snapped to their feet and headed off in a hurry out the door. While the door ever so slowly closed behind them, I could hear a police scanner buzzing and making scratchy noise in between bits of spoken information from field officers and the dispatcher. It made me feel right at home because we always listened to police and fire scanners in the newsrooms where I had worked.

When Hans Schmidt and Tony Kaye were brought in, they looked really ticked off that I'd given their info to the FBI. The cops took their film and went off to make copies. A short time later one of the officers came back and told the filmmakers it was going to take until the next morning to get their films back to them. They offered to cover the hotel rooms for them or to overnight the films back. Kaye said they would stick around in town and the cops could just return them to the hotel, "But be careful with them; we cahn't replace them," he said in his distinguished Anglo accent.

Agent McFaul advised us that it might be wise for the three of us to leave town just in case Hill or his allies got wind of what we had done. I said that I thought Hill or Burt might be able to figure out that I was the one who tipped off the authorities because of the unique confidences they had shared with me, but that the radicals had no way of knowing about Hans tipping me to the presence of the guy with the guns. I thought he and Tony were still safe. After a brief discussion, they all agreed, and so it was decided that I would not stick around for the "something big," but that Hans would. I half-jokingly repeated the words of John Burt, "Cover it, but not too closely." Tony wouldn't be around because he had to head to South America to scout an exotic location to shoot a new TV commercial.

McFaul walked us out to the door as though we were guests at a party. After shaking our hands, the last thing he said to me was that I should call in during the week so he could tell me how they were progressing, and that I should try to stay in contact with the radicals and their friends via the phone to see if I could garner any more details.

As the door closed behind us and we started down the doublewide sidewalk toward the parking lot, Tony said, "You know, mate, I really didn't appreciate being brought into all this in this way."

Before I could reply, Hans added, "Yeah, vhy did you have to give them our names?"

I apologized for causing them such inconvenience, but said that when I mentioned the guy with the guns that Hans told me about, they wanted to see the films. Hans said, "Seeing dose musclebound SWAT guys fillin' up the doorway vhen I opened it at the hotel was scary as hell."

I said that it all seemed like an episode of some detective show mixed in with *The Twilight Zone* and some religious programming tossed into the mix. Tony commented that this mix of guns and God seemed to be growing in America. Hans said, "Only in America do Christians run around vith guns, and the government says it's okay. It's a good thing. They have the right to bare their arms or arm their bears or something." Then we started to laugh about the absurdity of the whole situation.

It had been three and a half hours since I first arrived at the police station and I was feeling punchy. To make up for keeping me there so long, the FBI was picking up the tab for my motel room. Since we were all getting a free night in town, we decided to make the best of it.

We stopped off at a local watering hole and had a few drinks and talked about all the things you're not supposed to talk about—religion, politics, and sex. And, of course, we talked about the "something big" and took guesses as to whether or not the feds could stop Paul Hill and his pals in time if they did try something. I felt confident that the feds could handle the situation. And I had been very impressed with the SWAT guys. Hans quipped, "Dose guys could just crush the bad guys in their bare hands like Ah'nold Schvarzennegger in de *Terminator* movie."

There was something about Hans's accent and the tension that we'd all been under that made us laugh very hard at that silly little observation. It may have been a slight case of gallows humor.

TWENTY

Ring, *ring.* The phone sounded annoyingly loud as I rolled over in my bed the next morning to answer it. I said hello, and in reply I got, "Are you still sleeping? Vake up!" I recognized his voice and accent easily by now.

Hans wanted me to come over to their hotel to give Tony a chance to film me. He had a bunch of questions for me, and they wanted me to come to brunch with them before filming. I looked at the clock; it was 10:30. I told Hans to give me time to shower and shave, and then I'd come over.

He told me to hurry, but I took my time. We had spent enough time together during the week of the trial that I was used to Hans barking for me to hurry by now. I had told him earlier that he must've been drinking too much caffeine. In retaliation, he gave me the nickname "Pokey." I laughed and told him my father used to get just as annoyed with my pace; his nickname for me was "The Flash."

When I arrived at their hotel an hour and a half after he'd called, Hans greeted me at the door and said, "Here's Pokey, over in a flash." But it turned out that I was glad I hadn't come over earlier, neither of them was ready to go. As it was, Tony was on the phone, long distance, so

we had to wait twenty minutes for him to finish. We had another break-fast buffet, but this time it was at the hotel instead of at Shoney's (so of course it wasn't as good).

Then we returned to the hotel and got the camera. Tony led us down to the pool area to shoot the minimovie in which I got to play the star-ring role of the "talking head" so frequently featured in documentaries. For almost two hours, we set up in different spots and filmed segments.

In bits and pieces I rehashed the string of events that had led me to eventually go to the police, and in turn to the FBI. Tony was completely fascinated. He said, "This is a bloody great story, and you tell it extremely well. Let's get some of your background story, too. I won't use the whole thing, but it will help me to know all this, all right mate?"

Filming with Tony was a strange experience for me because he wanted me to keep looking ahead while he moved all around me, even shooting the back of my head at some points. I wondered if he knew what he was doing. Later, I would see his unusual one camera shooting style used in TV shows, movies, and commercials. And when I saw his major film-directing debut, *American History X*, I realized that I had been filmed by a brilliant talent.

But at the moment, I was thinking more about the discomfort of trying to look straight ahead while someone kept moving away from me, and the sun was blinding me and there were people looking out their hotel windows at us and pointing. Still, I wasn't one to let less-than-optimal conditions stop me from reporting my story, even if this time it was literally my story.

Tony wanted me to give him a feel for what I experienced back in Buffalo when Operation Rescue brought its national protest to town and I became the media coordinator. "Take me inside of the Operation Rescue protest you took part in, make me feel like I am there from the moment the protest started," he said from behind his camera.

I told him how I first entered the world of Operation Rescue.

"It was on the most somber of all Christian holy days, Good Friday, 1992, when the infamous Randall Terry was coming to preach at the pulpit of his good friend, Paul Schenck, my senior pastor. My wife and I walked from our house over to the church for the special evening ser-

vice, because we lived just around the corner from the church and school complex where she taught and the kids attended school.

"It should have been a pleasant little amble that evening because the weather was good, but there were figurative, if not literal, clouds on the horizon. We could hear horrible sounds coming from the church parking lot as we approached, and we could see protesters in the distance, standing near the entranceway to the school hall where we entered to get to the sanctuary.

"As we got closer, we saw a mob of strange and unruly people, some with green or purple hair, their genders almost indistinguishable in many cases. Some had rings through their noses or nipples and others had tattoos on their shoulders or necks. Leather and denim seemed to be everywhere, and many of the picketers held signs with shocking slogans, like 'I fuck to cum, not to conceive.'

"As we tried to get to the door, a large African American woman with a do-rag bandanna on her head came toward us, spinning like a whirling dervish out of all control. She held a hanger in her hand as she spun round and round. She missed my face by inches as I ducked from her approaching swing.

"She stopped suddenly and said to the manly looking woman next to her, 'Oh, boy, look at this. We got a giant Aryan boy, Hitler's dream, right here in our midst.'

"The he-woman with her responded, 'Yeah, you got that right. He's a big, blond, butch Nazi!'

"My wife tugged at my sleeve, signaling that I should not respond. She had been volunteering recently as a sidewalk counselor and part of their training included when not to respond to the other side. We hurried the kids through the gauntlet of noisy picketers, whom we would later find out were from an out-of-state radical group called NWROC, the National Women's Rights Organizing Coalition.

"Once we got inside I was asked to go right back out again as part of a group of men who were serving as volunteer security guards to get churchgoers safely into the building on this sacred day. I noticed that the cops were arriving in two squad cars, but I knew they'd need more help to keep this situation under control.

"Just then I saw an elderly man staggering toward me with blood flowing down his forehead. I rushed over to him and his wife said, 'Some crazy woman with a hanger sliced his skin open.' I knew right away who she was talking about, because that would have been me had I not ducked so quickly.

"I told the woman to describe the assailant to the police while I took her husband down to the men's room to wash up. After washing the wound and holding paper towels to it, he said he was not in need of any further assistance. He went out to find his wife, and I followed.

"The cops had moved the crowd of picketers off the private property and into the street. It was causing quite a commotion in the quiet neighborhood, with its fastidiously manicured little lawns and abundance of elderly residents.

"I had missed the hullabaloo that accompanied Randall Terry's arrival while I was inside helping the older gentleman take care of his forehead. Once I saw that the situation in the parking lot was under control, I went inside and made my way to the sanctuary.

"When the time came for Paul Schenck to introduce the featured speaker, he called Randall Terry a 'great man of God.' Terry received thunderous applause and a standing ovation from the several hundred pro-lifers who had come from far and near to hear their shepherd's voice.

"Terry began his message by reading the gospel account of Jesus being tried in front of Pontius Pilate as the bloodthirsty mob shouted, 'Crucify him, crucify him!' Almost on cue, the protesters who had been moved to the street rushed the church all at once like an angry herd of wild animals. They banged on the clear glass windows of the sanctuary running from floor to ceiling at the back of the church, and we turned around to see their hate-filled faces hissing and spitting and screaming in rage.

"A chill ran down my spine at the sight. It was overwhelming, it was as though we were witnessing a mob guided by the very same spirit that two thousand years ago had driven another such mob to call for the blood of an innocent one. And it couldn't have worked out better for Randall Terry's message.

"He was a master of improvisation, anyway, and so it was easy for him to work the scene into his sermon. He pointed out the parallels between these people and the bloodthirsty mob in Christ's day, but then he took off on that theme.

"In Randall Terry's version of the gospel, Pontius Pilate washing his hands was our Supreme Court in the *Roe* v. *Wade* decision to legalize abortion. Judas was now the liberal church that supported the pro-choice argument, and Peter, the one who denied Jesus three times, was now the conservative Bible believers who looked the other way while four thousand babies a day were being slaughtered. Terry's cadences and delivery style created a kind of hypnotic motion that drew us into his control. We were in the palm of his hand as he drove home point after point after point.

"Only later would it occur to me that if Terry's analogies about each of the gospel characters held up, then the part of Christ was today played by the fetus. The blood of the fetus had replaced the blood of the lamb for Randall Terry. It was his defining mission, his reason for being, his one true master.

"His was a strange and twisted theology that created the warlike mood of the movement. The weird reaction we were witnessing by the young radicals was a direct response to the actions Randall Terry himself had taken. As they say in science, for every action there is an equal reaction. Terry had set the agenda, the tone, and the style of the rescue movement. He had sown the harsh seeds from which we were now seeing such a bitter harvest.

"Terry also trotted out his standard stump speech, the theme he has returned to time and time again. He'd say, 'Imagine that this is the year 1959, and someone tells you that within a generation, prayer will be banned from public schools and condoms will be given out instead. Imagine that in 1959 someone tells you that sodomy and baby killing will be respectable, while mentioning God at public events will be the civil sin of the day. Imagine that in 1959 someone tells you that euthanasia and assisted suicide will be gaining in popularity, while the traditional family is being destroyed at every turn by the out-of-control liberals, and that half of all marriages in the nation are going to end in divorce. And all of this is going to happen within one generation. Just one generation. You would never believe it, but folks, it's happening right now even as we speak. And if, in the last generation alone, things got this bad, can you imagine how bad they will be a generation or two from now? Pray for your children and your children's children. As we approach these last days we will see more mockers of Christ than ever before. The crowd outside the windows of this church is proof enough of that.'

"Turning around again, I saw the mob back out in the street. As one of the young men made eye contact with me, he quickly flipped up his middle finger; it seemed like an exclamation mark to the point that Randall Terry had just made.

"Later, when I saw Terry in the back room after the service as we waited for the mob to disperse, he seemed like a different person than the raging demagogue who had held the crowd in the palm of his hand. He looked smaller and his ways were a little bit nerdy. His jokes were cornier and he looked like he'd just like to kick back for a while. I felt a little like Dorothy in *The Wizard of Oz* when she saw the man behind the curtain."

TWENTY-ONE

After making the long ride home, I was glad to be back in Houston with my family and my regular routine again. Everything felt so good, so normal, after the strange cast of characters and limited amount of sleep I'd lived with the week before.

I called Agent McFaul on Thursday, March 10, and he told me something incredible. He said that two federal agents had gone to John Burt's house and told him that they had evidence that he had knowledge of a potential plot in Pensacola. Burt denied it, of course. However, the two agents warned him that he had better cooperate right at that moment because in the event that an act of terrorism took place he would risk being charged as an "accomplice before the fact," which could earn him the same sentence as the perpetrator, possibly life in prison. Burt freaked at the thought of going to prison forever, so he gave the agents the name of the man who had bragged about having the guns.

"You're kidding!" I said.

McFaul laughed and said, "I'm telling you, he squealed like a stuck pig."

I was amazed, and it took me a moment to regain my composure enough to ask him who the man was. McFaul said that the full name of the man I had been calling Dan or Dave was actually Daniel Ware, who at first seemed to be just a mysterious drifter living out of his van. They started investigating his background and it turned out he is a convicted felon, a former convict who had spent four years in a Texas prison for counterfeiting. There were unconfirmed reports that he was involved in a right-wing militia group. I asked McFaul about that and he was purposely vague because he did not want to reveal more than necessary.

I later found out that some of the militia groups had used counterfeiting to finance their weapons purchases and to undermine the U.S. currency at the same time, as a part of their long-range plans to subvert the federal government. Many of the militia groups considered what they called "the alphabet soup of federal agencies"—ATF, FBI, IRS, HHS, and so on—to have so corrupted our national government that it was time to "water the tree of liberty with the blood of patriots," a phrase supposedly adapted from a Revolutionary War slogan.

The FBI got a federal arrest warrant issued against Ware because his possession of firearms was a violation of the conditions of his parole from prison. But when I asked if they had arrested Ware yet, McFaul said that, unfortunately, they were so far unable to find Ware and were under the suspicion that he might have fled. He asked me to call Donald Treshman and see if I could find out anything further.

I was reeling when I got off the line. My wife came in and asked me what was wrong. I told her about the conversation I'd just had, and she said that she wished I'd stay out of the whole mess. After we discussed it for a while she said, "I don't see why you're putting all of our lives on the line for abortionists. I personally am not going to shed any tears if they all croak."

I was shocked, but I realized that she had been too close to the battle lines to keep her perspective. When we were in Buffalo, she had taken part in a small rescue blockade that was just for female pro-lifers, set up as part of a reaction to the negative press the male-dominated movement had received in the wake of the big Spring of Life protest.

Unfortunately, things got a little rough. One of the pro-choice escorts, decked out in his identifying bib, grabbed my wife by her sweat-shirt and threw her down the stairs. It was a small set of stairs, but when I saw the video I was outraged. I went with her when the man was brought to trial, but was disappointed as we watched him get nothing but an action contemplating dismissal judgment that basically meant as long as he didn't do it again for six months, he was home free.

Sue had been a dedicated "sidewalk counselor" trying to dissuade women from entering the clinics and offering information on adoptions. But both of us had been influenced by our time at the Schenck brothers' church more than we knew. We had lost much of our perspective because the lens we were seeing the issue through was colored by the confrontational setting outside the clinics and inside the radical church.

Like a frog that is brought to a boil very slowly, we did not realize how much we were changing in our years with our pro-life friends until it was nearly too late. Later, when I read the books of Gary North and R. J. Rushdoony, the writers who influenced Paul Hill, I realized that had I read them right before I went into Operation Rescue, I might have agreed with much of their point of view. As horrible as it was, I had to admit to myself that under certain conditions I might have become a sympathizer to the violence.

I think that's what Paul Hill felt about me, too. I was closer to his way of thinking than I would have wanted to let on. Fortunately, I had the other side, the commonsense side, which made me realize we were going in the wrong direction. And, eventually, my wife would see it clearly, too.

Later that same day, I called Don Treshman. I was very uncomfortable about it because he was right in the same city with me, which was much too close for comfort. And I wasn't sure if he would start to figure out that I must've been the one who informed. Fortunately, I caught Treshman in a talkative mood, and I told him a lie. I said, "My boss wouldn't let me stay in Pensacola for the Abortion Providers Conference and I couldn't persuade him because, after all, I couldn't very well tell him that 'something big' was going to happen. If I did, I might have got in trouble afterward, you know, with the law."

Treshman told me that Burt had just gotten in trouble with the law for the same kind of thing. I played dumb and asked, "Really? What happened?"

Treshman groused, "Those damn federal agents came like storm troopers" into Burt's house and scared the living hell out of him. He said that somehow they got wind of "things that were supposed to be going on," and turned the heat up on Burt. He gave up the name they were looking for, "which he shouldn't'a done," but at least he had stopped there and offered no further information. Treshman said that Burt had called him the moment the feds left. "I told him he shoulda kept his mouth shut. Jeez, he didn't even call a lawyer."

I asked Treshman if Paul Hill or any of the other guys were getting grilled by the feds. He said that all kinds of things were going on. Cars were getting "torn apart in illegal searches" by the ATF and FBI, and people like Hill, who lived in Pensacola, had the "jackbooted thugs" showing up at their doors, too.

Treshman also complained that all the pro-life people were getting trailed very obviously by the feds. "It's all about intimidation," concluded the Rescue America boss. He was angry that people who hadn't done anything yet were being "treated like criminals."

I couldn't have been happier to hear what he was telling me, but I tried to sound sympathetic. I said that this was obviously going to go on from here on out, and I wondered if that would destroy the plans for the Abortion Providers gathering. Treshman said that from what he was hearing, "Probably nothing is going to happen."

As soon as we finished, I called the FBI agent back and told him what Treshman had said. He hoped I was right that nothing would happen, but he asked if I had found out anything about Ware's whereabouts. I told him that since Treshman hadn't brought up Ware's name or the fact that he was on the run, I couldn't really ask. He said he understood, and thanked me again for helping.

I was greatly encouraged by the way the federal agents had used their power to discourage the radicals from taking any violent action without really going after anyone except the man with the illegal weapons. Sure, they had intimidated Burt and the others, but that is what it sometimes takes to keep the peace. Given the fact that there was not enough evidence to arrest anyone for criminal conspiracy, I thought that the way things were progressing was about as good as we could hope for.

But I wondered where Ware was. He was the missing link in the whole deal, and then I suddenly realized that we didn't even know if he had his weapons with him or if he had left them with his newfound friends in Pensacola.

I found out the next morning. First, I called the FBI again. McFaul told me that they had just arrested Ware in an early morning bust. He was arrested back in Houston, not far from my home, in his cab outside the Hobby Airport in Houston. He had in his possession at the time of the arrest a 9 mm pistol, a 30-30 rifle, and a .357 magnum revolver (Dirty Harry's weapon of choice).

I was thrilled to get the news, but asked, "What about the two bags full of automatic weapons?" McFaul said that they didn't have a clue where those were. I said, "I think that's kind of important, don't you?" McFaul readily agreed and suggested I call Treshman again.

I was very nervous calling back the very next day to Treshman, but he was once again glad to fill me in on what was going on. I told him that "through my friends in Pensacola"—I was hoping he'd assume I meant Burt and Hill when I actually meant the FBI—I had heard about Ware's arrest a short time ago.

Treshman said it was a shame that they had busted him, and that, "He was a good kid who had gotten in a little trouble before." Of course, I knew that the "little bit of trouble" had been the felony conviction and four-year sentence on the whole counterfeiting mess, but I wondered why he called him a "good kid." I would soon find out that it meant he did what Treshman told him to. Treshman said, "As soon as John [Burt] told me that he had given Danny's name to the feds, I called him and told him that it was time to end the trip. I told him to pack his bags and get on a Greyhound and get his butt back here to Houston."

I told Treshman another lie, "I saw on the AP wire at work that the feds think Danny had two duffel bags full of automatic weapons with him, and that's why they were looking for him."

Treshman said, "Well, all I can tell you is that I saw two duffel bags when he got off the bus, but I wasn't about to look inside, ya know?" He laughed the dirty insider's chortle again.

I suspected that he was saying he had not looked because he already knew what he would find. I told that to Agent McFaul, and added, "Besides, if he is the one who ended this guy's trip by ordering him to come home, I wonder if he ordered the guy to start the trip."

McFaul said, "That's a good point," but neither one of us could provide the answer. I agreed to keep in touch with the radicals and to keep the FBI informed if I found out anything else. The next morning I picked up the *Houston Post*, and found a small story tucked away halfway down the page on A-24, where I had to really look for it. There I found a brief blurb entitled, "Cabby with ties to antiabortion group arrested, charged with arms violation."

The article said, "Daniel Raymond Ware, 40, was arrested Friday morning by federal agents." It quoted a federal spokeswoman saying that "three informants in Pensacola tipped federal officials that Ware was seen in Florida carrying a large number of weapons." I chuckled quietly to myself as it dawned on me that she was referring to the two filmmakers and myself.

Anyone else who read the reference would never be able to guess that the three were a news reporter who used to be a conservative activist, a Hollywood director, and a frail young cameraman. We may have been the most unlikely trio since the Lion, the Tin Man, and the Scarecrow.

That little passing mention of the incident in the paper was going to be the closest we would ever come to a public recognition of what we had helped avert. We would keep the secret to ourselves from that day until now.

Later, I'll explain why I'm spilling the beans after all this time. This story is not just about what happened way back then, even though on the weekend of the National Abortion Providers conference, when Hans told me over the phone that everything went off without a hitch, I thought the story was over.

Boy, was I ever wrong!

Defrocked minister Paul Hill looks at his family one last time before the jury recommends the death penalty in his murder of an abortion provider and his escort. Hill's small band of zealous followers dubs him "The Reverend Saint Paul Hill," vowing to avenge his death when it comes. (Photo credit: AP Photo/Mark Foley)

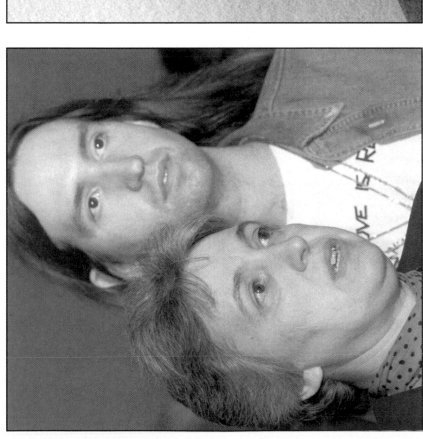

Eleanor Smeal, president of the Feminist Majority Federation, and David Gunn Jr. talk to the media in Pensacola, Florida, on March 5, 1994, after a jury finds Michael Griffin guilty of murdering Dr. David Gunn. (Photo credit: AP Photo/Mark Foley)

Randall Terry, founder of the militant antiabortion group Operation Rescue, uses the front steps of New York City Hall to spout his political views. Billed as a moral voice for the nation, he would later be excommunicated by his church because of inappropriate relationships with women. *(Photo credit: AP Photo/Mark Lennihan)*

Rev. Paul Schenck is taken into custody at a 1992 national antiabortion rally in Buffalo, New York. Despite a long history of arrests and a conviction for lying under oath in federal court, he is now the administrative director for Robertson's American Center for Law and Justice (ACLJ). *(Photo credit: AP Photo/D.Cappellazzo)*

With a dead fetus in his hands, Rev. Rob Schenck confronts members of the National Women's Rights Organizing Coalition, the most controversial group at the 1992 protest. On a later occasion, he was arrested for approaching President Clinton with a similar fetus while screaming about dead babies. *(Photo credit: AP Photo/D.Cappellazzo)*

Don Treshman, national leader of Rescue America, talks to the media about his move to the Washington, D.C., area from Houston after losing expensive lawsuits brought by pro-choice organizations. (*Photo credit: AP Photo/Hillary Hoffman*)

Ralph Reed, who conceived the Christian Coalition with Pat Robertson, developed "stealth campaigns" in which born-again Christians would run for office while hiding their true agendas. Reed would later boast of his supposedly nonpartisan organization's ability to influence the GOP, referred to as "God's Own Party" by many Christian Coalition members. (*Photo courtesy of Jerry Reiter*)

Pat Robertson founded the Christian Coalition, with its stealth campaigns and powerful influence in the Republican Party. An attorney on the staff of his ACLJ offered the "justifiable homicide" argument in defense of antiabortion assassin Paul Hill. (*Photo credit: AP Photo/Marty Lederhandler*)

The FBI continues its manhunt for James Charles Kopp in connection with the 1998 murder of Dr. Barnett Slepian in Amherst, New York, as well as four other attacks in the United States and Canada. Kopp is appreciatively referred to in Operation Rescue training manuals as "the Atomic Dog." *(Photo courtesy of the FBI)*

Pat Buchanan struts his stuff at the famous O.K. Corral during the 1996 Republican presidential primary in Arizona. Buchanan, whose most outspoken supporters include racists, militia members, and conspiracy theorists, left the GOP to run on a third-party ticket in the 2000 election. *(Photo credit: AP Photo/Eric Draper)*

EXTREME DANGER

PART TWO

TWENTY-TWO

Something was missing for me after the arrest. I felt a vague sense of letdown. I wasn't sure why I felt that way, since what I wanted to see happen had indeed happened—the potential violence I worried about had been averted, and the man with the weapons was arrested. But it was becoming my greatest story never told because the potential plot was foiled, but not proven in court, and because I was concerned about my family's safety if the radicals found out what I had done.

I was glad I had been able to get away without them realizing I had spilled the beans. Still, somewhere inside I was feeling like the story had no real ending, at least not the way I felt it should have. Maybe it was because I was with two filmmakers from Hollywood when we talked to the FBI that I expected a more dramatic finish.

Hollywood endings come with a crescendo of violins and a rolling of credits that are visible for all to see at the end of the story, but in the real world there was only silence. And many of the "bad guys" were still out there, allowed to walk the streets as though nothing had happened.

Then I thought of the times when the bad guys get away in Hollywood films. Usually that means they're coming back for more action in a sequel that will feature some of the same villains attacking again, only with more devastating force than before.

Unfortunately, sometimes life imitates art. And it was about to in this real-life sequel. There would be some new elements thrown in, too, that would keep the story alive with more twists and turns than any fictional murder mystery.

In late April 1994, just one month after getting home from the murder trial in Pensacola, I received a call from a federal agent about a meeting coming up in Wisconsin in May that had the potential to be a brand-new development, and an extremely dangerous one at that. The agent said that they had been tipped off to a gathering that might set the stage for an unholy alliance between the radical fringe of the anti-abortion movement and the increasingly militant militia movement.

I was stunned at the thought of what that could mean. I had been reading a little about the militia groups, and I knew that many of them were well armed, from semiautomatic weapons to grenades and rocket launchers. Their weapons, combined with the radical antiabortion Christian soldiers' willingness to use them, could mean we would see a whole new level of violence.

I decided to go to the meeting, and it would lead me to attend several other key gatherings of the newly revised political party with the misleadingly innocent-sounding name, the United Taxpayers Party.

I had a bad feeling about the convention I was heading off to attend, even though I had virtually no chance to research the group before I hopped on a plane and flew off to Madison. Little did I know that this political group I had never heard of would, by the year 2000, claim to be on the ballot in all fifty states, one of only five parties to succeed in doing so.

In 2000, it would also change its name to the Constitution Party, and tone down the rhetoric to look more respectable on its Web site and press releases; but back in spring of 1994 I was about to see the raw revolutionary rhetoric of the early years in all its gory glory.

Arriving in the airport of the Dairy State's most progressive city, I bumped into a gray-haired man with a military uniform on, topped off by a circa-1959 crew cut. He introduced himself as Col. Jay Parker of the Montana Militia, which I would find out later was one of the biggest and most militant groups in the country.

I told him that I was a former Air Force officer, and he asked me several questions in rapid-fire succession. I seemed to pass his tests and he warmed up to me as we shared a taxi to the hotel where we both were staying.

Colonel Parker would turn out to be a most fortunate person to meet up with at the start of the weekend because he seemed to know all the leaders in attendance, and he introduced me to several of them. In talking with the various militia officers, I realized that they were as rabidly anti-government as the antiabortion fringe, but for different reasons.

They were a motley assortment of conspiracy theorists, former family farmers and other small business owners who blamed the government for their losses, a coterie of crackpots and some stray citizens who had gradually drifted into the militias after a steady diet of conservative talk shows and right-wing rhetoric.

I also saw some familiar faces, such as Operation Rescue founder Randall Terry and Rev. Matt Trewhella, one of Paul Hill's allies and a signer of the Defensive Action Declaration that Hill had circulated nationally.

I was surprised to see national antiabortion figures attending this supposedly statewide meeting, but it confirmed what the federal agent had heard from his sources. This was going to set the stage for a national alliance between the antiabortion radicals and the militias. Why else would Randall Terry, the leader of the antiabortion movement, be attending a state convention of a minor party in Wisconsin?

The political party had been growing substantially only since 1992, and by 1994 had been completely infiltrated by the militia membership to an even greater degree than the Republican Party had been infiltrated by the Christian Coalition. If truth in labeling were required of political parties, this group would've been called the Militant Party.

Many of the younger male attendees wore the close-shaved hairstyles that would soon be made famous by Timothy McVeigh. Surprisingly, it was a look that was going to spread to young men everywhere in America in short order.

There was an excitement in the air as the convention got underway with talk of how they were going to change the nation. At this meeting and the next few that I would attend, they actually worked on the platform that they would take to the American public. They called for our nation to be ruled by biblical law standards and scriptural principles. They wanted America to be an officially Christian country that would demolish the growing trends toward secularism, humanism, feminism, and other forms of modernism. Many of the speeches were laced with racist and antigay messages.

To me, this seemed like standard fare for the far Right, but we were about to be treated to some real red meat. One of the speakers, George Jensen of the Michigan Militia, went into a rant against the "black helicopters and mounting military plans of the United Nations," predicting a secret battle plan supposedly already in the works that would culminate with the UN troops taking over America.

At the notion of being taken over by UN black helicopters and the international storm troopers, the crowd booed as bloodthirstily as they might have back in the Coliseum in Ancient Rome, when gladiators fought to the death. And when the speaker denounced "the alphabet soup of government agencies" the crowd cheered.

Many of the speakers were also mad as hornets over the Waco, Texas, tragedy the year before that destroyed the compound of the Christian cult run by a man who called himself David Koresh. The way the militias saw the event was that the feds had invaded the safety and security of the private homes of Christian people whose views were not "politically correct." Many in the militias did not believe the allegations that Koresh sexually abused children, and saw no overwhelming danger in his dictatorial leadership of his "family." After all, they saw society's biggest problem as taking away a man's place as lord of his castle, and they deeply distrusted the federal government. One speaker repeated the now-common mantra, "From time to time it's necessary to water the tree of liberty with the blood of patriots."

Many of the militia members had good reason to be suspicious of the government; they had been evicted from their family farms throughout the 1980s (when Republicans happened to occupy the White House), sometimes after several generations of ownership. Often the orders to leave came from government agents or marshals who acted on behalf of the banks that had given out mortgages and business loans. They felt that the government was helping the big corporate farms at their expense, dispensing corporate welfare while cutting aid to farmers.

I did some research on it later, and there was a good deal of evidence supporting the argument that the federal government had adopted policies that were hurting small, independent farmers while assisting a handful of international corporations.

Small farmers were finding fewer and fewer grocery store chains willing to distribute the products of their family farms. Instead, customers were being sold produce and other staples from the largest corporate farms here and abroad. No wonder the evicted farmers were such receptive listeners to those who offered them the various conspiracy theories—after all, there had to be some explanation to cover what had happened to them.

The feeling of anger was palpable at the militia-led meetings. We were told horror stories again and again about how the banks had foreclosed on farms; how the government cut farm aid; how the IRS seized small businesses lock, stock, and barrel, often immediately after a family member had died.

The way the militia people saw it, the government was purposely involved in taking the family farms and family businesses away from them to help the wealthy corporations that donated big bucks to the politicians at every level of government. And after they felt that the trust with their own government had been breached, they were ripe for the panoply of other antigovernment propaganda being sold by marketers of fear.

Many of these farmers and small businesspeople were salt-of-the-earth folks who felt that their American dreams had been turned into nightmares, and they wanted to know who was to blame. These were churchgoing, God-fearing people who worked harder than all the corporate types who now owned the land and businesses where their families had worked and lived for so many years.

And these simple country folk didn't understand societal changes of the past generation. When the Christian radicals spoke of a moral decline in America, many farmers and shop owners just accepted the explanation that the evil in their lives had to have been inspired by the devil himself, and that somehow they must fight back.

Randall Terry explained what many activists felt: "Our goal is a Christian nation. We have a biblical duty, we are called by God to conquer this country. We don't want equal time. We don't want pluralism."

He quoted George Grant, a conservative Christian writer from Texas, to explain the ultimate goals of the conservative Christian movement:

> It is dominion that we are after. Not just a voice. It is dominion we are after. Not just influence. It is dominion we are after. Not just equal time. . . . World conquest—that's what Christ has commissioned us to accomplish. We must win the world with the power of the Gospel. And we must never settle for anything less. . . . All our political action will aim at nothing short of that sacred purpose. Thus, Christian politics has as its primary intent the conquest of the land—of men, families, institutions, bureaucracies, courts, and governments for the Kingdom of Christ.

Back in 1992 I had applied to produce Randall Terry's national radio show, but fortunately not been hired. My pastor, Paul Schenck, had personally recommended me for the post, and later, when Schenck became Pat Robertson's ACLJ administrative director, it brought Terry one more tie to the televangelist.

Terry, who also had ambitions of Christian TV stardom, was a frequent guest on many evangelical programs, and was hosting a national Christian radio show he humbly named after himself. It would eventually air on over four hundred Christian stations, including airings on the CBN Radio network owned by Pat Robertson.

In spite of his activism in the new United Taxpayers Party, Terry was still connected enough to the GOP that he would make more than one run for Congress on the Republican side from his home base in Binghamton, New York. Terry was getting more and more strident all the time with his rhetoric. Not that he hadn't always been harsh—at one of his rallies in the months before Dr. Gunn was killed, Terry called abortion doctors "baby killers," and "Wanted—Dead or Alive" posters were distributed with the soon-to-be-assassinated doctor's name and face on them.

Terry denounced the killing right after it happened, but glossed over the incident, saying that thirty million babies had been killed. He claimed no responsibility for his rhetoric, but said to his followers shortly after the doctor was killed that he was tired of all the politically correct talk about tolerance and compassion. As was widely reported at the time, he is quoted as telling his flock, "I want you to just let a wave of intolerance wash over you. I want you to let a wave of hatred wash over you. Yes, hate is good."

By 1994, it was becoming clearer that Terry was being heavily influenced by the most radical Reconstructionists, and was in fact becoming something of a spokesperson for them. During his speech at the United Taxpayers gathering, he called outright for imposing biblical law on all Americans.

Off the podium, Terry took the opportunity to build bridges with the many different state militia groups in which he found a sympathetic ear for most of his points of view. He would be a key part of this new effort to formally "marry" the militia groups to the antiabortion radicals.

The Wisconsin United Taxpayers Party also heard the Rev. Matt Trewhella. He electrified the crowd with his extremely pro-gun, anti-government rhetoric. This "man of God" explained how he took his church members on military maneuvers every Saturday to prepare for "the coming civil war." He told the emotionally charged-up group that all those who were loving parents "should buy their kids an AK-47 and five hundred rounds of ammunition for Christmas," so they'd be ready to defend themselves from the corrupt government.

And, in the pièce de résistance, he held up his sixteen-month-old son, and asked him to tell the crowd, "Which one is your trigger finger?" When the toddler wiggled his right index finger, the crowd went wild with applause, laughter, and cheers. For me, it was the worst abuse of a child I'd ever seen. He was being turned into a disciple of hate before he could even speak.

Later, Trewhella would tell one of my fellow reporters that the whole thing had been a big joke, but even though there was gleeful laughter at the stunt, it seemed to capture the mood of the movement more than anything else that happened in those early meetings. The innocent were being used as tools by the demagogues.

The militia members in the United Taxpayers Party were as dedicated as any zealots could be, and they would make their play to be a national force in the 1996 campaign. Their leaders lobbied hard to get Pat Buchanan to leave the Republican Party and head up their first serious national ticket.

Buchanan's people dismissed the overtures from the fledgling party, and when Buchanan himself was asked about going the third-party route, he said that he always had been a loyal Republican and he always would be. Of course, in the next presidential go-round four years later, Buchanan would jump ship from the GOP and head off for a third-party shot at the White House. He still didn't pick the United Taxpayers Party, which had by then become the Constitution Party. He went with the Reform Party and its $13-million war chest.

A short while after I returned home from the May conference of the militant party's convention, I called Paul Hill in Pensacola from my home in Houston. He seemed down, but he would not say what was troubling him. I couldn't ask him if it was about a certain double-crossed potential plot, but I did ask him about some of his friends that I had met.

He said that Donna Bray was helping him plan a new group to be called The Defenders of the Defenders of Life. By "defenders of life," they meant those who were on the run or in prison for using militant solutions to change the abortion situation. They were defending other radicals who agreed with their views.

Hill told me that otherwise things were not progressing much. He said that his friends were all a big bunch of talkers, but couldn't seem to make any concrete decisions. He said he was frustrated with them, but he joked, "We're gonna have trouble taking over the world since our group can't even decide where to go to lunch." I laughed, but it was one of those gut-check times when I wanted to say, "Doesn't that tell you something about your whole 'take over the world for Jesus' approach?"

Soon, I would deeply regret that I hadn't tried to challenge Hill. I had played it safe to keep him talking, but I had not used my dialogue with him to try to help him see the errors in his thinking.

I hoped at that time that the whole ugly, violent way of thinking would subside for Hill. I asked him if he ever thought of becoming a minister again, but he said, "No, at least not in the way you think." That enigmatic answer was all I got from him. It would make sense to me later when I came to understand how he saw his mission.

Paul Hill was not content to go quietly into the night after his fifteen minutes in the media spotlight. He gave interviews wherever he could get them. In a lengthy piece in *GQ* magazine, Hill was portrayed as the wave of the future for the antiabortion movement. The reporter who wrote the piece made him seem creepy, but darkly fascinating. I tended to agree.

Part of the reason I did not call Hill again in that period was that I could still feel his weird charisma, even on the phone. I wondered if that was what so many people felt in the presence of guys like Charles Manson.

In a photo accompanying the story, Hill's trademark smirk was slightly lowered into more of a sneer, but he was standing against an open sky, as though he had unlimited potential—"Nothing but Blue Skies."

The article also included a picture of Dr. John Bayard Britton, the sixty-nine-year-old obstetrician who had been hired to take the place of the slain Dr. Gunn in the women's clinic. The photo shows the gray-haired physician wearing the bulletproof vest he must don just to go to work in the aftermath of the shooting.

Hill, who had never been a rescuer or a picketer, became an almost daily fixture outside of the clinic where Dr. Britton worked. Hill's presence there unnerved everyone, from the staff of the clinic to the volunteer escorts.

On June 10, two weeks after President Clinton signed the Freedom of Access to Clinic Entrances (FACE) Bill into law, Hill began to show signs of getting more aggressive. Instead of just marching around with his sign and shouting from the sidewalk, he approached the clinic, a clear violation of the distance requirement and the restriction on the aggressive kind of shouting that was so often used by the so-called sidewalk counselors as they shouted out insults and warned the women, "Don't kill your baby."

Linda Taggart, the clinic director who had been physically assaulted by John Burt a few years earlier, decided that she had to act fast. She stopped performing a sonogram on her patient as she heard Hill hollering close to the window, "Mommy, Mommy, don't murder me!"

Taggart immediately phoned police; they advised her that they could arrest him for violating the local noise ordinance. She wanted him charged with violating the new FACE law instead. She couldn't think of a better person to be the first detainee under the new law than Paul Hill. She had plenty of witnesses and Hill himself scoffed at the law so much he seemed like he would likely end up incriminating himself as he bragged about his latest tactic. To Taggart it seemed obvious that Hill was putting the new law to the test, and daring them to try to enforce it.

An FBI agent came to look into the matter, but for some reason decided not to take action. A second screaming incident took place with Hill in the days that followed the first one. Again, Taggart called the authorities and pressed hard to have Hill arrested. The Department of Justice did nothing.

It may have been concern that Hill could win in a test case of the new bill, or it might have been the feeling that putting FACE to the test in a conservative southern state like Florida would be unwise.

At any rate, the result of the inaction had definite consequences. While it was frustrating and demoralizing for clinic workers like Taggart, it was emboldening for Hill. If they weren't going arrest him in broad daylight violating the new law in front of witnesses willing to testify, then he could do more and more. This was a new day for Paul Hill. A break point had been reached.

It's likely that the FBI agents who investigated the incidents with Hill did not have access to the report I had given to McFaul. For some reason, my information on Hill and company would not be distributed to other agents until after Hill took the ultimate step in lawbreaking, after it was too late to undo the damage.

Only then would the FBI blast-fax my testimony to every office in the country, and all the agents would begin to understand what kind of people they were dealing with. By that time, though, the information that was just a few months old would already be dated to a certain extent. The radical fringes of the antiabortion movement were already moving into whole new arenas, gearing up for more action than ever before.

In mid-July of 1994, Hill boasted of his open breach of the new FACE law when he attended a three-day seminar for the radical fringe in Kansas City. It gave him a more elevated status in a group that was tailor-made for him.

The official message of the seminar was how to become a full-time activist, and the unofficial one was how to ratchet up the terror in the hearts and minds of the weak link in the abortion industry, the doctors themselves. Now Hill was not only the leading spokesman for the most radical action possible, he was someone who could break the law repeatedly with total impunity, and the federal authorities did not dare to touch him.

Hill was practically worshiped by many of the seminar attendees. They saw him as a mighty prophet, like the ones they read about in their Bibles. Hill was a modern-day Jeremiah with his diatribes of doom for the enemies of God, and he was calling the chosen ones to heed the almighty call to attack any infidels who did not share their faith in the supreme sanctity of the fetus.

This was an exhilarating moment for Hill. He could taste the sweet, intoxicating blood of the lamb in a new way. He offered the seminar attendees a chance to join in recognizing him as the new "messiah of the unborn." He told them that weekend that those who were willing to pay the price could go all the way to victory in taking over the world for God.

For those who bought into Hill's new vision, the moment was their own version of the Transfiguration, the moment when the chosen few gathered together with their Master high above all others upon the peaks of the mountains where God lived. There they could listen to a prophet and catch a glimpse of all that could be. Together, they could look down from their mountain at all those poor souls who were beneath them.

They shared a vision that bonded them together in a brotherhood of Christian terror as they predicted the day would come when abortionists would be tried for murder the way Nazis were in Nuremberg. When Hill described doctors in his brave new world getting the death penalty for what they had done back in the bad old days when abortion was legal, cheers and applause broke out in waves. This was a message that was music to the ears of the "faithful remnant," the small band who saw the truth that eluded all others.

Hill was the new high priest of the movement, and now the question became, "When, oh great one, will you act to show the infidel that we are moving with the power and grace of God?" Hill knew there was a problem, though. In spite of his tough talk, he had not yet been willing to do what God was clearly calling him to do.

He so far had been unwilling to sacrifice the young tender life of his nine-year-old son (as well as the mere females in the family) on the altar of antiabortionism, the way that the biblical figure Abraham had been willing to destroy his only son.

In the mythopoetical account, Abraham felt God calling him to sacrifice his only son, Isaac, on the sacred altar of his day. In blind faith, Abraham took a knife in his hand, and took his unsuspecting child up to the altar. He raised his hand to kill his own son, but an angel of the Lord stopped him just in the nick of time.

The point of the story, the way the radicals saw it, was that being willing to kill for God is clearly the mark of a great and holy saint. To be willing to murder one's own most beloved child for God showed the highest dedication. God himself later demonstrated this very point when he was willing to sacrifice his only son on the bloody altar of wood and nails disguised as a Roman crucifix.

This God of bloody sacrifices must have felt conflicted over his supposed bloodthirstiness, because he is also quoted in Scripture as saying, "I desire mercy, and not sacrifice."

It was clear by the mid-July gathering which side of the mercy versus sacrifice struggle Paul Hill was going to come down on, as soon as he could muster the courage to act.

Many people saw the growing stridency of Paul Hill, and concerns mounted. Susan Hill (no relation to Paul), owner of a string of women's clinics, would later say, "He really telegraphed [his intentions] only no one would listen." Chicky Desmarais, president of the National Organization for Women's local county chapter, said frankly, "I was very frightened." She would have good reason to be.

Even with his bulletproof vest, Dr. Britton did not feel safe. He traveled into work with at least one escort at all times, usually armed. There was also an off-duty police officer to serve as a paid security guard. Dr. Britton's most faithful companion was an elderly man who sometimes brought his wife along. Retired Air Force officer James Barrett often saw Hill at the clinic while driving the doctor into work.

For Hill, life was now divided into two parts—his dramatic role as an infamous radical pro-life prophet speaking to the whole world through the mass media, and his dull daily routine of working at the car place. He also had a wife and three kids who were hard hit by his cut in pay and loss of medical benefits, not to mention his lack of standing in the community.

But the future could go either way. Hill didn't have to accept his current options as the only possible ways to go. He had other opportunities ahead if he chose to apply himself, and he was bright enough to— but did he want to?

He had changed since his days as a pastor. Back then he had a wide variety of interests, and he was willing to perform a great deal of service for others. Now he had a new perspective, a single-minded focus his enemies called fanaticism.

Hill loved his new life. He had risen so far, so fast from those humble days as a mere local church pastor, a shepherd whose voice was only heard by a small flock. Since he'd come out for justifiable homicide (and hired a publicist), he was doing countless print and broadcast interviews. After his debut on *Donahue*, he had appeared on CNN's issue-oriented *Sonya Live* and ABC's *Nightline* with Ted Koppel, who had (unbelievably) dedicated a whole program to the question of whether or not it was justifiable homicide to kill a doctor. On that broadcast, which followed the (nonfatal) shooting of a doctor in Wichita, Kansas, the argument was between those who wanted to stop abortion peacefully and those who wanted to use force, with Hill serving as point man.

Hill was thrilled by his role as a media figure. He was appearing on TV, just like the president or a Hollywood star would do. In a culture where even boys who murder their parents get fan mail, it doesn't matter what you're famous for; it only matters that you're famous.

Hill had broken out of the pack. He had no desire to return to the flock, and if the best job he could get with his level of education, a master's degree in divinity, was painting and fixing cars for a living, how could he hope to get himself a more stimulating position than he now had as the bad boy of the antiabortion movement? It was obvious that Hill did not see himself having to work for a living like a common peasant. He was obviously called to greater things. "From glory to glory, from victory to victory," he would quote the Bible.

His new role was absolutely addicting, and it worried his wife, Karen. He couldn't tell her what he was thinking, how he dreamed of actually picking up a gun and heading off to shoot it out with the bad hombres, who had apparently moved from the O.K. Corral to the local women's clinic.

Hill was itching to take action, but according to the couple's friends, his wife desperately wanted him to consider their three young children, their nine-year-old son and their daughters, ages six and three. She did not wish to be alone the way Patricia Griffin was. She did not want violence to come from the same hands that had caressed her body when they made love, the same hands that had held hers so many times in tenderness.

She knew that he genuinely believed in protecting the potential children who were not yet born, but she did not want him to damage and possibly destroy the three children already born to them, their very own flesh and blood. Surely, her husband would not disregard his own babies waiting for him there in their modest home. That would be akin to someone saying he loved humanity while purposely hurting his own family in the worst possible ways.

Hill knew that his wife would try to dissuade him from his thoughts. If he was ever going to go from talk to action, he would have to hide his intentions from his beloved.

In the months after the "something big" had fizzled, Hill was being egged on by the unlikely bedfellows of pro-life activists and reporters, who joined in taunting him as a man who talked the game, but didn't have the guts to do anything. No doubt the men who taunted him believed what they were saying, but for Paul Hill, it may have been the straw that broke the camel's back. As the Bible says, "Pride goeth before the fall."

On the morning of July 29, 1994, approximately four months after the murder trial and National Abortion Providers gathering, Paul Hill went to the clinic where he knew Dr. Britton would be arriving. He got there around 6:45, an hour and a half before the armed security guard.

He had to stand there waiting and waiting, second by second, minute by minute, for over an hour. Other men would have been nervous, but Hill felt a powerful calm come over him. It was the laserlike focus of adrenaline, and he found it transporting him into a higher state of mind. He was now transcending all the limitations of an ordinary man and tapping into his most primal self. He was a primitive hunter lying in wait for his prey, an ancient warrior waiting to ambush the stranger, and a thief who would take the most precious possession of all, life itself.

No one else was around yet at 7:45 A.M. when a blue-gray pickup truck carrying Dr. Britton, James Barrett, and June Barrett pulled up. Mrs. Barrett was the first to see Paul Hill. She thought nothing of it at first; he was always there these days.

She heard her husband, James, say quietly under his breath, "Get out of the way, Paul Hill. You know us. You know this truck." They started to slowly drive past Hill, who was on the driver's side.

In the version of Moses played by future NRA president Charton Heston in *The Ten Commandments*, God used the simple staff of Moses to bring forth miracles, but Hill did Moses one better. This preacher's rod and staff were the double barrels of a .12 gauge shotgun.

Hill reached into the large, round, brown cardboard tube where he usually kept his gory posters, and pulled out the tool God had provided him to deliver death to the disobedient. He tossed aside the tube; it fell into the grass nearby.

Then everything seemed to happen in slow motion for him and his victims. He raised the shotgun and took aim. He was as steadfast as could be as he directed the barrel toward the truck. A thunderous boom shattered the still morning air.

It didn't seem real as June Barrett watched Hill's gun recoil from the shot, and she shouted out, "Oh, my God, he is shooting!"

The sixty-eight-year-old grandmother was the farthest from the shooter. She instinctively threw herself on the floor and froze as the next shot went off. *Boom! Boom! Boom!* The deafening blasts kept coming out of the weapon in the hands of the once-caregiving minister.

Glass flew in a million tiny pieces as the windshield and side windows seemed to disintegrate and then fly across the cab. June Barrett was so terrified that she could do nothing but lie motionless on the floor of the silver truck as the shots kept coming and coming.

Then as silence suddenly returned, Mrs. Barrett quietly said, "Doc, are you okay?" There was no answer. The frail, diminutive woman forced herself to open her eyes, and as she did, she saw blood dripping between the seats, and a pool of blood forming fast. "Oh, no, Doc is not okay," she said aloud.

It suddenly dawned on her that she was bleeding, too. The burning pain of bullet wounds flashed into her consciousness; she had been hit in the forearm and the breast. Blood flowed from her body, but she would survive.

She still could not see her husband from where she lay. To see if he was okay, she had to get out of the truck and walk around to the side where Hill had been shooting just moments before. Her heart was still racing.

She got to the door on the driver's side. Her husband was hanging upside down with his head on the ground, his body riddled with bullets and soaked in blood. He died right there before the ambulance could arrive.

For June Barrett, it was a tragedy in a life that had known too many tragedies. She was widowed from her first husband, and her son had died of AIDS. She had fought back from the pain of losing a child by giving of herself as a volunteer for the county's AIDS Service and Education program and in PFLAG, the Parents and Friends of Lesbians and Gays.

That was in addition to helping see the doctor through the dangerous situation at the women's clinic day after day. She was willing to take the risk and proud of her husband for being willing to give his life for the sake of a woman's right to choose. She said so from her hospital bed even after her dear husband had paid the ultimate price, and she vowed that she herself would go back to the front lines even after the cowardly attack. The tiny woman was braver than the biggest bully the radical Right could throw at her.

Hill had opened fire repeatedly on three unarmed civilians who had done nothing illegal, nothing threatening to him, nothing they did not have a right to do. But he blasted them into oblivion, anyway.

Hill had called his national group Defensive Action, but no one outside his cultlike following could see anything defensive about the shootings. The little vehicle with the unarmed victims looked more like a sieve than a truck when Hill was finished with it.

However, it was all legitimate and justifiable action to Hill. A trial had been held in the dark recesses of Paul Hill's brain, and all three of his targets had been pronounced guilty of being "enemies of God." And in Hill's religious court, he was judge, jury, and executioner. It didn't matter that two out of the three people he shot never had performed an abortion, just being there with the doctor made them guilty of being "accomplices."

He alone was the arbiter of the brand of justice he would dole out. He alone was the protector of truth. He alone knew what was right for those women in the clinic, and he alone knew it was time to play God and take those two human lives.

"Not the church, not the state, women shall decide their fate," cried the pro-choice protesters, but Hill's inner slogan had become, "Not the church, not the state, only I shall decide their fate." As a mighty modern messiah, he was above the mere laws of the civil government, and above the laws of the church to which he belonged. It was up to others to follow such mundane restrictions, not a brave soldier called to be a general in the army of God.

And where was the mighty warrior of God after the slaughter? He had put the shotgun down right at the scene, and walked slowly down the street with his hands outstretched so the police would see he had no weapons. He later admitted that he wanted to make sure the cops didn't open fire on him, and that right before the shooting he had said a special prayer that God would allow him to live through the attack. He didn't mind taking someone else's life, but he wasn't about to lose his own.

It was a complete perversion of the gospel message that he had been ordained to preach. Jesus had said, "There is no greater love than this, to lay down your life for your friends." Hill corrected Jesus in his own mind to fit in better in a culture that was more likely to revere Rambo than a meek carpenter's son. Hill's version of the gospel message was, "There is no greater love than this, to shoot up three unarmed senior citizens you disagree with on one issue, and to keep your own butt safe from the cops." Amen?

He was arrested within minutes and taken into custody as meekly as a lamb. The bully always becomes a coward when greeted with greater force.

In Hill's mind, things were going well. The authorities thought they had him now, but he would surprise them by rising up to become the great shepherd of a flock that was thirsting for more and more blood. The amazing thing was that Andrew Cabot told me after the shooting that Hill's small band of disciples began to refer to him as "The Reverend Saint Paul Hill."

His new disciples of "pro-life death" shouted war cries at innocent passersby, starting at the funeral of the slain doctor, when Hill's allies sang his praises and called the doctor (rather than Hill) a killer. They had their signs and their bullhorns and their ghastly screams of condemnation to spew forth at all who could hear.

To most people, the idea of barging in on someone's funeral to sell your ideology is truly abhorrent, but it was completely justified in the minds of the pro-life radicals, because they did not see the grieving family members as people, but as objects to be used to get publicity for their cause. The radicals were just parroting what they had heard and seen done at Dr. Gunn's funeral. This was one of their new traditions.

Starting from the time of the shooting, all across the country, those on the radical fringes felt stronger and safer knowing that they had Paul Hill showing them the way to do God's will. Those who had been longing for a sturdier shepherd to guide them through the Valley of the Shadow of Death than Michael Griffin had turned out to be when he was broken in prison could not have been happier. Now they had a minister who spoke God's word with a shotgun, and who would continue to advance their cause from his cell.

Donna Bray, the sister-in-law of bomber and radical author Michael Bray, told me that Paul Hill was doing remarkably well in prison in the months following the shooting. Because of his high profile and expected future trip to death row, he was being isolated from the other prisoners. Ironically, this helped him to avoid the kind of brutalization that had so thoroughly devastated his predecessor in the cause of doctor killing, and allowed him to hold onto his harsh beliefs. Donna Bray seemed to see this as a result of divine intervention.

I thought of the biblical story of St. Paul the Apostle when he was in prison—for preaching, not killing—in which an angel of the Lord shook the jail to its foundation and forced the doors open, miraculously setting him free and inspiring the jailer to become a convert right on the spot. In the case of "The Reverend Saint Paul Hill," God had apparently lost some power, because the best he could do was get his chosen one a cell away from the other prisoners.

Even Hill himself seemed to presume that his God was not as strong today as he had been in the ancient times. Hill obviously did not believe that God could act to stop major injustices nowadays. No, it was up to the self-proclaimed prophet to "help" the Almighty do what he should be doing. Without Paul Hill, God could not take action to protect his "little ones" and give them what Hill believed they should have.

Hill later sent the Brays a lengthy letter that revealed his thoughts leading up to the shooting and its aftermath. He asked if it could be read to his legion of zealous fans from across America at the White Rose Banquet near Washington, D.C., an annual event launched by Bray in order to honor the men who were bombers and shooters for Jesus. They even developed their own technologically advanced (if morally crippled) Web site, calling men like Hill "Prisoners of Christ."

Hill wrote this epistle to his scattered flock from prison, the way the earlier St. Paul had written some of his letters. But instead of such lofty words of that first St. Paul saying, "Without love, I am a noisy gong or a clanging symbol . . . without love, I am nothing," this new St. Paul wrote, "Why I shot an abortionist."

Here are some excerpts from the rambling, single-spaced seven-page letter from "The Reverend Saint Paul Hill," offering a powerful revelation into his mind. Note that in the first paragraph below, Hill admits implicitly that he is a "terrorist."*

All of the lines of reasoning that I had seen as justifying Michael Griffin's previous shooting of an abortionist converged in my own mind as I considered acting myself. I was struck with the encouraging and inspiring influence such an example would have on the upright and the terror it would bring to those involved in killing the unborn.

With some difficulty I finished my work that Thursday afternoon [when he started premeditating the murder] and went home. I continued to secretly consider the idea, half hoping it would not appear as plausible after I had given it more thought.

The next morning, Friday, as was my practice, I went to the abortion clinic. I arrived about eight o'clock, the time that many of the mothers began arriving. I was usually the first protestor there but that day another activist had arrived first. What was even more unusual was, after discrete questioning, I learned he had been there when the abortionist had arrived, about 7:30. More importantly, I discovered that the abortionist had arrived prior to the police security guard. This information was like a bright green light, signaling me on.

For months my wife had planned to take our children on a trip to visit my parents and to take my son to summer camp. She planned to leave that coming Wednesday morning and return the following week. I would have the remainder of that day and all of Thursday to prepare to act on Friday—eight days after the idea struck me. All I had to do was hide my intentions from my wife for a few days until she left. If I did not act during her planned trip (since I could not keep

---

*The full text is available online at www.mttu.com/POC/PHill-l.htm.

my feelings from her for long) she would almost certainly develop suspicions later and my plans would be spoiled for fear of implicating her. I could not hope for a better opportunity than the one immediately before me. God had opened a window of opportunity; it appeared I had been appointed to step through it.

Saturday afternoon, the second day after I began considering action, we went as a family to the beach. My wife, Karen, and I enjoyed the beach in the afternoon. We arrived a couple of hours before sundown; it was beautiful. No one was on the stretch of beach we chose. The sand was sugar-like and clean, the water clear with gentle incoming swells. It was the perfect end to a busy week and a hot day.

Our three children were delighted in the outing. My son was nine and my two daughters were six and three. We dug in the sand, splashed in the water, and walked along the edge. All the while I weighed my plans in my mind, being careful not to raise suspicion. This was a heartrending experience. I doubted I would ever take my family to the beach like this again. I would be in prison, separated from my beautiful wife and children. The sight of them walking along the beach, so happy and serene, and the contrasting thought of being removed from them was startling, almost breathtaking.

I could not allow my emotions to show. To retain control I lifted my heart to God in praise and faith. As long as I responded to the pain in my chest with praise I could rise above it and still see things clearly—and what a strikingly beautiful sight it was. Somehow, responding to the stabbing pain with praise turned it to joy, a joy as clear as the sand and the sky. As I lifted my heart and eyes upward I was reminded of God's promise to bless Abraham and grant him descendants as numerous as the stars in the sky. I claimed that promise as my own and rejoiced with all my might, lest my eyes become clouded with tears and they betray me.

All my paternal instincts were stirred as I played with my children. They enjoyed their father's attention. I took them one by one, each in turn, into water over their heads as they clung to my neck. As I carried and supported each child in the water it was as though I was offering them to God as Abraham offered his son.

I also admired the beauty and grace of my wife. She is a remarkably fine and capable woman. I knew that, by God's grace, she would be able to cope with my being incarcerated. But it was soul wrenching to think of being separated from her—though I knew our relationship would continue. Though I would almost surely be removed from my precious family I knew God would somehow work everything out. I would not lose them, just be separated from them. The separation would be painful but the reward would be great, too great to fathom, it was simply accepted in faith.

After the sunset we brushed the sand from our things and walked back to the car. Neither Karen nor the children seemed alerted to anything. I enjoyed watching them through eyes unknown to them, like a man savoring his *last supper* . . . [messianic imagery]. The decision was agonizing. I would be leaving my wife, children, home and job, but I felt God had given me all I had that I might return it to him. I felt that *the Lord had placed in my hands a cup* whose contents were difficult to swallow, but that it was a task that had to be borne [continuing the messianic imagery].

The path lay before me, all signs pointed ahead. The only alternative was disobedience—neglect of the very worst kind—turning my back on a vast multitude as their lives were being brought to a cruel end. This was unthinkable; I had no other choice. . . . It did not occur to me at the time, but now I wonder how Abraham felt as he walked up Mount Moriah to kill his son. Surely his heart was heavy, very heavy, and his blood ice cold—mine was.

Paul Hill admits he committed the multiple murders in cold blood. That is what made him the new "messiah" of the movement that called for killing in the name of life. He would now be enshrined in the history books, and when his brothers in Christ found the courage to follow him into the fight, he would be listed as the man whom God had selected to spark the new uprising.

He had said to me a few months earlier that he would be to the "coming civil war" what John Brown was to the first civil war, the one who foresaw the need for war and took action before his comrades did. It was an interesting analogy for him to choose since many historians view John Brown as a dangerous and unbalanced man who was mentally ill and out of control when he launched into his orgy of violence.

TWENTY-THREE

Hill's assassination case was red-hot in the media from the moment it happened until he went to trial in November 1994, just five months after his shooting spree. This time I stayed home, though. I had had enough of "pro-life" murder cases.

Hill wanted to be able to have his legal defense provide him with cover for what he had done. He did not dispute the fact that he was indeed the triggerman, but he did dispute whether his actions were a crime or not.

Most conservative Christians, then and now dismiss shooters like Hill and Griffin as being lone, crazed killers who are merely unfortunate aberrations in otherwise good Christian groups. They supposedly have no connections to "respectable" conservative leaders.

Yet there are some very interesting ties between the radicals and the respectables. For instance, former Republican presidential candidate Pat Robertson, the politically powerful televangelist who founded the Christian Coalition and whom many are claiming was the kingmaker in the nomination of George W. Bush during the 2000 Republican primary, has an interesting connection to Paul Hill.

When Hill was looking for an attorney to help make

his case for "justifiable homicide," Pat Robertson's ACLJ attorney, Michael Hirsh, was there for the shooter. ACLJ stands for the American Center for Law and Justice (the biblical way). It is Robertson's legal machine, his parody of the American Civil Liberties Union.

ACLJ attorney Michael Hirsh wrote the actual justifiable homicide legal briefs that matched the notorious assassin's theories perfectly, even though they would never be used in court. It was a remarkable situation. Here you had a paid staffer of Pat Robertson, the televangelist who publicly maintained the usual denouncements of violence, actually writing the defense for an antichoice assassin.

Robertson realized he would have a problem if word of this got out, so he quietly transferred Hirsh to a smaller regional office in Illinois for a few months and then, when no one was looking, let Hirsh go. At least that's what Hirsh himself told me when I met him the following year after I had become an FBI informant.

Hill submitted Hirsh's justifiable homicide defense to the court in Pensacola, but it was, of course, rejected by the judge, who saw it for the vigilante nonsense it was. According to the law in real-world America, justifiable homicide applies to self-defense, when one's life is in imminent danger.

Hill's argument was that you have the right to violate the law in order to save a life, for example, trespassing to save the life of a drowning child. The judge explained that ever since *Roe* v. *Wade* in 1973, the law of the land said that on such difficult gray areas as when life begins and whether a pregnancy should be carried to term, had been moved from the public arena of one-size-fits-all legislative rulings to the privacy and individuality of the woman involved in the decision, in consultation with her doctor.

After the judge rejected the zealot's defense so ably written by Pat Robertson's "mouthpiece" (as they used to call lawyers), Hill knew that his goose was cooked. He sat sullen and silent through most of his trial, unable to launch into his extremist sermons. He spoke only to cross-examine an occasional witness. He had decided to act as his own lawyer, and give himself a fool for a client, to paraphrase the old saying.

His one moment of glory came when he got to throw in a few references to his reasoning (or lack thereof) in his final remarks to the jury. It was definitely a case of too little, too late.

Two days after the jury came back with a recommendation for the death penalty, I was awakened at home early in the morning. My son came in and shook me, saying, "Dad, Paul Hill is on the phone for you." I jumped up, grabbed the portable phone, and hoped I could snap out of my drowsiness.

Hill said that he heard I'd been asking questions about him to his friends. I said I was working on a book idea, and that I wanted to interview him at length. I wanted to know about his background before all this happened and who he was as a person, so I could better understand how he came to arrive at his controversial conclusions.

Hill was extremely cautious, and asked me questions about where I was going to church and what I thought of justifiable homicide. I candidly admitted that I still did not agree with the shooting, but I was more than willing to listen to his side of the story and write his words accurately. I made the case that I also had a better understanding of the pro-life movement in general than most other reporters. I didn't mention that by now I was beginning to question the whole movement's legitimacy.

Hill said that he was only going to grant short interviews and that he was already working on big ways to get his views out. He saw me as small potatoes now that he had shot to the top, and could get major networks to grant interviews.

I said, "John Burt told me that Michael Griffin was right in killing Dr. Gunn only if God told him to do it, and he wasn't sure if God had spoken to Mike or not. What about you, Paul, let me just ask you that one question. Did God tell you to do it?"

He wouldn't answer it, though saying, "God told me to do it," was a common thing to say in his religious tradition about major decisions in one's life. Hill said he was comfortable with his decision, though, and knew that God was blessing him greatly. I then asked if he thought he was doing good for the pro-life movement, or if the critics were right that he was hurting the cause.

Hill changed his tone as he began his explanation. He slid slowly into that euphoria I had heard in Andrew Cabot when talking about killing for Christ. Hill's tone added to the frightening concepts he advanced, "I am going to be the one who causes the abolition of abortion in America. It is my call. I am called to be a martyr. My death will cause the righteous to rise up and take to the streets and say 'no more' to the baby killing, 'no more' to the sin. When I am executed unjustly, you will see an uprising that will shock the nation."

Hill said that he would not even take the last straw of hope, the appeals process. He said that he did not wish to extend his life. "Won't that be hard on Karen and your three young kids?" I asked. He acknowledged that it would not be easy for them, but he had something else to consider. He felt he had a rendezvous with destiny in his "sacred call" to be a martyr.

"But, Paul, even St. Paul the Apostle used every legal defense he could when he was arrested. He appealed all the way up to the Emperor of Rome, the highest civil authority. Why wouldn't you do the same?"

Hill said that some men are called to be martyrs, and he was one of them. It was his divinely ordained mission. He said, "Ours is not to question why, ours is but to do and die."

I had heard that saying before, but it never sounded so creepy as at that moment. Hill was so far gone I didn't feel that there was any rational way to reach him. That is the trouble with fundamentalism in any religion—appeals to love and logic simply can't get through the shield of dogmatism or the armor of self-righteousness.

I felt that Hill was using the same kind of thinking that the Pharisees and other religious conservatives had used against Jesus two thousand years ago, able to justify all kinds of narrow-minded cruelty and judgmentalism in the name of God. Caiaphas, the high priest, in calling for the execution of Jesus, used the exact same logic Hill did in justifying the execution of the doctor: "Better for one man to die than many."

But I made one last futile effort to get Hill to reconsider his decision on the appeals process, because I was concerned that he might be right that his small but zealous crowd of followers might do "something big" after he was executed in the electric chair.

"Paul, even Jesus himself did not wish to die," I said. "The night he was arrested he had been praying so fiercely that he might be allowed to live that the Bible says he wept blood. So if Jesus himself did not want to die, why are you running toward death as though it were your savior?"

Hill said that death was welcome and was going to lead him to his Savior. He quoted Scripture: "Those who want to save their lives will lose it, and those who lose their lives will find it in the kingdom."

I thought to myself, Paul, how did you get everything so upside down and backward?

Hill had to get off the phone, but before he went he gently said, "God bless you, brother." Once again, I was stunned. I started wondering if there were anything I could've said back before the shooting that would have convinced him he was on the wrong track. I had been so cautious at times, simply letting him talk and not challenging him.

Then, when I first heard the news about his shooting spree, I had felt somewhat guilty. I thought that maybe I could have done something more to stop him. I had risked my safety to stop the potential "something big" at the abortion providers gathering, but after that I did not really press on to try to get Hill to see where he was off the track because of my concern for my safety.

I knew that most likely he would not have listened to me no matter what I said, anyway, because he had not listened to his church board and he had not been deterred by his own wife's longings for him to avoid violence. Yet still, I felt strangely sad and thought about what might have been.

If Hill had been convinced of the error of his homicidal theology, he might have gone back to a productive life, and raised his children the way he should have. Instead, he would leave his babies on their own while he spent his time in prison, granting as many interviews as he could.

It occurred to me that Hill would likely have had more children had he not gone on the shooting rampage. He, like many hard-line pro-life people, did not believe in birth control, so he almost surely would have conceived new lives with his wife, Karen. But, ironically, Hill aborted his own family while caught up in his obsession with taking away the rights of others to limit the size of their families.

Now, instead of the pitter-patter of little feet, he will have his patter in prison about what a great and glorious thing he has done. Hill purposely abandoned his wife and children; they will have to make their own choices on how to live their lives. And they will never get to know their brothers or sisters who might have been born had Daddy not made a choice to become a murderer and a misguided martyr.

The stark halls of Florida's Starke Prison, north of Orlando, where Paul Hill paces as he awaits his magnificent martyrdom seem a world away from the corridors of power where Pat Robertson travels, jetting off to Republican Party pow-wows that steer the nation. But Robertson has talked the talk of hard-line theology, and he cannot just wash his hands of any responsibility for his rhetoric.

Those biblical literalists who took such talk just as literally as they interpret their Bibles (unlike Robertson, who is shrewd enough to amass a fortune from his "ministry"), felt compelled to do something. Reconstructionism motivated the lone, crazed killers who shared Robertson's brand of conservative Christianity.

It saddened me to think about it, because Robertson had been someone I had admired since I was in high school. My inspiration to go into broadcasting had come while I was a teen, watching Robertson hosting the *700 Club*. And I had loved the book about his conversion, *Nine O'Clock in the Morning*. Robertson's political ideas had guided me even before I helped the small group of people who gathered together in the embryonic days of the Christian Coalition. Now I wondered why I had not seen the whole picture.

In 1991, the very first year we got the Christian Coalition up and running in New York, the president of our political machine, Pat Robertson, released a new book, which I did not read at the time. It was called *The New World Order*. It fed the fears of conspiracy theorists, like the ones I'd met in the militias, about a United Nations takeover of America, the rise of an antichrist in the very near future, and the coming end of the world as we know it after a showdown in Armageddon between the armies of God versus the armies of this world, as controlled by Satan.

Robertson had started the Christian Coalition to give himself his own army of Christian soldiers for the coming spiritual warfare. But when his executive director, Ralph Reed, came to train me and my small group for political activism back in February 1991, using a great deal of military rhetoric, I didn't take the phrases seriously enough.

Reed spoke of "flying under the radar" while running a "stealth campaign" in which we would camouflage our full agendas until elected. Military rhetoric did not shock me because I had heard such talk before. When I went to a Republican Party campaign school, the leader of the seminar built the entire weekend seminar on a foundation of principles from the book *The Art of War*, by the ancient Chinese teacher of battle strategies, Sun Tzu.

It would be many years before I realized the impact that such thinking had on society. Only later, when the accumulation of horrors I witnessed forced me to become open-minded enough to consider the possibility that I also had been wrong in my assumptions, did I see the evidence that made it clear there were some awfully dark undertones to our brand of Christianity.

Pat Robertson revealed the actual goals of his wing of the Republican Party as steered by the Christian Coalition, writing in *The New World Order*, "There will never be world peace until God's house and God's people are given their rightful place of leadership at the top of the world. How can there be peace when drunkards, drug dealers, communists, atheists, New Age worshipers of Satan, secular humanists, oppressive dictators, greedy money changers, revolutionary assassins, adulterers, and homosexuals are on top?"*

And Robertson has said on his TV show that it is not just the non-Christians that he objects to, it's anyone who does not agree with his entire agenda. It's not enough to be a Christian, you must be *his kind* of Christian.

The televangelist, who also holds a law degree, was a Baptist min-

---

*Pat Robertson, *The New World Order* (Nashville: Word Publishing, 1991), p. 227.

ister until he quit his ordination when God told him to run for president back in 1988; he complained on the *700 Club* that people say, "You're supposed to be nice to the Episcopalians and the Presbyterians and the Methodists and this, that, and the other thing—nonsense! I don't have to be nice to the spirit of the antichrist! I can love the people who hold false opinions, but I don't have to be nice to them!"

Somehow that doesn't sound like the man Robertson claims to represent. Jesus spoke of compassion, meekness, and love. But Robertson's version of Christianity is a much more muscular one. Like Paul Hill, Pat Robertson seems more comfortable with Rambo than with Jesus.

TWENTY-FOUR

By the end of 1994, I had put the strange and dangerous world of antiabortion violence behind me—or so I thought.

When I went into work in the early morning hours of Saturday, December 30, and sat down at my computer in the offices of Shadow Broadcast Services in Houston, a disturbing news report from United Press International came onto my computer monitor:

> Brookline, Mass., Dec. 30 (UPI)—A gunman dressed in black opened fire with a rifle inside two abortion clinics in a Boston suburb Friday, killing two women and wounding five other people, two of them seriously. Police and FBI agents were reportedly searching for a 23-year-old man from New Hampshire.
>
> Planned Parenthood, which operates one of the clinics, said it had asked the justice department two weeks ago to post U.S. marshals at the facility because of repeated threats from anonymous callers. The clinic is a federal test site for the French abortion pill R.U.-486.
>
> . . . all seven victims were gunned down within minutes early Friday at the Planned Parenthood and Pre-Term Clinics, which are about a mile and a half apart in Brookline, just west of Boston.
>
> State and local police and FBI agents immediately

mounted a massive manhunt for the gunman, who was described as white, about 6 feet tall and dressed in a black coat and black pants.

Antiabortion demonstrators were holding protests outside both clinics when the shootings began and several protesters were questioned by police, but no arrests were made.

Because the shootings occurred within such a short period of time, there was speculation there may have been more than one gunman, but investigators were quoted as saying they were confident both were committed by the same man.

WBZ-TV in Boston said authorities were searching for John Salvi, 23, of Hampton, N.H. . . .

The report went on to say that the two fatalities from the shootings were not abortion doctors, but two young women who were office workers. One was twenty-five-year-old Shannon Lowney, the receptionist at the Planned Parenthood Clinic, and the other was thirty-two-year-old Leanne Nichols, an office worker at the Pre-Term Clinic. Two of the wounded were volunteer escorts, and of the five injured people who had to be taken to Boston hospitals, none were abortion doctors.

I realized as I read the news report that even Paul Hill's simplistic argument that killing a doctor was equivalent to saving the lives of unborn children was no longer being used as the focal point of the "defenders of life." It appeared that Salvi was playing a game of "follow the leader" and acting in the new style that Hill had used just five months earlier.

Since Hill's shooting spree, the goal of the radical fringe of antiabortionism had become all-out terrorism, no different from what happened in the IRA bombings and shootings, the same thing Hill had cold-bloodedly predicted back when I joined him for iced tea and sandwiches in the cozy café in Pensacola during the trial.

In other words, Hill himself never really believed in the concepts with which he was publicly identified. His Defensive Action petition had only called for stopping doctors, not gunning down office workers, volunteers, and senior citizens.

Hill and Bray's new organization said their goal was to defend those who were "defending life." But they should have called the group Defenders of Cowardly Terrorists.

Salvi's act of madness, which was again was being called the act of a "lone, crazed killer," left a feeling of déjà vu. There were echoes of so many past acts, disturbing patterns once more rushing to mind. I thought of as many similarities as I could:

- Just like in the Christmas Day clinic bombings in Pensacola, two attacks were launched so close together that they briefly confused officials at the scene as the perpetrator(s) made a quick getaway (pretty good strategy for a "lone, crazed killer").
- The classic diversion created by protesters out front was just like what had happened when Griffin opened fire.
- Police questioned antiabortion leaders, but no arrests were made, also like what repeatedly happened in Pensacola.
- There was a reason for one of the clinics to be a particularly appealing target to antiabortion leaders rather than just a randomly chosen site by a "lone, crazed gun-man." In this case, the clinic was the one where the controversial birth control drug R.U.-486 was being tested, and in Pensacola Dr. Gunn was Burt's favorite target and shot at the clinic where Burt was celebrating his tenth anniversary of picketing.
- Just like in Pensacola, a God-fearing, gun-toting Christian citizen was doing his part to make America a better place. Praise the Lord and pass the ammunition.
- Salvi had carried his weapon into the clinic in a duffel bag, just as Daniel Ware had carried his duffel bags of weapons to Pensacola.
- Griffin and the earlier bombers had acted after being "inspired" by the teachings of a veteran of the abortion war. Could a veteran of the abortion war have inspired this shooter?

The report said that a nationwide manhunt was underway to capture this Christian terrorist. Instead of going into hiding, as you might expect, John Salvi decided to travel across several states to get to a particular clinic in Virginia.

When he got there on Saturday, December 30, he found that he could not get inside, so he opened fire from outside, hitting walls and windows but injuring no one. Police arrested him at the scene and took him into custody. Inside his pocket they found the name, address, and phone number of a minister. No one knew the possible significance of that name in the pocket. No one, that is, except me.

I thought about it for several hours before I picked up the phone and placed a call to FBI agent Fred McFaul in Pensacola, Florida. I found out he had retired, and the person I spoke to suggested I call the FBI in Washington, D.C. I did, but only got more runaround.

From Washington I was directed to Houston to speak to a special agent who worked in domestic terrorism, and who was gathering information for a new task force being put together by United States Attorney General Janet Reno on antiabortion violence and an investigation into a possible national conspiracy. I had thought of the Clinton administration and Janet Reno as the tools of Satan just a couple of years before, but now I was ready to deal with the devil to try to stop God's assassins from striking out at innocent people again.

I spoke to the special agent on the phone and we agreed to meet at a fried chicken restaurant in an out-of-the-way location. I arrived early and had to wait for the agent, who did not look a bit like Fred McFaul from Pensacola. McFaul had been a huge, husky guy about to retire. This agent was a trim and beautiful blonde who was also a single mom.

She entered the restaurant and smiled at me right away, as though she had always known me. She came up to me in the sparsely populated place and said, "Hi, I'm Beverly Lovelace. You must be the guy I'm looking for."

I laughed and said, "I'm Jerry Reiter. Nice to meet you." We got some fried chicken and fixings, and then sat together at one of the tables in the corner. While chewing our chicken, we chewed the fat, and where the conversation went surprised me.

The agent ended up telling me as much about herself as I was telling her about my background. She told me right away that she just couldn't imagine how people could come to think about things the way I was describing these Christian terrorists. She said, "It even sounds funny to say Christian terrorists, although we say Islamic terrorist and think nothing of it."

I told her that I saw these guys in very much the same light as Islamic terrorists. There really is no difference in the thought processes involved, and their use of the holy book is the same as what the Koran has inspired in some of its extremists.

Agent Lovelace said she had never experienced that type of religious thinking. She told me that she had been raised as a Unitarian Universalist, a church that didn't believe in the traditional teachings of Christianity on such harsh things as original sin or hell or damnation, but believed in the good in all humanity. I said that sounded great, but Lovelace now thought she had been a bit naive about the world. Her work in the FBI had shown her too much of the dark side of life to see humanity the way she once had.

There was something about her that seemed particularly vulnerable beneath her tough talk. She joked that she wanted to get away from everything into a perfectly peaceful place where a special condition would be required of any who wanted to come around. She called the rule of her ideal place, "NIAA," which she said stood for "No Idiots or Assholes Allowed."

I realized that though she laughed and joked, she was burnt out by her tough job. She wanted a kinder, gentler life than the one that came with chasing bad guys. Her specialty in dealing with domestic terrorism put her into contact with organized crime, drug gangs who conspired to kill the competition or the cops, militia groups in multiple states (and we'd talk plenty about that), and an assortment of other vile and dangerous characters.

Now she was learning about a new world—the antiabortion fringe. She was out of her element and had to get up to speed quickly. She was part of the national effort to investigate the wave of violence that now reached from Florida to Canada and from coast to coast with bombings and shootings in the name of life.

I told her why I had contacted Washington: "It may not lead you to anything, but I think it's worth investigating. The name, address, and phone number that were found in John Salvi's pocket when he was arrested belong to Rev. Donald Spitz; he was at the murder trial I covered in Pensacola where a potential plot I investigated was underway."

I started to explain, but she interrupted because she had already seen my testimony on Hill and his friends from the now nationally distributed FBI file.

Lovelace asked me about the connection between Spitz and Salvi.

"I'm not going to be able to be that helpful to you directly on this because I don't know for certain how close Salvi and Spitz were, but I would suspect that someone who is living under the threat of a nationwide federal manhunt would not go to see a stranger with the urgency that Salvi showed."

Lovelace agreed with my point and said she'd follow up on the suggestion. Then I told her that I had seen a young man in Pensacola at the courthouse whom I believed was John Salvi, only I was not 100 percent certain because I only met him once and he was part of the group around Hill. I was certain that I had seen Spitz there, and further that Spitz was a friend of both Don Treshman and John Burt of Rescue America. I explained about Burt's role with Griffin and the bombers, and wondered aloud if Spitz might have had a similar relationship with Salvi.

The agent said she would check into it, and then she started asking me other questions about relationships between Operation Rescue, Rescue America, the Christian Coalition, and so on. I filled her in on names, dates of events, and how people knew each other. She was thrilled and asked if I could help her improve a national directory that would show the web of relationships for people whose names and roles they did not yet know. She had data from Washington, but they had missing links in the web of contacts.

"Yes, I can do that," I said. "I want to help because I don't want to see all this violence going on. The death toll just keeps going up on religious violence in this country, and we've got to find a way to turn it around."

Lovelace seemed genuinely touched by my willingness to help for altruistic reasons. Later, she'd tell me about the unseemly informants she often dealt with in the underworld of crime and drugs that was her bailiwick. She said that many of the informants were only helping because they had been caught and wanted to cut a deal.

No wonder she took an immediate liking to me. I must've seemed like a breath of fresh air. However, she seemed to feel more than casual friendship for me. When she assigned me my secret code name, which she gave all her informants for our own protection, she gave me the name of a character from a movie. I went to the video store and found the flick. My character, the one I was named after in the secret code, was a handsome stranger who rides into town and sweeps a single mother off her feet while also ridding the countryside of bad guys.

This made me suspect that there was more than professional interest on her part, but she never crossed over the boundaries of her duty as a federal agent. She and I met many times over the next five months, and in the course of helping her build up the national directory of Christian antiabortion terrorists, I made a multitude of calls to radical and religious leaders around the country. I began to see some patterns developing.

In one of our secret meetings at the local restaurants where we discussed antiabortion violence, I mentioned to Agent Lovelace two things that were disturbing me. I had found out since I had met with her last that both my former tipster, Don Treshman of Rescue America, and my former pastor, Rob Schenck, were moving across the country to the Washington, D.C., area, at about the same time.

Don Treshman was coming from Houston, Texas, to be near Rev. Michael Bray, who was based in Bowie, Maryland, about fifteen miles east of D.C. Rob Schenck, the former outreach minister at the church I attended in Buffalo, had been invited to pastor the newly created National Community Church, in Washington, D.C. (right near the Capitol Building), made up of antiabortion extremists, mainly members or alumni of Operation Rescue. I thought about the Reconstructionists' call for a national church and wondered if this was the goal of the new church my old pastor would lead.

Even more ominously, I wondered if the sudden moves to D.C. indicated a growing effort in that area for the antiabortion fringe to take direct action against the government they hated so much. Agent Lovelace and I discussed the possibility of my going down to Bray's church or Schenck's church, to join undercover. I thought I could gather some good information because those places were obviously as connected to the radical fringe as much as any congregations in America could be.

As sponsor of the White Rose Banquet, where shooters and bombers were honored as heroes and saints, Bray's church was the place where the Reconstructionists were most likely to have contact with one another. Schenck's church would focus on political protests. At the Democratic Convention in 1992, Rob was detained by the Secret Service and arrested for rushing President Clinton while screaming about abortion and waving a fetus.

I knew that Rob Schenck was more radical in his speech than his brother, Paul, who came across as the more mature older brother, even though they were twins. Given the escalation of violence among the radicals and the way that mentioning the Schenck brothers' names seemed to open doors for me with the advocates of force, I wasn't sure if Rob was more likely to become involved with violence himself or not, though I suspected that if he did get involved with it he would be one of the shrewd ones who gets someone else to get rid of targets he did not like, rather than being one of the doofuses who takes the fall.

Still, I thought that Bray's church would be the better source for the most radical activity around. And I worried that Rob Schenck might somehow suspect that I was no longer a "true believer" for his cause. I had never said anything to him or his brother, but there was still the possibility that somehow he had gotten a clue.

I thought more highly of the idea of visiting Bray's church, and mentioned that I had been invited to come there by Rev. Michael Bray's sister-in-law, Donna Bray, after talking to her on the phone recently. Lovelace offered to help me get a job in the area and pay my moving expenses if I wanted to live in the community and actually join the congregation undercover.

I talked with her about what would be involved, but soon said that it would not be possible. I did not want to move my wife and kids to Maryland to pretend to go along with the radicals for months at a time. I said to the agent, "I'd feel like my life were turning into a John Grisham novel, caught between the bad guys and you FBI types."

She said that she might not have been able to get it approved, anyway, because of my career in the media. She said there were very extensive restrictions on journalists as informants, because the government had to keep a line between its need to know information and interfering with the freedom of the press. I was glad to hear that the federal government, in which we in the Right had such a low trust, was trying to look out for the rights of the press.

As we talked further that day, it became clear that there were going to be some interesting gatherings of radicals at upcoming weekend events and special seminars that could help her get the information she needed for the task force, and help me reach my goal of stopping the violence. I could justify going into the groups for a short time to work undercover. It would be only one step past where I had gone the prior year with the trips to United Taxpayers Party get-togethers.

I knew it would be extremely interesting, but after having been face-to-face with the increasingly armed Christians, it made me less than enthusiastic about going back into the radical Right, especially to serve as an informant for the FBI. I had literally gone underground into the secret communication and command center of Operation Rescue back in 1992, but then it was because I believed in the pro-life cause. Now it would be to try to stop "pro-life killers."

The first event that Agent Lovelace wanted me to attend was in Wichita, Kansas, in April 1995. The group I would infiltrate was the newly forming American Coalition of Life Activists (ACLA), formed by antiabortionists who were angry about the rest of the existing major pro-life groups' denouncements of violence.

Our plans were carefully and painstakingly made. Agent Lovelace would attend the conference with me, and there would be other federal agents on-site should I get into trouble. That sounded good, but as it turned out, none of those things happened. I ended up going all alone, feeling like a potential target.

And I had good reason to fear. Just nine days before the ACLA conference in Wichita, something happened in nearby Oklahoma City. On the morning of April 19, 1995, the second anniversary of the federal government's bloody showdown with Waco cult members, an incredible explosion tore apart the Murrah Federal Building, killing 179 people and injuring many more.

Shock waves instantly reverberated throughout America, and questions went up about who had done this and why. There was a great deal of speculation that Islamic terrorists from overseas must have committed this heinous deed. But I remembered the significance of the date and suspected that it might have been someone from one of the groups I had known.

And, sure enough, it would turn out to be not a foreign Islamic group, but an all-American Christian boy who had served his nation in the military, and who had been exposed to the teachings of the radical Right and the militias.

He had read *The Turner Diaries*, a fictional story that covered the conspiracy theories about the United Nations taking over America and installing the New World Order on good Christian folk. Timothy McVeigh had actively associated with militia groups, and had apparently become the militia's version of the "doofus-as-pawn" in the national militant movement that wanted blood.

He seemed to epitomize the people I associated with in the radical Right as I did my investigations. He was the kind of Christian soldier I would have expected to find in the United Taxpayers Party or in the new group I was going to infiltrate, the ACLA.

McVeigh also happened to be from the same region I was a native of: Western New York. He had grown up in Pendleton, a suburb not far from my base in south Buffalo and West Seneca. It's an area where Roman Catholicism predominates, and McVeigh, like 65 percent of the local residents, had been raised in Holy Mother Church.

It was a place where you played by the rules, did what you were told, and hoped God would give you a break or two now and again. But in McVeigh's case, the breaks didn't seem to come his way. The troubled lad, who had been deserted by his own mother, went into the Army with a gung-ho determination to make the special forces, but wound up leaving with a chip on his shoulder. The incendiary rhetoric of the radical Right fueled his anger and inspired his actions.

Shortly after he used massive amounts of explosives, I called some of the people I knew in the militia movement. Many seemed to think that McVeigh was well-meaning but misguided. But just like the antiabortion leaders, they put the focus on the many injustices of their opponent—in this case, the federal government rather than the abortion industry. The principle was the same in the blame game.

Within a year, as public sentiment solidified against McVeigh and the militias, the militias would spin their story. They would convince themselves that McVeigh had not actually done the bombing, but had been framed by the federal government so President Clinton could get some antigun laws he wanted. It was a sign of their growing isolation and desperation.

But in the immediate aftermath of the Oklahoma City bombing, all that I knew for sure was that we had reached a dangerous new place where reality was matching red-hot rhetoric, and there was no telling where it all would end.

I almost didn't go to the ACLA conference, but I decided at the last minute that I would in spite of my wife's good advice not to. She thought I was crazy for going, since the FBI agents would not be there to protect me.

Instead of a group of agents nearby listening in to my wire, as originally planned, I was given a phone number of the local FBI office as my only backup. This was a potentially dangerous situation, and had I known who I was going to meet I would not have gone. But I pressed ahead, pushed on by my natural reporter's curiosity to see where the story would turn next.

When I flew into the Wichita airport on Friday, April 28, I had a little extra trouble getting a rental car. In the aftermath of the bloody bombing nearby, the rental companies were making sure they knew exactly who they were renting to since McVeigh had used a rented truck to hide his explosives.

I was late in arriving at the Christian school where the ACLA was meeting, and came in on a talk by Joe Scheidler, the granddaddy of the radical element of the antiabortion fringe. Ever since his terror-based book, *99 Ways to Close an Abortion Clinic*, had come out, Scheidler had been widely recognized as a national figure on the antiabortion front lines.

I scurried to find a seat on one of the wooden folding chairs in the auditorium to hear Scheidler denouncing the situation with the pro-choice administration in Washington. He felt that "it's time to do whatever is necessary" to end legalized abortions, and he said of antichoice assassin Paul Hill, "We need to stop arguing over whether what he did was right or not. We need to gather together and take action in whatever way we can. Thirty million babies have been killed since *Roe* v. *Wade*, and there's no end in sight right now . . . but by God we will turn this thing around."

His implied theme—that we don't condemn or condone what Paul Hill and the other terrorists had done—would be a mantra repeated to the attendees and the press over and over again although, as far as the media went, I was the only press person inside the meetings other than at press conference time. I was not asked to leave because I had told the person who preregistered me about my ties to the Schenck brothers and Operation Rescue.

Scheidler was obviously frustrated with the pro-life movement's lack of progress, and his anger over the Clinton administration's pro-choice stance was painfully clear. He spoke derisively of "Hillary and the NOW gang" of femi-Nazis. Scheidler's off-the-cuff style played well with the ragtag gathering of about sixty people. His height added to the heaviness of his message as he leaned in over the microphone to make his main points and wave his finger at us as though we were all his children. Although we were indoors, he wore his trademark hat, a narrow-brimmed fedora. He had a deeply lined face that had edges of the cruelty I had seen on John Burt, but he could also appear grandfatherly at some moments.

As Scheidler grumbled and growled his way through his talk, I glanced down at the simple photocopied paper that served as the program for the event. I recognized many of the speakers' names, from Ed Martin of Florida, a friend of John Burt and Don Treshman, to attorney Michael Hirsh, the man who had worked for Pat Robertson's ACLJ headquarters when he wrote the legal defense for antichoice assassin Paul Hill.

Also in attendance at the event were Andrew Cabot, whom I had met with Paul Hill at the Griffin trial, and Joe Foreman, leader of the radical group of antiabortionists in Michigan, Missionaries to the Preborn. The FBI agent seemed particularly interested in having me spend as much time near Foreman as possible.

But the biggest shock of all was that another man who had been with Paul Hill, the man who had been arrested for weapons possession after my tips to the cops and FBI, was also there. Daniel Ware had been released from prison after a year and a half and was already back with his old allies in the radical Right, showing up at the most radical new group possible just a very short time after gaining his freedom.

I found his presence immediately terrifying because if he ever knew that I was responsible for sending him to prison, there was no telling what he would do. But I calmed myself enough that later that first day of the conference, Saturday, April 30, I asked Ware for a ride in his van as we went out to "take action."

Part of the program for activists was to do something during the conference rather than just talk. The conference was broken up into three groups of varying sizes for different projects, and my group was assigned to shut down an abortion clinic in downtown Wichita. A group of six of us hopped into Ware's beat-up van and started down the road.

A blonde named Becky Black introduced herself from the back of the van and asked me who I was. I told her my name and that I was a former member of Rob and Paul Schenck's church. Once again, I had said the magic words. Four of the six knew the Schenck brothers and thought they were wonderful. One man even said he had been arrested along with the Schencks during a big rescue protest in Atlanta.

Our little group was assigned to have four people picketing directly in front of the main doors while two of our squad would go directly into the clinic to try to intimidate the clinic workers, or as we put it at the time, "Help them see the light." Since I was a former member of the Schencks' church, they figured I was an old pro at all this. I must have made a good impression on the radicals I was pretending to go along with, because I ended up being chosen as one of the two to go inside the clinic.

I pretended to be brave and acted like it was all old hat, but I had never taken part in the clinic raids in my life. My heart was pounding a mile a minute as we pulled up to the brick building that housed the abortion clinic. I hadn't realized that this was going to be a part of the deal. Now I was truly acting as an undercover informant for the FBI.

As adrenaline rushed through my veins, I jumped out of the van, hit the pavement, stepped up onto the sidewalk, and hit the front door. I opened it up and let Becky go through first.

She was the real McCoy, not afraid one bit and loving every minute of our confrontation as it started. I rushed to keep up with her as we headed across the main waiting area for the clinic and straight up to the counter, where a white-uniformed woman with strawberry blonde mixed with gray hair looked startled to see the two of us charging toward her.

"Why are you killing babies in this clinic?" demanded Becky.

The woman was visibly shaken as she said, "We don't. This is Dr. Smith's OB-GYN office. There are no abortions here. None."

The facts didn't stop Becky. She was on a mission from God. She continued even more forcefully, "We know Dr. Smith has a big practice and part of it is baby killing. We don't believe you, anyway."

I interjected, "That's right."

Becky continued without missing a beat, saying extra loudly, "You, and all of you who work here, are accomplices to murder. Someday you will have to answer to Almighty God on judgment day. And today this office is being shut down in the name of all the innocent babies who need to be protected."

I said, "We have our group outside and we are all committed to doing whatever it takes to stop abortions from ever taking place here again. Do you understand?" I said it with such intensity, and my large frame leaning toward her was so intimidating, that I could see she was trembling and fighting back tears.

Just then we heard a police siren, wailing louder and louder as it approached. I instinctively followed Becky out the door and we dove into the van where our waiting counterparts helped pull us in as Daniel Ware hit the gas and we took off.

"Wow, did you see that? The cops were just around the corner. It was a good thing we were on the side street or we'd'a been busted for sure," exclaimed one of the guys from the back of the van.

One of the women said, "Yeah, well the Lord provides for our safety." A bunch of halleluiahs and amens followed, and talk of Jesus and God mixed with talk about how great it was to terrorize the clinic workers and pregnant women.

"That old lady was gonna burst into tears if we'd'a had just one more minute, and you're so big you really put the fear of God into her," Becky boasted on behalf of our efforts. I couldn't show it at the time without blowing my cover, but I felt bad and thought that anyone who got off on doing this had to be seriously twisted. But I could definitely tell what they were getting out of it. The adrenaline pump going in, the power struggle inside, and the quick getaway from the cops all felt like we were inside a living action movie, and Becky and I were the pro-life version of Bonnie and Clyde as we pulled off the job and jumped in our getaway car. It was electrifying in a totally insane way.

One thing was certain, though, I had made myself an insider in the radical fringe. I could now go anywhere inside the new militant elements and be believed. But I didn't like it. I hated it when I had seen the Operation Rescue people lying on the telephone, like the leader who had said, "Truth is the first casualty of war, and this is war, brother." Or when the Christian Coalition publicly said they were against the illegal tactics of Operation Rescue while loaning out their offices for the group. Now, I had to ask myself the question, was I any better?

Lines had been crossed. At the other events I covered, I was myself, a friendly reporter who had been a member of the Schencks' church and an Operation Rescue media coordinator, but I didn't take part in any of the radical activities. Now I was playing a part as a "true believer" and taking part in an action that left emotional scars on women. It was disturbing, and I wanted out, but I was determined to finish the weekend first.

When we got back to the school, we joined the others who were already down in the basement cafeteria. We made sandwiches and drank soft drinks as we talked about our exploits. I saw Andrew Cabot across the room and went to talk to him.

At first he didn't recognize me, but I reminded him of our get-togethers the previous year in Pensacola and our talks on the phone since. We talked for a while, and he told me about something very strange. "I recently had a run-in with the FBI," he said.

I said, "You're kidding! What happened?"

He explained, "I noticed I was being tailed when I was on a trip to see my fiancée, so I pulled over to a restaurant. Afterward, there was no sign of the feds, but I started getting suspicious. I pulled the car off to the side of the road, and took a look underneath. I found a damned tracking device down there and pitched it. That was the end of that."

By this point there were others listening to his story, and a great deal of commiserating went on with everyone complaining about the intrusiveness of the federal government. An older woman said, "What right do they have to tail you, a private citizen?"

I was the only person who knew the answer to that question. Cabot had told me during one of our phone conversations that he was planning a trip out of state that was "really important." Since he never told me what it was all about, I passed the info along to Agent Lovelace.

Later I would confirm Cabot's story with Lovelace. Sure enough, it had happened exactly the way he described it. The agents had egg on their faces after the device was discovered and they came to realize that Cabot had only gone to see his girl. But I felt it was only a case of "better safe than sorry."

Even now, as I write this story down and Andrew Cabot is not suspected of a single crime, I can't figure out why he was so filled with rage and hatred at our government, the media, and women's rights groups. However much he may have seemed like the next one to snap, he turned out to be the barking dog that didn't bite.

Maybe that's all that Joe Foreman was, too. As instructed by the FBI agent, I sat right in front of Foreman that day as soon as I knew who he was. We had a speaker after lunch who did a lot of comparing current-day America with Nazi Germany. He talked about the abortion policies of the Third Reich. He kept comparing Bill Clinton to Adolf Hitler. He kept musing on how different things might have been in Germany if Hitler had not been around. He went on and on about how the nation did corrupt things when they had a corrupt leader like Hitler. The speaker asked what the solution might be for a nation with a corrupt leader.

"Take him out," said Foreman to a friend. I was stunned. I slowly turned around just in time to see Foreman smiling at the companion to whom he'd made the remark. Given the setting I was in, I felt he was probably serious, but there was no way to tell for sure. But I knew I would have to pass the comments along to the FBI.

A man near the front of the basement meeting room we were in asked the speaker, "Isn't it true that if the president and vice president were both killed, we'd get Newt Gingrich, the Speaker of the House, as president?"

The speaker said yes, that the Speaker of the House was indeed second only to the vice president in terms of succession to the presidency.

It all was really giving me the creeps. Were these people going to try to pull off a double assassination? What the hell had I gotten myself into? I had now entered the darkest recesses of American terrorism, and it was rotten to the core.

I felt a little better when the speaker at the front of the room decided it wouldn't be such a great idea to have the Speaker of the House as president. I felt more hopeful until I found out why.

Most of the people at the conference had given up on both major political parties and were determined to see an officially Christian government installed. The conference speaker who got the most applause was Michael Hirsh, the ACLJ attorney, when he predicted a future in which Christians would take over, and abortionists would face Nuremberg-type war trials for their "crimes against humanity."

Hirsh ranted against birth control, too, challenging the audience to have "as many babies as God gives you." He called Paul Hill a hero who had been let down by the church. "God will hold us accountable if we do not act," he declared. Hirsh came down from the podium and headed for the door. I followed him and caught up with him in the parking lot.

I told him my name and that I had been a member of the Schencks' church. That's when he told me that his best friend at the ACLJ was my old pastor, Paul Schenck. Hirsh said that ever since my old pastor had been hired as Pat Robertson's administrative director for the ACLJ, the two of them had spent a great deal of time together. They both had extremely large families (no birth control allowed), stay-at-home wives, and a deep concern over the abortion issue.

I asked Hirsh if he was assigned to the case for Hill. He knew where I was going next, so before I asked him about Robertson, he said that he was convinced that Robertson would deny knowing that he was writing the legal briefs if asked. "Plausible deniability, like in the White House, is the operative phrase," joked Hirsh. He said that he had written his graduate thesis on justifiable homicide while at Robertson's university. It had created quite a stir, and Robertson's legal arm hired the young attorney fresh out of law school.

It was clear to me that Hirsh liked his role as a rabble-rouser, even though it had cost him his job and the future was not too bright for someone with his extreme views. He would have to raise "as many children as the Lord gave him" on a very meager income. He did not seem likely to be concerned about such material matters; his focus was on the exciting world of extremism. I suddenly had a pang of sympathy for the wives of all these guys, not to mention their litters of little ones hungrily awaiting the basics of life while their dads went off to play a pretend war against their own government for its failure to enforce the morality they chose to believe in.

The ironic thing was that the government they were railing against was more reluctant than ever to get involved in investigating their groups. That's why I had been left to my own devices right after the Oklahoma City bombing.

You might think the government wanted to crack down on terrorists right after the horrible event, and they did, in a way. But they wanted to be extra careful how they did it. They realized they were perceived as having been partially to blame for the incendiary reaction they got at Waco (though they wouldn't admit any wrongdoing for years) and at places like Ruby Ridge, Idaho, where a radical's wife was gunned down by federal agents.

In both instances their confrontational style seemed to confirm the apocalyptic fears of the extremists, leaving the wackos feeling they had no choice but to defend themselves or die. Several weeks after the Waco fiasco, the FBI got a new director, Louis Freeh, who knew he had to find ways for his beloved bureau to be more effective at controlling the extremists without being provocative or perceived as heavy-handed. It was a difficult tightrope to walk, especially after the Oklahoma City bombing, which had clearly raised domestic terrorism to a new level.

Still, at the ACLA conference, just before Freeh came into power — it seemed that the FBI was temporarily paralyzed in the aftermath of the mass murder in the Murrah Federal Building. I can't say that I blamed them, after seeing their coworkers and children blown apart by one of their own citizens. But I didn't like being at this crazy conference all by myself, either.

Humor for the ACLA group consisted of sharing the *Bottom Feeders Joke Book*, a knock-off of the nastiest lawyer jokes, ethnic jokes, and other examples of cruel humor and pretty much anything in poor taste, but all with one purpose. This joke book had an intent that made no one else laugh, it was designed to intimidate young medical students in the OB-GYN field from choosing to enter the training necessary to offer abortion services.

The bottom feeders in the book were abortion providers, and one of the tamer examples was, "What do you call a thousand abortionists chained to the bottom of the sea? A good start." What made this different than when it was told as a lawyer joke was that antiabortion extremists had mailed a copy to each and every OB-GYN student in abortion service classes in every major public university in America.

Their receipt of the book was no joke. It seemed to imply, "We know who you are. We know where you are. We know how to get to you. We are part of an antiabortion extremist group, and if you don't pick another field of work, this is just the beginning of the campaign of terror that waits for you, and maybe one of these days there will be a bullet or bomb coming your way instead of a joke book."

At the ACLA conference, news that med students were choosing to go into the abortion field in smaller numbers than before were greeted with cheers and jeers. "This means that what we're doing is working," said one middle-aged man in the session. And to a certain extent, he was right. Terrorism did have a certain effectiveness in intimidating people. As long as you didn't mind being a brutal bully for Christ, it was an option you might choose.

The joke book was one of the few moments of levity during the weekend, though. Many of the radicals were clearly worn down by the long battles they'd had in the street theater over abortion. Some of them had been protesting and blockading clinics since the mid-1980s, and they felt they were worse off now than when they started.

When the first day's events ended, we were free to go off to our motel. Most of us who preregistered were booked into the same flea-bag motel near the site of the conference. Only the leaders were staying at a finer hotel. This was no egalitarian group and didn't pretend to be. As one of the attendees had commented about the corruption of American democracy today, "The Kingdom of God is not a democracy."

Amens and acclamations followed his observation. I was in a sub-culture that saw the American way as the enemy, and religiously inspired terror as the solution. I thought back to an account I'd read about a freethinker roughly four hundred years earlier. A man named Giordano Bruno had been arrested by the church for refusing to blindly accept its authority as the sole font of truth. Bruno was fascinated by the then embryonic science field and, though he was a cleric, questioned the church. When he refused to recant, he was dragged through the streets with a nail through his tongue so he could not speak his "falsehoods" that someone other than the Catholic Church might have something worthwhile to say.

I suspected that had these people I was meeting at the ACLA conference lived back in those days, they'd have been among the blood-thirsty mob cheering when the church tortured anyone who did not blindly accept the teachings of the one true church. Sure, the church had changed overall, but not voluntarily. It was because it was forced to change by the secular government and the wall of separation of church and state.

That separation turned out to be a good thing for the churches because it gave them back a mantle of respectability as they focused again on their evangelistic efforts, including caring for the poor, once their legal power was stripped from them. However, the group I was with wanted to return to the old days and old ways with a vengeance.

The surprising thing was that if I had met these people at a church function under more normal circumstances, they would have seemed like your regular, dedicated churchgoers. Most of them had close-knit families and lived personally moral lives as far as their sexual practices and basic honesty. But they saw nothing wrong with imposing their morality on others; indeed, they felt obligated to do so.

I ended up going to dinner with a small group of people that included Daniel Ware. He sat across from me as we ate burgers and fries. He talked about how much he was enjoying his freedom and how he had hopes of getting a full-time job someday in a Christian ministry. "God is so good, and I want to help people any way I can," he said.

I was surprised as I listened to him talk. Had he become a more gentle person than the man who had been convicted on felony charges of counterfeiting, and then years later on weapons charges?

He seemed to truly want to live a simple life of service, but his plans sounded fuzzy. He spoke of the fact that he had not had enough formal education to be a minister or a teacher in a Christian school, but he felt he could do something worthwhile. Then he said that he hoped there was time left "before Jesus comes back" to do the things he wanted to do.

One of the predominant things that would inevitably come up when I talked long enough with any conservative Christian, including this group, was how awful they thought this modern generation was, and how convinced they were that things were only going to get worse. Most of them were convinced that it was all part of God's plan "in these last days."

That "end times" teaching has been standard thinking for as long as I could remember in my Christian days. I had become born-again back in 1971, and even then most fundamentalists were predicting that we were about to see the imminent return of Jesus to the earth. I was one of the few born-agains who chose not to believe that particular doctrine. It just made no sense to me, but I was in the definite minority.

Hal Lindsey's 1967 book, *The Late, Great Planet Earth*, had done a great deal to popularize this teaching, which I would later find out had been around for at least a hundred years. Back in the late 1880s, the end times teaching had inspired many new churches to form, including two that are still around today, the Seventh-Day Adventists and the world's fastest-growing religion, the door-to-door faith, the Jehovah's

Witnesses. "The end is coming" had been a staple of the Pentecostal churches, too, since they started in the early 1900s.

The world seems like a different place when you believe that God Almighty is forcing the whole planet to go on a downward spiral that you cannot do anything about. It's a far cry from the modern scientific idea that we are evolving, and that positive change is possible.

That night, as I listened to Daniel Ware, I thought how different his life might have turned out if he had been taught to think for himself rather than to blindly follow the vile hate mongering that had been fed to him by all these Christian extremists. Like Paul Hill, he had a basic human decency that flashed through at times, but the power of the ideas he had come to believe was too overwhelming for him to resist.

On the second day of the conference, I saw that the local paper, the *Wichita Eagle*, had run articles over the last two days on the conference.* One said it had gotten off to "a peaceful start." That surprised me, since I had been part of the clinic attack.

But even more shocking was an earlier article. It was about Daniel Ware, and it told how he had recently been released from prison after being convicted on weapons charges right after leaving Pensacola. But then it went further. It told how he had been suspected of being part of a "Beirut-style" terrorism plot on the National Coalition of Abortion Providers. I was stunned because I had never seen anything along those lines in print anywhere except the FBI report that I had instigated.

I suspected that the reporter either had contacts in the FBI or in a pro-choice group with excellent intelligence gathering. At any rate, I realized I could now talk to Daniel Ware about the incident without obviously pointing to my own role in the matter. I decided to risk bringing it up.

I sat down with him during a break in the conference in a spot far enough from the others that they could see us but not hear us. I tried to hide my nervousness as I broached the topic. "Hey, I see you're getting some media attention these days," I wryly observed.

"Yeah, but it's not the kind I wanted. The liberal media is sticking it to us pro-life Christians again." Then he added that he did not want any part in violence.

---

*These articles appeared in the *Wichita* (Kans.) *Eagle*, Friday, April 28, 1995.

I pressed on. "Did you go to that national abortion thing, though?"

Ware was visibly uncomfortable, but sheepishly admitted that he had gone there. "Ya know," I said, "I've talked to Michael Griffin on the phone, and he is a mess, just a big mess, from all of that. I don't think that people realize how horrible it is to have to go to prison for life."

Then Ware gave an answer I was not prepared for. He had seemed so docile, and even a little bit simple in his thinking up to that point. But he looked me right in the eye, and said, "I know [how hard life in prison would be]; if it was me in that situation like Mike [Griffin] or Paul Hill, I would never be arrested. I would rather go out in a blaze of glory with my guns in each hand, and taking out as many as I could possibly get."

I froze. I could barely maintain my composure. So much for his denials about the article's accuracy. Any lingering doubts I had about his dangerousness went out the window. I realized I was in the company of someone who had been fed so much vile garbage that he was primed to potentially be the next doofus to be used.

It made me angry that this simple soul had been so twisted by demagogues that he could go from being someone who wanted to help people to someone willing to go out with guns blazing. I asked him, "Do you carry guns with you?"

He said of course he did. "I'm a big believer in the Second Amendment, and they ain't gonna get my guns unless they pry 'em from my dead, cold fingers."

He then offered to show me his guns. I said okay, and we walked out to the back of the building to the parking lot. His old, rust-infested van was near a tree. He opened the back door of the van, lifted the rug to the spot where the spare tire would have been kept, and pulled out one, then another drab olive duffel bag.

I couldn't believe it. This was what I had only heard about back in Pensacola, but here it was and about to be opened up. The thought rushed through my mind that I'd better hope he didn't know what I did to him or I might be dead in two seconds.

Ware lovingly lifted each weapon up for me to see. He told me their various makes and models, but it meant nothing to me. He was particularly proud of a Smith and Wesson rifle for some reason, but I was too numb to write it all down after we got back inside.

I was literally in shock. This was just too much. The whole situation in Pensacola was more real to me in that moment than it had been when I was there. Between the paper publishing Ware's willingness to take part in the plot at the abortion providers event and Ware's intensity about his guns, I could actually feel for the first time what a good thing I had done in Pensacola by turning Hill and him in. And I could feel the horrific possibilities that might have unfolded if I had not acted.

But I also realized that Ware was more dangerous now than ever before. He was so infatuated with his weapons, and they were all he had. He had been unable to get his old job back when he got out of prison, and he had become a drifter, sleeping most nights in his van. What would keep someone who had nothing left to lose from longing to go out in that "blaze of glory" he talked about so enthusiastically?

I didn't know what to do, but I knew I was in over my head. I retraced my steps to the parking lot, got in my car, and drove to a phone booth a couple of blocks away. I called the local FBI agent, but only got an answering machine. I called the FBI agent in Houston, and at least got a human being, but she was unable to reach Agent Lovelace for me. I was on my own.

I left my number at the motel with the FBI in Houston and went back to my room. I decided to skip the rest of the day's events unless I heard from one of the agents. About a half hour after I got into my room, I got the call I was waiting for.

"Hi, Jerry, this is Beverly Lovelace. What happened?" I explained to her about the guns and my feelings and the story in the paper. The words all tumbled out so quickly that she told me to calm down and relax for a moment, reminding me I was safe. She also reassured me that I had done the right thing by getting away from the situation.

After we talked awhile I felt a lot better. I told her I was going to go back to the conference for the last day, Sunday, after all. She told me a couple of times that I was under no obligation to do so, but I told her I was going to go anyway.

I went out for dinner and felt more relaxed when I returned to my room. At around 9:45 that evening my roommate, a quiet guy from Illinois, returned, and he had a surprise for me. He said, "I hope you don't mind, but I invited one of the guys to sleep here because he's been stuck sleeping in his van."

"Daniel Ware?"

He nodded yes, saying, "Oh, good, you already know him."

Just then Ware came into the room. "Hi, there, what happened to you at the conference? I didn't see you this afternoon after we talked at my van."

I couldn't believe this was happening. I stammered out a response as best I could, "Uh, well I wasn't feeling all that good. Musta been somethin' I ate, I guess. My stomach's been kind of upset."

Ware said, "Oh, I'm sorry to hear that. I hope ya don't mind me staying here."

"Well, we don't have anywhere for you to sleep. There are only two beds."

My roommate cheerfully responded, "Oh, that's okay. I already told him he can sleep in my bed—as long as he keeps his hands to himself." He and Ware laughed at the little joke. The best I could do was smile and turn away so that Ware couldn't see my real reaction.

Here was a living nightmare if ever there was one. How the hell could I get out of that room without tipping off Ware any more than my disappearing trick had already done? I was in a precarious position because I still thought it was likely Ware didn't know that I was the one who had tipped off the feds, which led to him spending a year and a half behind bars. But if I left the room in a hurry again, he might figure it out and follow me back to Houston, where he had told me he was staying.

Worse yet, if I was wrong, and Ware was just messing with my head by making his speech about going out in a blaze of glory and showing me his guns, I could be dead by morning.

Ware went into the bathroom to take a shower. Once I heard the water running, I asked my roommate why he had invited Ware to sleep with us. He said he felt bad for the guy, and added, "Wouldn't you want a shower and a bed if you'd been sleeping in your van? Try to put yourself in his place."

That last line about putting myself in Ware's place seemed haunting. It suddenly dawned on me. This could all be a setup. Was my roommate in on it? Now I was getting paranoid, but who could blame me given the company I was keeping?

I made an excuse to my roommate that I wanted to go get some Pepto-Bismol for my upset stomach, and I left. I called Agent Lovelace again, and got right through to her at home this time. She agreed with my assessment that Ware probably didn't know about my actions, but said she wouldn't blame me if I wanted to leave. "I'm not sure I could sleep in that situation," she admitted.

I still had my belongings in the room and I didn't have enough cash on me to get another motel room right then, so I went back in. I had to stop first and waste some money on Pepto-Bismol I didn't need. Even though I'd only been gone a half an hour, when I got back, Ware was already asleep and snoring.

I decided to lay down and try to stay awake as long as possible while pretending to be asleep. Minutes seemed like hours. The clock seemed to be stuck.

As I was lying there in tense anticipation, Ware got up from the bed and pulled out his Smith and Wesson, pointing it right at me. I jumped up and realized I had been dreaming. He was still asleep.

Fortunately, I had not awakened anyone else. But as I calmed myself, I realized that this kind of undercover life was not for me. And then I chuckled to myself for a moment, This is taking the "undercover" role to a literal level as I lie here worrying under my covers.

Realizing I couldn't go back to sleep and looking for a reason to get out of there at 5:15 in the morning, I pulled my running clothes on and went for a jog.

Then I went to breakfast. I picked up a copy of the Sunday morning edition of the *Wichita Eagle*. There was coverage of the ACLA conference, but not as much as I had expected.

One article that did catch my eye was entitled, "Haves, Have-nots Far Apart in U.S., Wealth-gap Worst of Industrial Nations." It started off with the point that most people think of America as an egalitarian nation, but that in reality it is the most economically stratified nation in the industrialized world. The article compared the concentration of wealth of the top 1 percent in America with other nations. It said that America's top 1 percent owned 40 percent of the wealth, compared with Britain, where the top 1 percent controlled 18 percent of the wealth. No other nation came close to the divide we have.

I realized that the figures they were using came from 1989, the last fiscal year of the Reagan-Bush era. Still, it was shocking to see that poor people in even tiny European countries were earning so much more of a percentage of the nation's income than they were here in America in supposedly good economic times.

The article explained that the powerful influence of money in the political process here had played a key role in tipping the balance of power toward the wealthy at the expense of the poor. In other words, our poorest citizens were getting screwed by politicians who were taking money from the rich. It was a reverse Robin Hood situation by our Congress and president. It shocked me because I had been a true believer in Ronald Reagan throughout the 1980s.

I looked at the day's schedule of events. The morning had largely been left free so people could attend the church of their choice. That struck me as odd for a couple of reasons. It would have seemed that a group as united in purpose as the folks at the ACLA were would want to worship together.

Instead they went their separate ways. And then it occurred to me that the Catholics and various Protestants who had gathered there could not share communion together. Each of their churches devalued the others, so they were divided on Sunday morning, the time that should have brought them together.

Their freedom to choose their own particular place of worship was a benefit that might not exist if they had their way in the future. Tolerance and pluralism could become casualties of their holy war on the nation if they ever seized the reins of power.

I returned to the conference for lunch and the man I sat next to got on a rant condemning the "homosexual agenda." He complained that a lot of people were talking about how we should be compassionate to homosexuals. He said, "Let's put it plain and simple: "God hates fags.""

He was hardly in the minority in conservative Christian circles. For some reason, homosexuality isn't seen as just another sin by conservatives; it's put in a category all its own. It's about the only sin short of murder that will get you kicked out of virtually all conservative churches.

At the end of the conference came the conclusive address by Joe Scheidler. He sent us off like we were his children leaving the nest. He encouraged us to "keep on fighting the good fight, and never give up." He seemed drained, though, and so did the whole group.

He got great applause, anyway, and finally we were out of there. I was so happy to get back home to Houston, and I was determined to never ever do anything like that again. And even though I would stick to that promise this time, I would find that dark world intruding on mine again.

I was only home about two weeks when the phone rang, and I answered it to hear the voice of Daniel Ware. He said, "How ya doin' brother?"

I said "fine," and asked how he got my number.

"Don Treshman gave it to me," he explained.

How ironic that the person who had given me the first tip about the "something big" way back the year before would now be the person to give my phone number and address to the weapon-carrying warrior I had caused to be arrested. Ware said that he was now living with some people who were not very far from me, and he invited me to get together with him. I politely declined.

When I got off the phone and told my wife about it, she said, "That's it; we're moving before this guy shows up here." And I knew she was right. Even though Ware had not threatened us and probably didn't know what I had done to him, it was time to get out of there.

I flew back to Buffalo a few days later and interviewed at my old radio station, WGR Newsradio 55. I was pleased to find out that Ray Marks, the kindly broadcast veteran who had helped me get my first national work as a regional news stringer, was now in charge. We had a nice lunch together, and I told him I wanted to return home.

I didn't tell him the whole big story of what had happened. I wished I had because I feel certain he would have helped me out if he had known what I'd been through. Instead he offered me part-time work, and I had to work fill-ins for the local office of Metro Traffic, subbing for days or weeks at a time on multiple radio and TV stations, but with no permanency.

Still, when we moved our family back to Buffalo, we were all glad to be back home among my large extended family. We were welcomed back with open arms by my six brothers and sisters, and my parents were ecstatic that we were back. Comparing our large family to the old TV show *The Waltons*, I was the John-Boy of the Reiter clan. We were back amid the guitars and banjo and drums and percussion instruments that popped up at some of our family gatherings and, just as though I'd never left, I was back in my role of telling jokes and stories, singing songs, and playing my guitar. My family called me "the one-man entertainment center," and it seemed that normalcy had returned to my life at long last.

But I should have known that no one could go through what I had and not have it impact his future. Like the Vietnam vets who returned from seeing too much in the war, I had returned from the culture war a different man. I just didn't know it yet.

TWENTY-FIVE

Fall 1995

I wanted everything to go back to the way it had been before I had gotten involved with the Schenck brothers, the Christian Coalition, and Operation Rescue. Neither my wife nor I could bring ourselves to get committed to another church, though. Who could blame us for being gun-shy at this point?

We didn't return to our old congregation at New Covenant Tabernacle or to our friends at the Christian Coalition. We occasionally attended church somewhere, but nothing seemed right. I started checking out the local Unitarian Universalist church, the denomination that Agent Lovelace had told me about.

Sue refused to go because she was still more influenced by the conservative ways of thinking than I was. I found the UU church, as they called it for short, appealing in its broadmindedness, but a bit dry after the charismatic style I was used to taking part in.

The liberals I had thought were so dangerous back in my conservative days now seemed a little bland. I wondered what the big fuss was all about. Though I no longer saw liberals as the enemy, I didn't quite fit in with them, either. But, because I was more at ease with people across the political spectrum, I decided to take part in a noble experiment a friend of mine was involved in.

Karen Swallow Prior, the woman who had served as the local Operation Rescue spokesperson for many years, starting even before I helped her and my pastors out in 1992's Spring of Life protest, invited me to join her as part of a movement that had been launched in reaction to the polarization of the protest.

The group was called the Coalition for Common Ground. People from the pro-life and pro-choice factions would gather together to dialogue. It wasn't a debate and nobody had to compromise his or her beliefs.

Karen brought me to one of the group's board meetings and I got a chance to take part in the dialogue technique firsthand. It surprised me that the topic that night was about the local school district rather than abortion, but Rev. Stan Bratton, a leader of the Common Ground group who was also head of the local Council of Churches, explained to me that the dialogue technique was used to help people discuss many different and difficult issues. He said that they were part of a national Common Ground Network, headquartered in Washington, D.C., and that the dialogue technique had been used to bring people together in such powder kegs as Bosnia and the Middle East.

The Common Ground method, a name that many other groups use far less effectively, brings people from the opposing sides of controversial issues together to listen to each other. They then feed back what was said to make sure they truly understand what is being communicated by their counterpart on the other side.

They compare the reality of their opponents' positions to what their preconceived expectations were when they arrived for the meeting (often opposing sides caricature or demonize their opponents). Then they purposely set aside their differences temporarily, without asking anyone to compromise, while focusing on the areas the differing sides do have in common.

It seemed simple, yet effective. I liked the process when I engaged in it that first night, and would be even more impressed when I saw it used on the abortion issue. Because of my media background, I was asked to help publicize the group's next public event. The dialogue workshops were kept private to ensure that people could speak freely. But to publicize the group's existence, they decided to hold a public sample of the process with two well-known public figures from opposing sides of the abortion issue.

I suggested that the best day to get media coverage would be January 22, the anniversary of the *Roe* v. *Wade* decision. It turned out to be excellent advice, and yielded coverage from most of the TV and radio stations in town, plus some good coverage in the local papers. They had never before received so much media attention.

I acted as emcee for the night, introducing the various participants at our display of the process. We were in a large room at Daemen College, a private, formerly Roman Catholic institution. The meeting room was close to full as we started off the evening's program.

Karen Swallow Prior took part from the pro-life side, and Ann Gugino took part from the pro-choice side. Both women had been very active on behalf of their causes, though Prior had the more public role. Dr. Wally Hobbs, a retired State University of New York professor, took the part of facilitator, asking questions of the two sides.

The first thing he did was to ask each woman to simply tell her story, the things that had led her to her position. Karen started off and shared her story of a journey of faith that had led her to hold such strong convictions that she was willing to work very publicly for such a controversial group as Operation Rescue. She was very articulate in explaining her positions and her reasons for opposing abortion on moral and spiritual grounds.

Ann Gugino was then asked about how she had come to her position as a pro-choice person. She surprised most people when she said that in many ways she was just as pro-life a person as Karen was, that she also thought of each abortion as a tragedy that could have been avoided. But then she explained that she worked as a counselor with low-income women, and had seen the negative side of women keeping their babies when they were not equipped to do so.

"I once walked in on an apartment where there were three preschool kids cooped up in their cribs. The children were covered in feces and dirt, and they were crying. Their mother had been having some problems mentally and emotionally, but she kept getting pregnant anyway. I went to one of the babies and picked her up. She clung to me for dear life, and my heart was breaking at the sight, the smells, the horror of it all," Ann said, and told more about the situation she had seen firsthand. As she finished her story, some people were getting choked up. A few sniffles could be heard in the back of the room.

I realized as a journalist that a personal story could have more power on an audience than all the most articulate explanations of an issue. At the time, I wished that Karen had also shared such a story, but the only one on the pro-life side of the stage that night who had a powerful personal story to tell was me, and mine would not have helped our side.

That night was the first time I had ever sat in the same space with someone who was pro-choice and truly listened with an open mind to her side of the argument. That would have a very big effect on me, but it would take time before the full impact reached my mind and heart.

By the end of that evening at the college, Professor Hobbs had tallied ten areas of common ground between the women after he had asked them a series of questions. For instance, both sides agreed that there were too many teen pregnancies, and that young men should take more responsibility to prevent unwanted pregnancies.

At the end of the evening, I told the audience about the forum for preventing teen pregnancies that had been developed by the Common Ground participants of the past, and that it was hoped the dialogues of the future would offer even more positive actions. Professor Hobbs added that the dialogue itself was very powerful.

Over the next two years, I sat on the board of directors of the Coalition for Common Ground, and I experienced the power of dialogue many times. I finally understood why someone who found abortion morally repugnant could still, however reluctantly, support a woman's right to choose.

There were no simple solutions to the problem of abortion, but the rhetoric against President Clinton turned out to be incredibly overblown. I can remember telling a group in 1992 that abortion was going to be bigger than ever under Clinton, but the number of abortions performed in America consistently declined year after year while that "pro-choice devil" was in office.

Pro-lifers always focus on the loss of human life of the fetuses, and with good reason; but when abortion was illegal, it was shocking how many times the mothers and babies died during pregnancy or childbirth. That was back in the good old days when God was in charge, rather than modern medicine and humans making individual decisions on what is best for their own bodies and families.

I had read a great deal of literature from a Roman Catholic priest named Father David Trosch, who has appeared many times on national TV calling for the execution of not only abortion doctors, but any women who used most forms of birth control as well. He had a particular hatred for the birth control pill, calling it a possible abortifacient, meaning it can destroy a fertilized egg and sperm's chances for survival. And, of course, the Roman Catholic Church remains just as intractable in its position against birth control as it is against abortion.

When I finally told my personal story at a Common Ground gathering, the impact was very powerful. I confirmed the worst fears of the pro-choice side, and deflated the certainties of my pro-life allies, but I offered my own hopeful analysis that maybe someday abortion would be unnecessary. I'm just as horrified by abortion as ever, but I also realize that it is better for family-planning decisions to be left to families or individual women than the federal government. I had made the transition to being pro-choice, even while retaining my desire to see abortions dwindle or disappear. Interestingly, some of the pro-life people who heard about it said they knew that was going to happen once we started down the common ground process. That made me realize why some of them were afraid to truly listen to the opposition — it might make sense.

I now believe there is more hope in the future of making abortions much less common through advances in pharmaceuticals and birth control combined with better sex education than there is from the shrill cries of murder of the "respectable" antichoice groups, and certainly from the blockades, bombs, and bullets of the "pro-life terrorists."

TWENTY-SIX

November 1995

TWO months before I took part in the Common Ground display in January 1996, I received a call from an old political friend one night out of the blue. It was from Jeff Bell, one of the original members of the Christian Coalition back when we started the New York State chapter with Ralph Reed's guidance.

I had helped Bell out with his two campaigns for New York State Assembly, and now he was getting involved in the Republican presidential primary on behalf of Pat Buchanan. He asked me to come and join the campaign, and said that they would be looking for delegates for Buchanan who would go to the National Republican Convention in San Diego in the summer of 1996. He wanted me to become one so we could go to the convention together.

I really liked Bell, but I remembered Buchanan's infamous "Culture War" speech from the 1992 convention in Houston, and said no thanks to the offer. Bell said that he was going to be very involved in the daunting task of collecting the massive numbers of signatures needed from each election precinct, and would I consider helping him

229

slog through the streets to garner petitions. He and I had done so several times before for various candidates.

I really didn't want to do that. He persisted, and asked if I would at least come to a big organizational meeting they were having in a local hotel. He said it would give me a chance to see a lot of old friends I hadn't seen since before I'd moved to Houston in 1993. I reluctantly agreed to go.

When I got to the hotel and found the meeting room, I enjoyed seeing all my old friends. When I told them a few of my horror stories from Pensacola, they were shocked. None of them had ever been involved in any violent activities, and were stunned to hear about what I'd witnessed. I had been careful not to say too much, keeping my stories very brief.

The evening's presentation was given by two full-time staffers from the Buchanan campaign, and one of them was another former member of the Schenck brothers' church, Stan Sardonic. He had visited me at my house before, though I hadn't seen him since those days back in the early 1990s.

Stan would turn out to be a key influence in my life over the next two years, but we would prove the old adage that "politics makes strange bedfellows." We were as different as night and day, but fate was bringing us together in ways that would impact my life more than I could ever dream.

Stan was the prototypical behind-the-scenes player in politics, while I was best as the out-front guy. He was the ballot-access coordinator for Buchanan in New York, in charge of what looked to be an impossible situation. New York had long been notorious for its party-rigged rules that kept non-party-backed candidates from being able to get on the ballot.

Though there were several serious candidates that year, only Steve Forbes, with his personal fortune, seriously had a shot at getting on the ballot—besides the party's man, Bob Dole. Everyone in the press and political arenas said we were wasting our time to try to put Buchanan on the ballot.

It would only take four weeks because that is how the party had written the state rules. The period between Thanksgiving and Christmas, the time most people had no time, was the period the party picked for petitions to be gathered.

I liked Buchanan's personality, but I wasn't too wild about some of his policies. On the other hand, I hated the rigged rules. Bell played on my natural sympathy for the underdog and desire for fairness, and got me to sign on to the campaign. He didn't have to twist my arm too hard because I loved being back in the political game, even though I knew we had no chance. It was simply the love of the game that drew me. Stepping into that political meeting had the same effect on me that stepping into a casino would have had on a gambler.

Our little group succeeded in the impossible task, and I wasn't all that surprised. We used the same techniques I had implemented when I wanted our local Christian Coalition chapter to win the national contest for collecting voter data. We set out our goal in each district, mapped out a plan, figured out how many worker hours it would take, and recruited enough people to do it. We also had a few incredible workhorses.

Stan and the rest of the campaign were ecstatic, of course. Buchanan came to Buffalo to thank us, and I was introduced to him on three different occasions. I attended several meetings with the Buchanan Brigade, as they were called. What I found there shocked me. I ran into several members of a group I'd never heard of before, the John Birch Society.

They believed in the same kind of crazy conspiracy theories about secret societies and UN storm troopers that the militia people did. But the man who introduced me to the concept was an attorney from the affluent town of Grand Island, where I was living at the time. He began to drop hints about the conspiracy theories; I knew the routine by now. It always began with talking about how much our constitution was being ignored today. Then he would offer some twisted logic, and I'd ask about it only to have him say, dismissively, "Just read your Constitution, then it will all start to make sense."

He dropped off some magazines from the groups he was involved in at my house one day. They were filled with all kinds of insanity about secret societies ruling the earth for the last couple hundred years. I could understand how a farmer who had seen his family's land taken out from under him could fall prey to such simplistic fear-mongering, but I couldn't believe that an attorney trained by the State University of New York could fall for it. But he was far from alone. There was a whole group right in my little town of twenty thousand people—a lawyer who had run for judge, and businesspeople, too.

I also met several openly racist radicals at Buchanan's meetings, as well as a man who hinted he might be part of a militia. I began to think that the Buchanan campaign was even worse than its critics had charged. I started to look at my friends with suspicion. I knew they didn't believe in that kind of stuff, but what did it say about us to be on the same team?

Buchanan lost in a landslide to Dole in the GOP primaries that year. But right after Buchanan dropped out of the race, Stan was hired by a local congressional campaign as its manager. He asked me to come on board as press secretary. We were in another impossible-dream situation, working for a very nice unknown.

A year later, in 1997, I ran for legislature, I gave a series of inspirational speeches, and was well received, eventually pulling down more votes than any other candidate had against the incumbent in fourteen years. But during my own campaign, I began to question the message I was delivering. Some of the local Democrats were actively involved in promoting regional government, but I took the popular party line at the time that we didn't need more and bigger government.

As I made the arguments, warning that our kids could be bused to regional schools and we could have to pay the bills for the city's mistakes, I gradually became aware of the hidden racism in my party's message. I was using racial scare tactics to make my points—though I never considered myself a racist at all. Like George W. Bush and other mainstream Republicans, I was using code words whose implications I myself did not fully appreciate. When I spoke of crime concerns and busing, I was playing into the fears of white voters who equated the city and crime with blacks. That was just one example. It was too painful to admit to myself at the time, but I would see more examples later.

Don't get me wrong; my style was not intentionally dark or sinister. I struck everyone as an upbeat and compassionate conservative. That's the problem. Even those of us who weren't as dark and brooding as Buchanan, even those of us who considered ourselves sunny-side-up Reagan Republicans, were guilty of class and ethnic divisiveness more than we would have thought, and certainly more than we would ever have admitted.

Reagan himself had given the first speech of his first presidential campaign on the same fairgrounds where the Ku Klux Klan had been born. He may not have been aware of it, but why did he just happen to end up there? I guess we'll never know. Over the following years I would see more troubling signs in the mainstream of the conservative politics of which I was such an enthusiastic supporter.

After my campaign ended, I was elected Republican Party Chairman for the town. But then an unexpected twist of fate would pluck me from the local scene and make me a player on the national stage instead. It happened in the most unexpected way.

A friend of mine called and asked me to help publicize a tax reform group he was trying to launch in the area. He wanted to help launch a local chapter of a tax reform group in Western New York. He gave me the number of their national field organizer's assistant, who was in town for the group's first meeting.

I didn't know it at the time, but the tax reformers had hired one of the world's largest high-powered PR firms, Ketchum Public Relations Worldwide, of Washington, D.C., to handle their national launch.

And the other thing I didn't know was that Ketchum's hand-picked national field organizer had failed to meet the media goals in nearly every city before Buffalo, and Ketchum was in danger of losing the contract.

When I attended the tax reform group's meeting the week before the press conference, they asked me to be lead speaker. I wrote my own speech, got their approval, and went to bat. We got all three network TV stations, the radio news stations, and the two daily papers from Buffalo and Niagara Falls to show up and cover us.

The guy from Washington pulled me aside afterward, congratulating me and asking if I thought I could repeat my success in other cities. I said sure, and within a week I got a call from the Washington office of Ketchum. They had fired the old national field organizer and decided to offer me the job. I could continue to live in my house in Western New York, and they would fly me around the country.

I spoke to groups from Harlem to San Jose, using a lively, political-rally style at the events. It was grandstanding, but it was fun. The crowd had been dragged off by friends to hear a talk on taxes, and ended up getting a revival meeting thrown in. It went over great, and when I asked if anyone had had a bad experience with the IRS, hands invariably shot up all around the room. Horror stories followed, and I let the group convince itself that my proposal might be worth taking a look at after all.

Public speaking had been a big part of my life since I was a teen speaker for youth groups and adult religious groups. The only time that my abilities were used for darker purposes was when I spoke to the Operation Rescue people. I could whip up the crowd the way that Randall Terry did, and I could feel the power in having that kind of control over a crowd.

It was an amazing, intoxicating rush but I saw how easy it was to play into the worst instincts of the mob. It scared me a little to realize that had I been so inclined I could have been one of the biggest demagogues around. And there was one very small part of me that found it tempting. But overall, I'm too easygoing and balanced to have stayed in that surreal world for long.

Shortly after I was hired at Ketchum, I was allowed to hire an assistant to travel on the road with me. They said they'd try to find someone for me as soon as possible, but it wasn't going to be easy to find someone who was knowledgeable about taxes and grassroots politics and very detail-oriented. I recommended my friend Stan, and they agreed to hire him.

When Stan and I flew into Washington to get him trained, we ran into Pat Buchanan waiting for his luggage. Stan went over and reintroduced me, and we talked about the sales tax. Buchanan said it would never fly. He told us that he had taken a look at the plan, and that his own mother, like other retirees, would end up having to pay way more in taxes than under the current system. Buchanan said, "But don't let it get you down, it's a good ride for as long as it lasts. Have fun with it. I wish you luck."

Within a short period of time, I realized that our tax reform meetings were drawing a disturbing percentage of respondents from militia groups. I was having strange conversations again about black helicopters and the UN I was really sick of it, and wondered why these people were popping up at all the conservative gatherings.

Stan and I often laughed about some of the oddball characters we met while we were on the road. Most of the time it was an incredibly great experience as we traveled all over the country, with me giving speeches to fire up the troops, coordinating our consistently successful press conferences in city after city, and doing radio and TV debates and interviews, while Stan was answering technical questions and convincing people to write the letters to the editor in each city.

The times when we were alone and talking politics, which both of us loved to do, turned out to have the biggest impact on me in the long run, though.

Stan was very critical of the Republican Party, and I had always been such a staunch loyalist who had recruited many friends and family members into the party. Stan, had a more international perspective. He was a devout pro-lifer, but otherwise he didn't think much of the Republican platform or the Christian Coalition's agenda.

Stan had been influenced by the more egalitarian and socialistic approaches of Europeans on one hand and, on the other, by those who believed that no government could provide what the Christian Coalition was looking for. Stan was right, of course, that no Christian government was going to create the kind of utopia that the radicals were looking for, but I was not about to join him in the Buchanan Brigade, either.

And Stan was sort of fatalistic in his cynicism about government. To Stan, the Communist Chinese government that had nearly arrested him while he was on a missionary journey was not that much more detrimental to the advancement of Christianity than the corrupt capitalism of upper-class-controlled America, with all its crass commercialism.

I was shocked. I had never heard any Christian make such arguments against conservative Republicanism's view of America. I began to read books he gave me, some very serious ones that made me reflect deeply and others a little light-hearted, like *Rush Limbaugh Is a Big, Fat Idiot*. When he handed me that one in a bookstore I was surprised, but I took his advice and bought it.

As Stan and I rolled along in a rental car on the long ride from Los Angeles to Bakersfield, I read aloud the first section about the author, Al Franken, having an absurd exchange of letters to the editor with hard-nosed Republican hawk, Jean Kirkpatrick. It was hysterical, and we roared with laughter at the message, which would have seemed like blasphemy to me just a few years before. I had been a huge Limbaugh fan, and liked all the conservative talk shows.

But it was also a case of the arguments tapping into all the negative things I had heard along the way, and forcing me to focus on the big picture. My research took me in a completely different direction than Stan was going, though, and that made it incredibly ironic. He was trying to get me to be a part of the permanent Buchanan Brigade, and I ended up realizing, after I finished my full investigation of all the political options, that I was a Democrat. Stan joked that if I ever told anyone that he was the one who had turned me into a Democrat, he would kill me.

After voraciously poring through book after book that was critical of my conservative Republicanism, I had to admit that the unofficial main goals of the Republican Party were:

1. To consolidate wealth and power for the upper class through tax code changes and spending policies in the name of "freedom," such as increasing spending on incarceration while cutting education—supposedly to create a safer place for all, but in practice to keep the lower classes "in their place."
2. To maintain the societal status quo by stopping any new progressive social justice approaches, for example, cutting as much federal aid to housing, child care, education, and nursing homes as possible.

These unofficial GOP goals dovetailed most effectively with the main unofficial goals of the Christian Coalition:

1. To reverse the recent rise of the civil rights movements for minorities, including the most visible attacks on women (anti-choice, anti–birth control policies) and gays (anti–equal rights and prodiscrimination policies), mixed with the more subtle and unofficial put-downs of African Americans (the rise and fall of the Christian Coalition era just happened to be accompanied by a rise and fall in the burning of black churches nationwide), thus helping to keep Sunday morning the most segregated time of the entire week. The 1950s, as seen through the hazy glaze of nostalgia, were often painted as the ultimate destination for good moral Christians (even though that was only the case for those who were white, well-off, and conventional).

2. To "get the government off our backs" in terms of taxes and federal spending, for example, cutting federal aid to education, housing, child care, and nursing homes (without any awareness from the rank and file on the impact this would have on their own loved ones in terms of getting their kids through college, helping some family members get mortgage loans, and taking care of their elderly parents and grandparents when their health failed). Christian school vouchers and the removal of educational standards for home schoolers were seen as vital elements of the Religious Right's agenda of turning America into a Christian nation.

Ralph Reed had kept our attention away from hard, analytical questions by keeping us focused on our fears, the usual tactic of the hardcore Right. He warned us that we were in a war according to the Scriptures, and we must be prepared for battle.

At the same time, he followed his own advice on hiding his true views, publishing two books that used stealth techniques to paint himself as a reasonable and respectable conservative. He led a public campaign in which he said that all conservative Christians wanted was "a place at the table." He later called for incremental changes in abortion laws in his version of the Republican Party's Contract with America that he called the Contract with the American Family.

It backfired for two reasons:

1. The press and the general public did not believe him.
2. The hard core wanted no talk of slow progress; they wanted action based on ideological purity and an all-out assault on the secular government.

Reed saw the handwriting on the wall and decided it was time to go out a winner. His organization had grown to the point where 65 percent of Congress agreed with all or part of his agenda, and his organization was an absolutely vital part of the Republican Party.

He was lucky to get out before the Federal Elections Commission could make a not altogether favorable ruling on the Christian Coalition, and before he could be devoured by his own hardcore radicals.

He took the golden parachute, making a very soft landing as a consultant to virtually all conservative Republican presidential candidates. He now makes more money as a consultant, and doesn't have to worry about being attacked by his own allies.

Robertson decided to split Reed's post in two after he left, at least in part to maintain more personal control over the organization. Funding dropped off drastically, though, after Reed left, and the organization is not anywhere near as widely supported as it was in its pinnacle period from 1994–1996. But Robertson is using it more and more baldly as a tool to enhance his own power.

Robertson's two hot-button issues in the Christian Coalition are opposing the advancement of privacy-based abortion rights and birth control rights for women and reversing the growing struggle for equal rights for gays and lesbians; and calling for draconian tax cuts for the wealthiest Americans while cutting federal programs for the poor.

It is a very shrewd combination because the first part draws the fiery passion of his hardcore reactionary religionists, while the second part makes the mainly unsophisticated "true believers" of the Christian Coalition tolerable to the "real Republicans," the country club patricians who otherwise control the party's levers of power.

When Robertson created the Christian Coalition, he went beyond the moral issues of concern to conservatives by adding "God's position on American tax policy" to the group's literature. That drew fire from many evangelicals and mainline Christians, but it was well worth the trouble because it has resulted in huge financial donations for the televangelist's coffers from wealthy industrialists who see Robertson's sheep as a means of getting the votes they need.

Unfortunately, the mainly modest-earning sheep have been led to believe it is their Christian duty to be shorn on taxes. If they ever get their entire tax and fiscal agenda in place, many of Robertson's sheep will find out too late that they are actually sacrificial lambs who will dearly pay the price to give the wealthy an even faster accumulation of money and power than they already have. They aren't aware or concerned about the fact that 1 percent of the population owns 40 percent of the wealth. A rude awakening may come at the next economic downturn.

Interestingly, Jesus—the supposed leader of the Christian Coalition—never spoke against homosexuality or abortion, but that became the mainstay, the red meat of the political machine. I know because when I was a regional leader of the Christian Coalition myself, I was as good as anyone at pushing the buttons of the activists. And though it has been painful for me to face, I now realize that the tone of our teachings in the Christian Coalition was as harsh as the preachments of any right-wing Pharisee that Jesus railed against.

The self-righteous, self-proclaimed "moral majority" religionists of Jesus Christ's day hated his association with the poor, the outcasts, the prostitutes, and the tax gatherers; yet those morally superior, separationist policies that the Pharisees advocated align perfectly with the message of the Christian Coalition.

Robertson's tax policies for Christians are a far cry from the teachings of Jesus, who seemed to see a wall of separation between church and state when he said, "Render unto Caesar what is Caesar's and to God what is God's." And Christ's fiscal policies called for his followers to take care of the poor in such teachings as, "I was hungry and you fed me. I was thirsty and you gave me drink. I was sick and in prison and you came to visit me. . . . Whatever you did for the least of my brothers, that you did for me."

There are many religious and nonreligious organizations that quietly do those helpful things every day, but the gospel of Robertson's grassroots organization has inverted and politicized those verses. The Christian Coalition's twist on the gospel reads more like this: "The poor are hungry, and so we demand that the rich get huge tax breaks. The poor are thirsty for knowledge, and so we demand an end to the federal government's role in education. They are sick and we cut back on health care and faithfully oppose any comprehensive plans to make it better. They are in prison and we call for an increase in sentences and more jails to house the poor (though some of us 'compassionate conservatives' want to say we know it is unfortunate that the 'residents' are disproportionately our black and Latino brothers)."

When someone calls himself a "compassionate conservative" now you know what he means: He supports the same programs as the hardliners, but he doesn't enjoy it. Of course, the man who wears the mantle of "compassionate conservative" on his sleeve, the man Pat Robertson put all his marbles behind, the man with the W. in the middle of his name, has run the state that is last in the nation with regard to health care coverage, but first in the number of executions.

"Thou Shalt Not Kill" is one of the Ten Commandments that the Christian Right wants to see on every school and public building, but George W. Bush is proud of his role in well over a hundred executions in litte more than one term as governor of Texas. At a time when the rest of the civilized world has banned executions, Bush, who could have pardoned anyone he wanted to on the Lone Star State's death row, chose not to be "soft on crime." As the "father figure" of the state, he has shown his toughness and willingness to dispense "justice."

I thought of the story Jesus told about the prodigal son, and how the father in that famous fable quickly executed his son when he returned. Oh, wait, correct that. He forgave the son and welcomed him home, and helped him get back into the family and rebuild his life. I'm not saying that we should just forgive criminals; I'm suggesting that we make the effort while our children are young to educate them, and I don't mean just our own biological children. We need to be our brother's keeper as part of a community.

But now you know why the Christian Coalition never really let the compassionate Jesus into its stealth army of warriors—he was too liberal with his love!

TWENTY-SEVEN

For two years I continued to stay somewhat active with the Common Ground group, and when I told Karen Swallow Prior from the pro-life side of the Common Ground group about some of the ways my thinking was changing, and how I still had many unanswered questions about the role my former pastors, the Schenck brothers, might have played with the advocates of violence, she said, "I think you owe it to them to talk directly to them about what you heard rather than trying to surmise the truth from the observations of others."

She gave me Paul Schenck's number and I left a couple of messages, but never heard back from him. Then I ran into his twin, Rob, at a local event in Western New York. He was heading back to Grand Island and was going to ride with a family member until I asked if I could drive him so I could talk to him about something important. He agreed and got into my car.

As we drove down the expressway, I told him about some of my experiences in Pensacola. And I told him that every time I mentioned his and his brother's names people would open up to me like I'd just shared a secret password. He said that many people knew of them because they'd been so highly visible in the pro-life movement.

I pressed him on his nonviolent stance because I had seen the difference between the public and private stances of many men, from Pat Robertson to John Burt. Rob said, "Paul and I have debated these guys who advocate violence on TV shows, Christian ones . . . and we disagree totally with what they say and do. Killing is wrong, plain and simple."

I was glad to hear him say so, and really wanted to believe him, but I was a bit skeptical after all I'd observed. I could have really pressed him that day, but I decided that I had done all that I could reasonably hope to accomplish in a face-to-face meeting with one of the brothers Schenck. If they had a secret agenda, they certainly were not going to share it with me, no matter what I said.

But I was a little bit worried. I had told them for the first time that I turned in the planners of the potential Pensacola plot, the "something big." And even though it had been roughly three years since I'd last heard from the gun-loving Daniel Ware, I was still a little concerned about repercussions. If my worst fears were true, something violent could happen.

On October 23, 1998, I was celebrating my birthday with my family in a restaurant in Amherst, New York, while at the same time in the same town a man dressed all in black was lying in wait.

I had no way of knowing that a mysterious stranger was hiding in the backyard of his intended target's home. He decided to duck behind the family's swimming pool and wait for the man he would shoot to come back to his home. The sniper-to-be was very quiet and calm as he waited to do his dastardly deed. No one in the neighborhood suspected a thing.

When the shooter saw his target, he put his eye up to the scope of his high-powered rifle, took careful aim and then squeezed the trigger. *Pow!* His bullet shot out of the barrel and headed through the plate glass window and into the body of the man he'd come to kill.

The man fell to the floor and his wife rushed to his side, but it was too late. He was dying in her arms as their children watched helplessly. The family called the police, and an ambulance rushed to the nice suburban home, but no one was able to help the victim in this case. Dr. Barnett Slepian was dead.

I was horrified when I heard the news that night on the way home from my birthday celebration. I did not know Dr. Slepian, but I instantly remembered who did. My old pastors, Rob and Paul Schenck, had been the ones who brought the national leaders of Operation Rescue to the very doors of the home where Dr. Slepian would later be killed.

The Schencks and their allies had taunted the entire Slepian family for years. Some of them hollered to the Slepian children, "Your father is a murderer, a butcher, a baby killer!" Paul Schenck called Slepian "a pig!" That is a particularly offensive term to a Jewish person, as the Schenck brothers knew; their own father was Jewish. A strange sort of self-loathing seemed to accompany such episodes.

Picketing and taunting of the Slepian family went on for a decade until Dr. Slepian was assassinated. The Internet Web site where the advocates of violence posted the targets they would most like to see "executed" included Dr. Barnett Slepian.

An obscure physician from a midsize city like Buffalo, New York, would not likely have been on such an extremist national shortlist unless he had been rated a high priority by some very heavy hitters in the secretive corridors of antiabortion terrorism. It was impossible to say with certainty who had put Slepian on the secret list, but it was possible that the national leadership would not have known about Slepian at all if it had not been for Rob and Paul Schenck. They were the first to choose him as a target for antiabortion protestors.

Days later, with Slepian's body barely in the ground, I was surprised to see a live news report on TV of Rob Schenck stepping off a plane from Washington, D.C. He looked surprised to see the media there, though I would find out the next day from Karen Swallow Prior that Rob had sent press releases to every news station in town.

While he was in town, he went to the office of the doctor he had tormented for so long, and he made a very public, pious, and pompous display of placing a wreath at an impromptu memorial site for the slain man and his family. He also sent flowers to the widow of the man who had so often been the victim of his torments.

Lynne Slepian was disgusted by what appeared more like gloating than expressing sorrow. She said she held the Schenck brothers partially responsible for her husband's death and she sent the flowers back. In the package, Rob had included a flower for Slepian and each of the children, and one extra one, a white rose.

A reporter asked him about the extra flower, and he said the white rose was for good luck. I had never heard that white roses meant good luck, but I knew that Rob and Paul Schenck prided themselves on their ability to use symbolism in some pretty powerful ways. I thought of a different possible explanation than the one Rob had given.

What if the white rose was a code message to all the members of the White Rose group, which held its annual banquet to honor the shooters and bombers who were incarcerated? Was it possible that my former pastor was telegraphing a darker message to the disciples of terror than what he was telling us in his public statements?

As of this writing, the FBI had still not caught the man they suspected of the cowardly act of cold-blooded murder. The FBI spokesman in Buffalo said that it was obvious that the suspect, James Charles Kopp, was getting shelter and support from people within the pro-life community.

Kopp had been arrested in city after city where the Schenck brothers were also arrested—Atlanta, Georgia; Cherry Hill, New Jersey; Pittsburgh, Pennsylvania; and so on. They were part of the same little brotherhood of hardcore protesters.

Rob Schenck told me that he and his brother didn't know the man, and had never heard of him until the FBI announced him as a suspect. I was shocked, because I personally had heard of James Charles Kopp on just my second day in service in the Operation Rescue "bunker" with the Schencks back in 1992. He was written about on the first page of the Army of God manual that was given to me on that day in the secret headquarters.

James Charles Kopp is called the "Atomic Dog" in the manual, and he had been well-known for a long time as one of the most rabid of anti-choice supporters. Like John Burt, the Schencks don't know an awful lot of things you would reasonably expect them to know, but who can say what goes on in the inner recesses of another man's mind?

The terrible thought flashed briefly through my mind that maybe my former pastors had been able to arrange the Slepian matter to happen on my birthday as a warning to me to keep my mouth shut, but I realized there was no evidence for that. However, less than a week after Dr. Slepian's funeral, Rob Schenck and his ally Rev. Bob Behn held a press conference at Slepian's office.

Behn announced that the Spring of Life protest that Rob and Paul Schenck had led back in 1992 would have a reunion in Buffalo in 1999. They would invite all the pro-life activists from all over the country to come to gather and march in the town where Dr. Slepian was now buried. It seemed incredibly ghoulish, as though they were all going to take a victory lap around the slain man's grave.

And the date they picked to start their reunion was also spooky — April 19, the same day as the Waco tragedy and the Oklahoma City bombing, a date that had the most powerful symbolism possible for all militia members across the nation.

As the date drew nearer, the Schenck brothers suddenly announced that they would not come to the new protest. They admitted the timing looked bad, and they bowed out. It's possible they were truly having a change of heart, but I also wondered if they were cynically making pious proclamations and keeping their distance so they would not end up as "the first suspects" (using John Burt's phrase) if violence occurred. Their claims of innocence and nonviolence actually made me more ill at ease as the event approached.

I felt torn between a duty to speak out against what they were doing and the duty to protect my family's safety. I settled for a small step as a compromise. I told my background as it pertained to the planned protest reunion to a local freelance reporter. He was so afraid of printing it while the radicals were taking part in the protest that he published it only after the radicals had left town and only under a pen name.

It made the cover of *Buffalo Beat*, an alternative newspaper in town, and caused quite a stir. Karen Swallow Prior called me at home and asked me if I had written it myself under the pen name J. Davis. I told her no, but she sounded like she wasn't sure whether she should believe me. She said it contained information I had told her before. I admitted that I had given information to the reporter, but asked her not to tell anyone. She was upset about the article and claimed it was inaccurate. I thought that overall the paper had done an excellent job, but I did not argue with Karen. She never told me what she thought was inaccurate.

I was still safe in my anonymity overall, though by that point the Schenck brothers and Karen Swallow Prior were both unhappily aware of my change of heart. Karen then told me something very different than what she had said before. She made the revelation that Paul Schenck was her best friend. When I had inquired about him in the past, she acted like she hardly ever spoke to the man.

It's not that I blamed her for publicly keeping her distance after what had happened. Paul Schenck, who carried himself with great dignity and righteous indignation over the immorality of pro-choice people, had lost some of his luster ever since it came out that he had lied to a federal court. My senior pastor, the man I had been willing to follow into the Christian Coalition and then Operation Rescue, pleaded guilty to lying under oath, admitting he had lied on the witness stand about his activities in a minor incident during antiabortion street theatrics with his twin brother way back in 1991.

That incident had not hurt his career, though. Instead he had received a huge promotion, from being a local pastor and volunteer antiabortion leader to being hired as the administrative director of televangelist Pat Robertson's national legal center, the ACLJ. To the people who do not share the muscular Christian Reconstructionist view, it may seem ironic that a man who lied under oath while testifying before a federal judge was plucked from obscurity and placed upon the national stage as a leader of the American Center for Law and Justice.

At Schenck's trial, Assistant U.S. Attorney Martin J. Littlefield Jr. said the Justice Department took Reverend Schenck's admitted action very seriously, because "lying under oath goes to the very heart of the court system. The whole system is based on the integrity of people who are testifying under oath. This kind of activity really undermines the court system."

Maybe Schenck's experience "undermining the federal court system" was not seen as a total negative by Pat Robertson. One would have to look far and wide to find someone with as long an arrest record, combined with a conviction for lying under oath, as Reverend Schenck has accumulated. Maybe that didn't matter since all of it was done for the right cause.

Paul's brother Rob had an interesting spin on the whole thing. He wrote in a letter to the editor of the *Buffalo News* about Paul's behavior: "Never did he admit to 'lying.' What he did was concede to a bully. He did so for the sake of his family. If you decide to condemn him for that, look at the One whom my brother takes as his role model: Jesus Christ. It is of Him that the Bible speaks when it says that for our sake 'He counted His reputation as nothing, but emptied Himself . . . and accepted death on a cross.' "

Like Paul Hill turning the call of Jesus to lay down your life for others into a call to kill others and protect your own life, Rob Schenck had twisted the facts of the situation so that he claimed his brother was not guilty of lying (even though Paul had admitted it already), but that the judge was crucifying an innocent and holy man. For some reason the Jewish word *chutzpah* comes to mind.

Karen also told me during the same phone conversation about the *Buffalo Beat* article that her best friend, Paul Schenck, had recommended her for a job working for the founder of the Moral Majority, Rev. Jerry Falwell in Virginia, and she was going to take it. She was going to the televangelist's power base in Lynchburg (gotta love that name for one of the radical Right's key locations).

On the bright side, she may do some good at moderating Falwell's views. It wouldn't surprise me if I found out that she had something to do with Falwell's recent attempts at finding common-ground areas of discussion with gay people. She has that ability to bring diverse groups of people together to begin to dialogue.

I will continue to hope that my former friends are trying to find their way out of the extremism for which they were once known. I have written of my former pastors in sadness and out of a sense of duty. I have no delight in having seen them fall for such garbage, and hurting the many more dedicated average working people who did not know what they were buying into.

The leaders of the Religious Right just keep falling, though. In March 2000, I found out about a case of sex scandal, lies, broken oaths, and hypocrisy involving America's leading antiabortion figure. Operation Rescue founder Randall Terry, a close and friendly ally of both the Schencks and Pat Robertson, was publicly censured and excommunicated by his own church—just like assassin Paul Hill, but for other reasons.

In a letter dated November 6, 1999, Terry's former pastor and church board at the Landmark Church in Binghamton, New York, rebuked him in the harshest possible way for these two of their four reasons (and I quote here):

1. For leaving his wife in preparation to divorce, annul or otherwise dissolve their Christian marriage, and for his unwillingness to repent of this sin we do hereby censure him.
2. For a pattern of repeated sinful relationships and conversations with both single and married women we do hereby censure him.

I nearly fell off my chair when I saw the document from the church. This was the same Randall Terry who had called President Clinton every vile name in the book over his adultery, and now Terry stands accused by his own pastor of the past fifteen years and his own church board of committing the very same offenses in an ongoing pattern!

From the description they gave in their letter, and corresponding documents since made public on the Internet by Operation Rescue (which recently changed its name to Operation Save America), he may have been doing it more often than the man he has so viciously vilified countless times.*

Did Terry the good Christian Reconstructionist stop when church authority told him he was wrong and sinful and needed to repent? No, he warned of legal action with the civil authorities against his church— absolutely incredible hypocrisy for a man who is building his career on the teaching that our civil government is so morally corrupt it should be replaced by a Christian government overseen by the one true church. When he got into trouble, he found the government a more reliable ally than his church.

---

*www.OperationSaveAmerica.org

I can't wait to see how well the one true church idea is going to work out when its own key advocates ignore the church authority they are currently under. No word yet if Pat Robertson will offer Terry a job now, but Robertson himself has long been criticized for submitting only part of his vast empire to the Evangelical Fiscal Responsibility Board, the one that many other ministries use to keep their books audited by independent sources for the sake of the public, particularly those who donate. Robertson has a very complicated mix of ministries and other ventures.

Speaking of donations, in the same letter about adultery, Randall Terry was also censured for his fund-raising letters. The church leaders said some of his statements were misleading, and that "this lacks integrity." They admonished him to "cease soliciting funds until such time as his public persona and his true manner of living are known to be the same." It sounds to me like they are implying hypocrisy on top of adultery and lying.

They went on to describe Terry as a man on a downward spiral for the last three years. Their credibility was helped by Randall Terry's own many public statements saying that his longtime pastor was a mighty man of God who was not afraid to tell the truth no matter the cost.

Over the years Randall Terry has been almost as vehement in his outspoken opposition to birth control as he has been to abortion. This raises two incredibly interesting questions:

1. If Randall Terry has been engaged in the adulterous affairs with "single and married women," as his church's accusations allege, did he himself use birth control?
2. If not, and there are no known cases of a woman bearing his illegitimate child, is it possible that the founder of the most radical antiabortion movement in the nation has had his own fetuses aborted by the women he loved and left?

Randall Terry's wife and children, meanwhile, were left behind in Binghamton, and the pastor there said the church was having to take care of them. Flip Benham, Terry's eventual successor in the militant antichoice group, has published on the Internet his recollection that Terry told him he was going to slow down and take time to put his life in order, starting in the beginning of the new year in 2000, because of the church's serious disciplinary action.

But then Benham says, "Since January, however, he has announced plans to run for U.S. Senate, he is storming the gates of the homosexual agenda in Vermont, he is selling his mailing [donor] list, and is engaged in yet another fund-raiser. He never had nor does he now have any intention of pulling back."*

Sounds like Terry and Schenck will continue to have a lot in common, at least as far as their ends-justify-the-means approach to the truth. It should not have surprised me as much as it did—since way back in my first week inside Operation Rescue, a national antiabortion leader had looked me straight in the eye, after I observed him lying, and said, "Truth is the first casualty of war, and this is war, brother!"

This kind of hypocrisy and lying is not limited to the radical element in the Religious Right. We saw so many of the most "respectable" Republican congressional critics of President Clinton's adulterous activity having the same skeletons in their own closets in the 1999 impeachment fiasco.

Terry, after ditching his wife and kids, hurried off to condemn gays, in a state where he is not even a resident, for their "immorality." What kind of moral watchdog does this guy think he is?

The whole mess is not exactly a high-water mark for "traditional family values" or other rock-rib Republican values. Any credibility that the Religious Right had on moral issues has long since been lost by that slippery slope of ends-justify-the-means morality that led to Christian terrorism and pro-life killing.

Given the instability and cutthroat methods of the men who lead the national Religious Right, I was fearful that my former friends might have allies who would want to make sure I did not do their already imperfect reputations further harm. Finally, I realized that the only way to break free of the worry I was feeling was to just tell the whole story. That way it wouldn't do any good for unsavory elements to do something to me or to my family. Attacking us after the story came out would only make the radicals look worse.

---

*www.OperationSaveAmerica.org

The Armageddon that some said would come at
the dawn of the new millennium passed
without a sound, but that does not stop fundamentalists
from preaching a gospel of fear and sometimes revolution.
On June 21, 2000, Christian Coalition founder Pat
Robertson advised born-again Christian viewers of the
700 Club that they should "think about revolt." Those are
potentially dangerous words, particularly given in the
wake of the antiabortion assassinations and the Oklahoma City bombing. And it did not take all that much to
get Robertson talking that way. The source of his frustra-
tion this time was his objection to the U.S. Supreme
Court's ruling that struck down the practice of broadcasting prayers over the loudspeakers at public high
school football games. The televangelist called the Court
"tyranny of an oligarchy" and a "dictatorship that's been
imposed upon us."

In a similar vein, Pat Buchanan is also sharply critical
of the Supreme Court. He scornfully asked the conservative Heritage Foundation, in a January 29, 1996, address,
"Who are the beneficiaries of the Court's protection?"
Answering his own question, he said, "Members of various minorities including criminals, atheists, homosex-

uals, flag burners, illegal immigrants—including terrorists, convicts, and pornographers."

In my opinion, to make such comments is to fan the flames of the deep distrust of the federal government already present in right-wing groups, and there is no telling what kind of reaction extremist groups will have to either man's comments. Both men have long track records of making similarly outrageous comments over the issue of abortion— even though the Court did not impose its will on anyone regarding that issue, instead leaving it up to women and their physicians to decide how to handle each individual situation.

Buchanan's status seems to have diminished since leaving the Republican Party, partly because of negative press attention some of his recent writings have garnered. However, the press and the public should pay more attention to the views of Robertson and his organizations. The former Baptist preacher has unprecedented power in the nation's politics through his role in the Republican Party because of the clout of his Christian Coalition political machine.

In July 2000, a doctor who provides abortions was stabbed outside his office in Vancouver, British Columbia. This same doctor had previously survived an assassination attempt at his home in November 1994. And more violence is sure to come at the hands of right-wing extremists. Paul Hill still sits on death row in Florida, and his small but extremely loyal band of followers have shown no sign of cooling off on their promise to "rise up" when "The Reverend Saint Paul Hill" is put to death.

The man antiabortion assassin Paul Hill most admired, leading Reconstructionist theologian Gary North, has actually written a book entitled *Backward, Christian Soldiers*, calling for turning back the clock to a time before Enlightenment-era advances in science and philosophy. He is not alone in his back-to-the-future thinking. Many fundamentalists want to ignore the mountains of scientific evidence in areas such as evolution, carbon and radiation dating, and many other areas to advance their theological ideas in the science classroom. More than a dozen states have altered their curricula on evolution since Kansas took the lead in 1999.

Fortunately, the extreme right wing is not strong enough in America to overthrow the government by force, as has happened in smaller nations in Central and South America. However, the "IRA-type reign of terror" predicted by Paul Hill seems certain to continue for the foreseeable future. And it may actually be worse under a Republican administration than a Democratic one, because of rising expectation for changes that will probably not come on the hot-button social issues. That is what happened in the Reagan administration; bombings of abortion clinics were more common during Reagan's two terms—apparently because the radicals were frustrated that "their man in the White House" did not change the nation's policies on abortion and other issues important to them.

And in spite of Robertson's strenuous efforts on behalf of George W. Bush, it is not likely that the "true believers" will get what they want. The simple truth is that America is moving in favor of individual liberties, and a return to the tyranny of the majority will not happen in the foreseeable future. The Religious Right should be satisfied—as should all Americans—that they are allowed to believe what they want, live as they want, and share their faith with anyone who wants to listen. But the hard core of that group will not be satisfied unless they can also impose their beliefs and morality on others. Therein lies the danger.

Most Americans do not want the country to become an officially religious state—be it Christian or any other religion. Theocracy is an idea that has always led to intellectual stagnation when the true believers repress those with new ideas. Even such mainstream religious organizations as the Roman Catholic Church, still the largest branch of Christendom, are slow to accept many new ideas. For instance, it wasn't until 1991 that the church officially admitted it was wrong and that Copernicus and Galileo were right about the sun rather than the earth being at the center of the universe. Unfortunately, the scientists had died nearly four centuries earlier, so the church's apology did not help them advance their careers or escape imprisonment.

And the Catholic Church is not alone; conservative Christians tend to fear new developments in scientific or social thought. Conservative, Bible-believing Christians have opposed the abolition of slavery, the advancement of women's and civil rights, and the teaching of evolution. The saying goes, "God said it, I believe it, that settles it." The real-world result of this literalistic interpretation of the Scriptures is that all moral progress and development is frozen forever in the Bible-era writings of the men who wrote "God's word." Therefore, there is no need to think about new approaches in light of new evidence; the only use for the human brain is to learn how to be obedient slaves to our lord and master.

Many liberal Christians and liberals in other faiths reject this kind of blindness but continue to hold onto the basics of their religious heritage. Yet, ironically, these more progressive churches are losing members while the hard-line conservative congregations are growing. In this era of rapid change, there is something vastly comforting about being told that all the answers to life's hardest questions can be found in just one book. Unfortunately, not everyone gets the same answers from the Bible. My story shows just how wrong those who are truly committed to the Bible can go.

Obviously, the people I have focused on in this book were the most radical of the individuals I met, and I realize that there are many people of more reasonable temperament who have adopted a far less strident form of conservative thought. Conservatism is widely accepted today in the heartland of America. Many God-fearing Christians thank God for democracy, individual liberty, and a capitalist economy. While I acknowledge that each of these things has played a major part in our American history, conservatives fail to acknowledge that none of these things are promoted in their Bibles.

Indeed, in the gospels and the New Testament stories of the early church in the Book of Acts, believers in Jesus sold all that they owned and put all their money in a common purse. They lived in a community dedicated to a pacifistic life of service and sharing the message of their faith in a moral leader who they claimed rose from the grave. Today such people would not fit in with most churches or conservative groups; they would be called communists or cultists.

But, if he were here now, would Jesus applaud the harshness and judgmental approach of today's conservative leaders? Do conservative icons like Pat Robertson, Pat Buchanan, and Rush Limbaugh, who speak to more people in one day than Jesus did in his lifetime, have the kind of personal humility and meekness advocated in the Sermon on the Mount? And why is "tolerance" such a dirty word in American conservative society? An inversion of the words of Jesus, the unofficial motto of the new conservatives seems to be: "Keep looking for the speck in your brother's eye while ignoring the plank in your own."

I didn't come to these conclusions lightly. I freely admit to having been a new conservative myself, from the time of Ronald Reagan's first presidential campaign up to the time when the proponents of open violence forced me to begin to question how Christian conservatism could have spawned such creatures. Though I know that there are advocates of violence on the other end of the spectrum as well, I found it completely incongruous for the Bible to be the source of such actions. I did not and I do not wish to see a Christian fundamentalist version of the Islamic fundamentalists who perform violent acts of terror in the name of their god.

If nothing else, my story shows what can go wrong when advocates of "one nation, under God" take it upon themselves to knock down the wall of separation between church and state, trying to impose their morality on others—even if they have to "execute" people to do so. Many people don't see the connection between a government that executes people and a citizenry that also does. America is one of the few modern nations left that continues the death penalty, and it not so coincidentally has one of the most violent populations in the civilized world, with unprecedented rates of both intentional and accidental gun deaths in an era of peace and prosperity.

As I reflected on it later, I definitely noticed common strains of thought among the many diverse groups I met—from antiabortion activists to militias, and from Republican Party leaders to the many conservative action groups, be they inspired by the Bible or by the unique tradition of American thought that goes backward from Newt Gingrich's Republican Revolution to Reaganomics to George Wallace's segregationist campaigns, all the way back to the ideas that led to the development of the Confederacy. Although the concerns of the movement that eventually became the Confederacy were a hodgepodge coming from diverse groups and approaches, they became united by three main precepts in the mid-1800s. These were:

1. **A deep distrust of America's federal government.** Anecdotal evidence of misdeeds by the government was rampant. This was sometimes fanned into paranoid rage and hatred by the incendiary flames of red-hot rhetoric from demagogic leaders.

2. **Scapegoating targeted minorities, and using the Bible to justify doing so.** Many of the nation's problems at the time were seen as "God's judgment" because of perceived "immorality" surrounding and involving freed African American slaves. Many a sermon was preached on the evils of racial intermarriage, and the biggest fear tactic of the day was to tell wild tales of the horrors of white women being ravaged by black men.

3. **Seeing guns as a God-given way for alienated citizens to solve their problems and control the federal government.** Gun ownership was popular among many Americans, but particularly important among Confederates—not only for protection from intruders and wild animals, but as a part of the revered tradition of dueling for one's honor and for protecting oneself from the federal government if it went wrong. When the Confederate leaders lost the rational arguments over the issues of slavery, segregation, and the right of the states to continue those heinous practices, they called on their followers to take up arms against their own government.

Today's conservative movement is very diverse, and runs the gamut from the so-called compassionate conservatives (a term that some hardcore conservatives call an oxymoron) to those who pride themselves on being "somewhere to the right of Attila the Hun" (many people I have met from conservative action groups have used this expression themselves, considering it a playful boast rather than a put-down of their positions). But the three common strands of what I now call the "New Confederates" are the same as they were in the old Confederacy, just updated to fit the times. And this time their campaign is cultural rather than regional.

The deep distrust of the federal government, the targeting of minorities, and the advocacy of guns continues. Guns are seen not just as hunting or protection tools, but as part of a constitutionally protected, God-given right to ensure that the people can resist their own federal government.

This message has been seen on bumper stickers for years, with slogans like, "The Second Amendment is not about hunting." And whenever you press a hardcore advocate of Second Amendment rights, he will invariably say that he sees guns as the ultimate protection from the government should it go wrong. And many gun advocates already find a staggering number of things to criticize.

In May 2000, the NRA drew approximately forty thousand people to its annual convention, an astonishing and unprecedented number. Press materials from the NRA portray its membership as being mainstream America, but NRA president Charlton Heston used his reelection press conference to send a shrill message to the most powerful advocate of gun control in the nation. Holding up a shotgun, he said in harsh tones to the vice president of the United States, "Mr. Gore, you can take this gun from me when you pry it from my cold, dead fingers." Such radical talk should certainly get the attention of all truly mainstream citizens, and perhaps the Million Mom March in Washington, D.C., was the first sign that the public is beginning to awaken to the dangers of extremist rhetoric and actions by the gun worshipers.

The biggest difference between the old Confederates to the new ones, though, is that they can no longer openly use race as the main draw for the demagogues in their midst, although racists often feel perfectly at home attending the meetings of "respectable" religious and political conservative groups. At many conservative political gatherings, I bumped into the most dangerous racists. And it's not just in political groups—Sunday morning continues to be the most highly segregated time of the week, with the church trailing behind the rest of society in breaking down racial barriers.

Today's New Confederates deny any racist tendencies while cutting federal spending on any programs that might help people of color. At the same time, the New Confederates promote legal policies that have resulted in having one-third of all young African American men spending time in jail. As Jesse Jackson puts it, we spend more on incarceration than on education.

Our legal system locks up a higher percentage of its population than any major nation except Russia, and we have a vastly disproportionate number of nonwhites bearing the brunt of that policy. It's a legal system of apartheid, because whites have a much better chance of acquittal or reduced sentencing on many of the same crimes for which African Americans and Hispanics spend many years in jail. The racism of the old Confederacy lives, though usually in a quieter and more insidious style.

The old ways of lynching and terrorizing blacks are still brought back from time to time, most memorably in the case of James Byrd in Texas, but now these practices elicit a major outcry of horror from mainstream America. So now, to get hardcore activists of conservatism fired up, new scapegoats are offered up.

The main minority under attack now by the political and Religious Right is the gay and lesbian community. AIDS has been referred to as "God's judgment" by too many major preachers to list, and knee-jerk reactions against the rights of citizens who are attracted to the "wrong" person are rampant. When diminutive Matthew Shepherd was savagely beaten and left on the crossbars of a wooden fence in Wyoming to die, the lawyers of the two murderers tried to use sexual flirtation as justification for the crime.

Gays have been criticized for being promiscuous by radio and TV preachers as well as politically conservative talk show hosts. At the same time that these New Confederates rage against the promiscuity of the targeted minority, they oppose the legalizing of their lifelong unions—even though such unions would likely reduce promiscuity rather than promote it.

Senate Majority Leader Trent Lott has, on a number of occasions, compared homosexuality to deviant criminal behavior like kleptomania, and Congressman Steve Largent successfully launched the Defense of

Marriage Act—as though giving gays the right to marry would somehow destroy traditional marriage for the heterosexual majority.

Of course, the Right claims that gay and lesbian people can simply choose to "turn right and go straight," as the popular saying goes. I had my own encounter with the group Exodus, which claims to "heal" homosexuals. Back in 1992, when I was hosting a conservative Christian talk show, I wanted to interview members of a local group that said it was having success in this area. When I arrived at one of the group's meetings, I was surprised to see only a half dozen people there. I asked what kind of counseling or addiction recovery techniques the group used and was told that they used no modern psychological techniques at all. They simply distributed a list of Bible verses to read and prayers to say to guard against temptation.

Even at the time, I was highly skeptical that this would be enough to work, and those thoughts seemed to be confirmed when the young man next to me began slowly rubbing his leg against mine. I began to wonder if I was in a group that was healing gays or providing a place to meet new dates, and I began to think that doing the show on the "good news about gays being healed" was a bad idea. The clincher came a week or two later when I happened to see a PBS television special on the national organization Exodus, which reported that two men who had cofounded the group had to resign their leadership posts because they fell in love with each other. For me, that spelled the end of any credibility the gay-healing movement might have had. I never brought any gay-healing promoters on my talk show.

However, in 1998 and 1999, conservative Republicans across the country sponsored a national advertising campaign to spread the word that gays can be healed and "set free" through prayer and a commitment to religious faith. The ads, which ran in newspapers across the country, usually mentioned the group Exodus specifically. I have been unable to find any empirical evidence by neutral scientific groups to back up their claims. Apparently, medical professionals also disagree with the claims of the gay healers, and psychiatric professionals removed homosexuality from their list of abnormal behavior a generation ago.

Other groups are also targeted minorities. The largest target of the Religious Right is the roughly 11 percent of the population that is not religious. Out of ten thousand men and women currently holding elected state and federal positions, none were elected to office running as openly atheistic or agnostic persons. Contrast that to the 98 percent of all elected state and federal officials who are at least nominally Christian. Granted, not all the Christians are born-again, but by comparing the role of Christianity in American government to the plight of the nonreligious, you can see who is the unrepresented minority. Yet back when I had my first phone conversation with Ralph Reed in 1990, he explained that the Christian Coalition was to be founded on the premise that "Christians are a persecuted minority in America today."

How off-base that now seems in this age when religious faith seems to be a prerequisite to holding office in the nation—and the assumption that religious people automatically live by higher moral standards than those who prefer reason over revelation, science over faith, and philosophy rather than dogma—goes absolutely unquestioned in most communities. Even religious liberals often assume that those who do not commit to a supernatural belief system must have made that decision due to a sour personal experience.

I myself held that view until I met some nonreligious people who were so positive and compassionate that I was intrigued. In June 1999, I was asked to serve as a technical and programming consultant for a TV show called *The Humanist Perspective*. I was brought in by the program's host, Joe Beck, a certified social worker and humanist counselor. Through him, I met Dr. Paul Kurtz, founder of Prometheus Books as well as a number of humanist and science-based organizations.

I had always been convinced that a person had to be open to spiritual experiences to be truly human, to be truly alive and filled with what the Bible calls "the fruits of the Holy Spirit—love, joy, peace, patience, kindness, goodness, humility, and self-control." Yet I found all these traits in these two men, who did not believe in anything supernatural. It challenged some of my most profoundly held assumptions.

I feel like I have started a self-directed education program. I now believe that the difference between a good education and a blind indoctrination is that a truly educated person is comfortable asking questions that may not be answered, while a person who is indoctrinated is given answers he may not question.

There are both religious and nonreligious people at many of the events that I attend. I am constantly amazed by the intelligence and humanitarianism of many nonreligious people. But I think I understand why religion continues to be popular in this scientific age.

Religion offers a sense of continuity with the past, a sense of community for today, and a sense of hope for the future. At least until such time that secular humanist groups can rival that, religion will continue to thrive. There are some new humanist endeavors springing up trying to do just that, but they are only in the embryonic phases and remain largely a well-kept secret.

My hope for the future is that more of us will begin to understand that people of all faiths or no faith can be positive and productive human beings committed to living active and ethical lives, and that more of us will reject the idea that one group can have the sole franchise on the truth.

ON THE WEB

Abortion-related sites

Missionaries to the Unborn—www.mttu.com (contains
 links to many other controversial groups)
Planned Murderhood—www.plannedmurderhood.com
Prolife.org—www.prolife.org

California Abortion and Reproductive Rights Action
 League—www.caral.org
NARAL: Reproductive Freedom and Choice—www.
 naral.org
Pro-Choice Resource Center—www.prochoiceresource.
 org

Religion-related sites

Christian Coalition of America—www.cc.org
Christian Worldview—www.geocities.com/CapitolHill/
 1492 (a kiosk with links to Christian Reconstructionist resources)

The Anti–Pat Robertson/Christian Coalition Site—www.geocities. com/CapitolHill/7027/patrobertson.html (contains links to all major opposition sites)

Council for Secular Humanism—www.secularhumanism.org

Unitarian Universalist Association—www.uua.org

Militia-related site

The Militia Watchdog—www.militia-watchdog.org

BOOKS BY

Gary North, including *Backward, Christian Soldiers* (Tyler, Tex.: Institute for Christian Economics, 1984), *Christian Reconstructionism: What It Is, What It Isn't* (Tyler, Tex.: Institute for Christian Economics, 1991), and *Lone Gunners for Jesus: Letters to Paul J. Hill* (Tyler, Tex.: Institute for Christian Economics: 1994).

Pat Robertson, including *The New World Order* (Nashville: Word Publishing, 1991).

Rousas John Rushdoony, including *God's Plan for Victory: The Meaning of Post Millennialism* (San Jose: Chalcedon Foundation, 1997).

Karen Armstrong, including *The History of God* (New York: A. A. Knopf, 1993).

Rob Boston, including *The Most Dangerous Man in America? Pat Robertson and the Rise of the Christian Coalition* (Amherst, N.Y.: Prometheus Books, 1996) and *Why the Religious Right Is Wrong About Separation of Church and State* (Amherst, N.Y.: Prometheus Books, 1993).

John Shelby Spong, including *Rescuing the Bible from Fundamentalism: A Bishop Rethinks the Meaning of Scripture* (San Francisco: HarperSan-Francisco, 1995) and *Why Christianity Must Change or Die* (San Francisco: HarperSanFrancisco, 1998).

*Some names have been changed